Essays on the Pleasures of Death

Essays on the Pleasures of Death

From Freud to Lacan

by Ellie Ragland

Routledge
New York   London

Published in 1995 by

Routledge
29 West 35 Street
New York, NY 10001

Published in Great Britain by

Routledge
11 New Fetter Lane
London EC4P 4EE

Copyright © 1995 by Routledge

Printed in the United States of America on acid free paper.

Library of Congress Cataloging-in-Publication Data

Ragland, Ellie,
    Essays on the pleasures of death : From Freud, to Lacan / by
Ellie Ragland
        p.   cm.
    Includes bibliographical references and index.
    ISBN 0-415-90721-7—ISBN 0-415-90722-5 (pbk.)
    1. Lacan, Jacques, 1901– . 2. Freud, Sigmund, 1856–
1939. 3. Death instinct—History. 4. Pleasure principle
(Psychology)—History. 5. Psychoanalysis—France—
History. I. Title.
BF109.L28R34 1995
150. 19′5′ 092—dc20   93-26977
                                                            CIP

**British Library cataloguing in publication information
also is available**

For my beloved Caroline, my life

Contents

Introduction

Traduttore emendatore: The role of translation and interpretation in exegetical renewal

We all know the proverbial Italian tag *traduttore traditore*: the idea that the translator—either by design or through incompetence—improperly conveys the letter and spirit of a text from one language to another, thereby betraying the original. I should like to consider yet another view of the translator: the role of translator as emendator. But such an idea immediately sounds treacherous. Translators are humble instruments of transmission, slaving in the mines of fidelity to the letter and spirit of a text, the very antithesis of emenders. Taken from the Latin *emendare*, an emender, in contrast, is one who takes out a fault or blemish, makes scholarly corrections, suggests a different reading.

My proposal becomes less audacious when considered within a Lacanian theoretical context. Representing himself as Freud's conceptual emendator, Jacques Lacan's exegesis of Freud attempted to paraphrase the original meanings implicit in Freud's texts within a larger framework. Lacan's emendations were meant to correct Freud's unresolved insights, or arguments that had gone astray for lack of sufficient contemporary knowledge to help him further in understanding the originality of his own discoveries. No less a problem has been the tendency of Freud's interpreters to read him in light of the nineteenth-century theories of mechanistic physics and neo-Darwinian biology by which he sought to explain his startling finds.

Although the German works of Freud exist in a *Standard Edition* in English to which I shall refer in more detail further on,[1] the Francophone world became seriously interested in Freudian psychoanalysis at a much later date than the Anglophone world. When the French finally took up study of Freud, they brought a different

1

set of presuppositions to psychoanalysis than had post-Freudians from Germany, England, and the United States. When the French psychiatrist/psychoanalyst Jacques Lacan publicly announced his "return to Freud" in 1953, and submitted the Viennese founder's texts to his own radical rereading, a set of new problems was posed for the Anglophone world: translating Lacan's reinterpretation of Freud's German into English.[2] Although Freud's body of theories had already possessed an English nomenclature for decades, Lacan's extensive French-language reworking of Freud's terms amounts to nothing less than a reconceptualization of Freud's theories (both early and late), requiring fresh translations of Freud's terms in English. Beyond the three-sided translation problem—how best to convert Freud's texts from German to English, from German to French, and from French to English—Lacan's work, taken as a whole, means that a new exegesis of Freud is required in any language into which he is translated.

Any commentator who renders terms or passages of Lacan's French into another language is, moreover, obliged to make decisions about how best to bring Lacan's innovations into that language within the expanding furor surrounding the meaning of psychoanalysis.[3] In the Anglophone world, paying attention to Freud's language is currently only one path taken in trying to ascertain an ever more correct interpretation of his texts. Indeed, certain efforts at "psychoanalyzing psychoanalysis" have taken specifically literalist and historical bents.[4] Not only do we have the literary critic Rose Marie Balmary digging up documents suggesting that Freud's father managed to keep one marriage secret, we also have the growing controversies surrounding the finds of Moussaieff Masson. Masson, formerly a professor of Sanskrit, has also trained as a psychoanalytic fellow at the Toronto Institute of Psychoanalysis in Canada. Masson has interpreted heretofore unseen correspondence between Freud and Fliess to mean that Freud's 1895–1897 literal seduction theory was correct. The cause of neurosis lies in *real* childhood seductions, not in fantasies woven around sexual configurations.[5] Moreover, Peter Swales, autodidact and former publicity hype agent, claims to have piled up adequate "proof" to convict Freud of having impregnated his sister-in-law (Martha Bornays).[6] Using the most spurious of arguments and the slimmest of historical evidence, both men claim to have discovered "empirical" proof that will shake the foundations of psychoanalysis, if not besmirch the reputation of its founder.

The examples mentioned above demonstrate, if nothing else, that in the Anglophone and Francophone worlds it is "open season" on psychoanalysis. Among the questioners seeking a "spiritual" renewal of psychoanalysis from within, I would also place Bruno Bettleheim. Demanding that the language of psychoanalysis itself be reconsidered, Bettleheim's doubts about the fidelity of Freud's translators (*Standard Edition*) to the spirit of Freud's discoveries might well be compared to Lacan's own scrutiny of Freud's German. Indeed, Lacan's scrupulous attention to Freud's language should warn anyone who tries to translate Lacan's French that in making terminological and conceptual judgments, any translator shoulders a large responsibility whether he or she wishes it or not. The translation of Lacan's French into English confronts the additional problem of unmaking and remaking an already solidly entrenched lexicon. In his book *Freud and Man's Soul*, Bruno Bettleheim impugns this lexicon.[7] Reviewers of Bettleheim's book who have not always been favorably inclined toward his efforts, paraphrased the book's thesis as follows (in a long review in the *Village Voice Literary Supplement*): "Freud's original texts were deliberately distorted by an occult group [Bettleheim] calls 'Freud's translators'; these villains set out with the intention of generating the hide-bound monstrosity that is American psychoanalysis today, and they succeeded."[8]

Another reviewer takes Bettleheim to task. Both a native speaker of German and a student of Lacanian thought, Helena Schulz-Keil argues that

> the only tools Mr. Bettleheim uses are his linguistic intuition, the *OED*, and *Der Duden*, a rather basic German dictionary. Armed in this fashion, he proceeds to show that 'in significant instances' the English translators distorted the meaning Freud sought to convey when choosing his terms. . . . Freud's language, [Bettleheim] contends, was deliberately metaphorical and ambiguous. It did not aim at scientific precision, but appealed to the heart or the *soul* of man. They [the translators] cleave to the Freud inclined toward science and medicine. . . . [9]

In Schulz-Keil's view not only is Bettleheim (Viennese born) found guilty of pursuing the phantom of the "German soul," he is also culpable on the count of placing excessive trust in dictionary definitions. If you have read Freud in his own context, she says, you will know that *Trieb* means "drive" and "instinct" means "species-specific impulse" (265). What does it matter if James Strachey translates *Trieb* as "instinct," says Schulz-Keil, as long as one has read Freud in his own context. Like any other concept used in a discourse, mistranslations disappear in the reading process itself and they yield place to translations which are *problematic*. Bettleheim's point is precisely that "mistranslations" do not disappear, but, on the contrary become the terminological chain upon which conceptual edifices are built.

Both Walter Kendrick and Schulz-Keil miss the importance of Bettleheim's book. True, he seems old-fashioned, dressed in archaic "humanist" garb: very out of style in a deconstructive, poststructualist era. But neither Kendrick nor Schulz-Keil pick up on the subversive gesture of Bettleheim's own deconstructive maneuver, all the more perverse when one grasps that Bettleheim desecrates the Psychoanalytic Holy Temple from within its very walls (not from its fringes like Masson and Swales). Bettleheim does not really have answers for the questions he poses in trying to understand the word *Seele* (soul) in terms other than that of the contemporary liaison of psychoanalysis with psychiatry and medicine. But in that he does understand the "soul" as *more* than bodily symptomatology (more specifically, sexual malfunction), he is close to Lacan's understanding that the power of words builds personalities, institutions, and gods, and divides the sexes as well.

Bettleheim, of course, maintains complete silence on Lacan's complex dispersion of the "soul" onto multiple planes. One might even say that Lacan continually divided up the soul—as, for example, in 1964—among what he termed the "four fundamental concepts of psychoanalysis."[10] The "drive" becomes desire for satisfaction that always exceeds itself, making dissatisfaction the lot of humans; the unconscious is the desire that governs the soul's archaic discourse; transference is the relationship with others where love and hate dialectics are engaged; repetition is the principle underlying the essence of human identifications, *jouissance*. In the essay "A Love Letter" ("Une lettre d'âmour," *Encore*, 1972–1973) Lacan says that people generally take the "beloved" other to be their very soul. He goes on to play on the diverse, often perverse, connections between the idea of soul and the unconscious knowledge one has about desire.[11] "In this world, the soul can only be contemplated through the courage and the patience with which it faces it [the world]. The proof is that up until now the soul has never had any other meaning" (155).

Bettleheim would probably not like to be placed anywhere near Lacan's epistemological camp. Nonetheless, just as Lacan chal-

lenges the inadequacy of the "knowledge" of Freud's day, Bettleheim challenges Freud's translators who, indeed, had Freud's approval to translate certain terms in a medical and scientific
direction. Thus, Bettleheim, without saying so, indirectly challenges Freud's own best judgment, accidentally exposing Freud as
an aging researcher who never ceased to covet acceptance by a
scientific and medical community to which he was himself mar-
ginal. In Freud's defense, however, one must add—as Bettleheim
does—that Freud never envisioned the powerful alliance between
psychoanalysis and the American medical establishment.

More disparaging in his attack on *Freud and Man's Soul* than
Schulz-Keil, Walter Kendrick compares Bettleheim's "dangerous"
humanist book to Samuel Weber's *The Legend of Freud*.[12] In his
Village Voice review essay Kendrick writes that while Weber's only
complaint against Freud's translators concerns their presumption
that Freud's " 'original' text knows what it is talking about, or at
least what it wants to say," Bettleheim, by comparison, seems to
view Freud's translators as "anarchists assembling bombs in the
basement" (Bettleheim, *Freud and Man's Soul*, 17).

The fact remains that neither Schulz-Keil nor Weber—both native
speakers of German—make any concession to the person who cannot read German. Weber's brilliant book keeps Freud's German
terms in German because "no precise equivalents exist for the
words in question" (Weber, *Legend*, 16). Making minimal conces-
sions to the translator, Schulz-Keil argues that "since meanings can
never be rendered directly, translations are bound to the materiality
of the alphabetic letter. They must remain *literal* to an extent which,
even though variable, precludes the wild troping of readings based
on an author's 'thought,' not his style" (Schulz-Keil, "Review," 265).
But if "the self is thought" (as Schulz-Keil says elsewhere) and
thought is an elaboration of language conventions and "self" (i.e.,
style), then how can one work on style without working on thought?
Seen from this point of view, Bettleheim's apparently innocent ex-
ercise in "translator bashing" becomes a serious enterprise in the
ongoing exegetical renewal of Freud's texts through the emendation
of translated terms, which gives rise to a conceptual body. Thought
is "rethought," word by word, word upon word.

Situating Freud's translators, both British and German, in England during a post-Hitlerian era, Bettleheim focuses on their desire
to portray psychoanalysis as a medical specialty. Everyday ordinary
German words were translated by medical terms and by learned
borrowings from Latin and Greek. *Fehlleistung,* meaning a faulty

performance (a Freudian "slip"), became *parapraxis*. *Besetzung,* meaning occupation by a strong force (perhaps a military one) or even occupation of a pay toilet (as in "occupied"), was translated as *cathexis,* a word invented by the translators from the Greek *catechein* (to occupy). Decrying the pseudo-scientific character of such translations, not to mention the loss of any ordinary (or literal, for that matter) affinity with Freud's German, Bettleheim does not portray Strachey as malevolent; merely as tendentious. Freud's concept of psychic energy (its source, aim, and goal) becomes cathexis, which supposedly translates *Besetzung.* And cathexis subsumes counter-cathexis, influx and discharge of energy, excitation, tension, and displacement. Thus cathexis bears the burden of joining obscure mental phenomena to the physiological data of the senses, which were said to determine mental phenomena. Going from physiology to psychology Freud relied on Fechner (the founder of experimental psychology), against the biological materialisms of his day.

Lacan's Language

Lacan's return to Freud can only be approached in terms of the language Lacan used. To call this language "jargon" implies that there is a classical language—a metalanguage—in which all epistemologies can be discussed. Such an assumption goes to the heart of the problem introduced by Lacan. Any systematized use of language is itself symptomatic (meaningful) of a desire to use language to close up an unclosable gap in thought. Lacan's redefinition of already established meanings works toward dispelling neo-Darwinian, neo-positivistic assumptions of a transparent relationship between language and the soul. Any attempts to render Jacques Lacan's texts into English will, therefore, continually run up against technical and conceptual difficulties. The moment one seeks to translate a text, one also takes on the burden of interpreting that text. One gives it a meaning, makes it into thought. Just as terms are finally inseparable from concepts, so is translation fused to interpretation, interpretation being—for Lacan—desire (or unconscious intentionality). At the very least one can say that the problem of interpretation is not solved by sidestepping translation problems.

Many already existing translations of Lacan into English are acceptable. In my view, others beg the question. For example, Freud's key terms *Ich* and *Es,* the first and third person neuter pronouns in German, were translated in the *Standard Edition* by their Latin equivalents, ego and id. Catherine Clément has commented on Lacan's claim that Freud did not always write *das Es* or *das Ich*, as Marie Bonaparte's translations of Freud into French implied. Bonaparte wrote: "Le moi [the Ego] doit déloger le ça" [the Id]. Instead Freud used the simple pronouns "ich" and "es."[13] Lacan also converted the German pronouns into nouns, but used in a personal sense. This lent support to Lacan's contention that Freud's post–1920 agencies—the ego, id, and superego—were concepts Freud evolved when he failed to grasp the concrete and individual nature of the unconscious as constituted by language, images, and the trauma of loss.

Contemporary post–Freudian thought generally views the ego as the conscious self, the id as an instinctual, pleasure-seeking combustion engine, and the superego as the agency of sociomoral censorship. Using the tools of modern linguistics, cultural anthropology, and mathematical topology, among others, Lacan argued against this post–1920 Freudian system. Returning to Freud's earlier idea that unconscious activities were organized in an intelligent and personally idiosyncratic way, Lacan took Freud's *Ichspaltung* (splitting of the ego) literally as a paradigm of the true nature of the human "subject." Freud's *ich* became Lacan's speaking subject, his *je/moi parlêtre*, and Freud's *es*, his *ça* or *jouissance*. By moving away from earlier French translations, not only was Lacan free to emend the concept of impersonal psychic agencies, he could also give full individual play to the terms *je, moi* and *ça*, functioning as an intertwined unit governed by the *objet a* (cause of desire whose source is unconscious). The *moi* symbolizes the uniqueness of each person's narcissism (or identity). And even though the person is unaware of the fictional (identificatory and linguistic) nature of his own "personality" composition, the relation of "being" (or unbeing) to the *ça* or *jouissance* is palpable.

But in translating *moi* and *je* into English one quickly realizes that the seemingly simplest of solutions opens up the most complex problem areas. Lacan's best-known English translator Alan Sheridan has solved the "problem" by translating *je* as the "I" or the subject, and *moi* as the ego or *Moi*, on occasion.[14] Although satisfactory as far as they go, these translations still do not give wide enough scope to Lacan's use of the words in French. Sheridan's *moi* seems an apparent unity—a subject of passion and belief—while Lacan showed it as paradoxically dialectical and contradictory within itself, made up of multiple voices, images, and refractive messages. Moreover, the *je*, as the subject of conscious speech and social conventions, and the *moi* as the subject of personality or identificatory relations, function alternately as subject or object of each other, as well as subject or object of the unconscious Other. They also "act" differently depending on which associational plane, with its attendant *jouissance*, is in focus: the imaginary, the symbolic, the real, or the symptom. Any linguistic reduction along subject versus object lines is, therefore, close to the "two-body" psychology of ego psychology or of phenomenology, both of which Lacan abhorred. Translating the *je* into "I" and the *moi* into "me," not only eludes Lacan's dynamic complexity, but also sounds unnatural in English. In French, on the contrary, *moi* plays the role of subject as a disjunctive pronoun. In addition, from 1583 on, *moi* has been used as a noun, first by Montaigne and later by Pascal (*"Le moi est haissable"*). *Je* became a noun at a later date.

Linguistically speaking, Strachey's translations of *Ich* as ego (subject) and *Es* as id (suppressed object) were natural solutions within English. Not only did they support Freud's second topology, they also followed the subject/object distinction already existing between the pronouns "I" and "me" in English. Perhaps this linguistic reality is one reason English translators of Lacan have seemed to gloss over the depth and scope of the translation problem raised by his splitting of the human subject into mutually interacting, yet contradictory, parts. His commentators usually translate *moi* as ego or "self," and *je* as *the* subject. But the insufficiency of these translations cannot be blamed on the structure of English grammar alone. Perhaps the recent infusion of phenomenological thought into the Anglophone academic arena has also laid the groundwork for an unconscious tendency to equate the *moi* with ego (a phenomenological "self" object) and the *je* with the subject of consciousness. An adequate translation of *moi* and *je* into English is further complicated by the autonomous meaning the French word *moi* has assumed in English. Taking its signifying departure from French Romanticism, the *moi* is thought to refer to a pathos of self, a private or hidden self, or an inner soul.

Lacan certainly meant none of the preceding things when he translated Freud's *Es* as the subject of *jouissance* and turned the *moi* and its ideals into those forms meant to stop loss and its effects: the object *a*. By redefining *moi* as the subject of *jouissance*, but an unwitting object of unconscious meanings, Lacan denoted the opposite of insight, introspection, or sensitivity. On the contrary, the *moi* has become the source of human identity *qua* resistance by a kind of stitching together of fragments of sound and sight taken in from the outside world into a seemingly unified fiction. Functioning as a symbol of "self" individuated in the world, or as a "descriptive narcissism," the *moi*, held together by tightly drawn threads, reveals the necessity of closing out unconscious fragmentation (the real of "death") if one is to live as an apparent ideal in the eyes and ears of the world.

The translation solution I would suggest in the case of *moi* and *je* would retain the French originals, but always modify them with descriptive phrases. *Je* becomes the speaking subject, or the subject of social conventions, or the intellect, not taking desire into account. *Moi* would be rendered variously as the subject of personality or individuality, or a representor or signifier of a "self" symbol, and so on. One should resist translating *moi* as "self" or "identity"—although this is often difficult—since both words have specific and complicated histories within English philosophy and psychoanalysis. Moreover, both terms imply a wholeness and unity of being which Lacan did not attribute to the human ego, despite its unified fictional fantasies.

A better known translation problem for Lacanian commentators is what to do about the term *jouissance*. Lacan used the term *plaisir* to denote sexual pleasure, thus freeing himself to use *jouissance* to describe things other than sexual pleasure, such as the earliest of human satisfactions and disappointments. From the start of life satisfaction and dissatisfaction are derived from the experience of incorporating the effects of partial objects that become associated with fulfillment only because the *jouissance* effect they give is lost. And the experience of losing *jouissance* makes desire a structure in being at the level where something always remains unfulfilled. Yet, *jouissance* retains both its sexual and psychic meanings in French. Noting that there was no equivalent word in English, Lacan recommended that *jouissance* not be translated. Still, one can read *Television* (1975) as putting forth a theory of *jouissance* as a meaning system based on three kinds of *jouissance*: an *essence* of being that guarantees stability (Φ) and serves alternately to give pleasure and to block pleasure; a *jouis-sens* of signifiers that constitutes unconscious thought or meaning as a set of beliefs or knowledge suppositions; and a *jouissance* of the body in which repetitions of drives try to annul lack through satisfactions, thereby seeking to fill the void in the Other [S($\varnothing$)].[15]

Although various context-specific translations of *jouissance* do exist (such as enjoyment), this term is generally left untranslated and without commentary. But since the concept is so central to Lacan's teaching, perhaps one could best follow its French usage by locating its position in relation to its precise functions in the real, imaginary, or symbolic, and in terms of corporal effect, desire, or fantasy. How does a given *jouissance* emanate from the *cause* of desire, only to return as a desire for repetition? Such a strategy may at least throw obstacles in the way of those who "understand" the term too quickly (i.e., translating it to themselves), thus reducing Lacan's multivalent concepts such as this one to only one meaning. Given Lacan's view of Freud's post–1920 theories as failing on the side of biological realism, thereby betraying the earlier insights Freud had in regard to language and symbols in their relationship to the unconscious, one would expect that Lacan means more than sexual pleasure by *jouissance*.

Moreover, Lacan's concepts always function in dynamic cadence with his other concepts. For example, *jouissance* is linked both to the Other and to the *object a*, as well as to the death drive. *Jouissance* comes from the Other, Lacan said in his essay "A Jakobson" (*Encore*, 19–27). That is, *jouissance* emanates from the Other's desire, as well as from loss. In the same essay Lacan uses the *object a* to denote the *plus-de-jouir* or surplus value in *jouissance* where the real of a symptom appears (21). We remember that the *a* stands for the myriad substitute activities and objects that provide temporary compensation for an incompleteness in human being, an incompleteness caused by all the losses that constitute the unconscious as a lost continent that "knows" all the same. But the *object a* also points to an unresolved tension in being that the symptom articulates. *Jouissance*, then, "is not a sign of love" (*Encore*, 21). It is, rather, a sign of the unconscious screening itself off from conscious life by means of fixations that give rise to repetitions. *Jouissance*, thus understood, can be viewed as a correlative of the Freudian libido. It is caused by an insatiable desire for the constancy of satisfaction, but is not reducible to any given satisfaction.

By translating *jouissance* as a sign of joy, satisfaction, Oneness, fulfillment, pleasure, bliss, glee, euphoria, or rapture; or conversely as misery, dissatisfaction, the impossibility of Oneness, lack, displeasure, depression, anxiety, or *malaise*, one conveys the idea of a feeling or sense of surplus or excess in desire itself: a "beyond" that persists in meaning and thought. We remember that Marx attributed value only to surplus. In a similar way, if the mysterious *source* of affect is explained as an excess that appears in language and being—a *jouissance*—this excess itself becomes one more proof of an absent/present knowledge governing human response. Humans misunderstand this experience, their illusion being that the other (be it lover, film, literary text, etc.) provides *jouissance*. Paradoxically, the source of the three *jouissances* lies within each person's intrasubjective circuit, each seeking a contradictory goal: to maintain narcissistic certainty by excluding any lack in being, body or meaning. That is, *jouissance* is felt as a oneness or consistency that maintains itself against myriad foes: the discontinuities of life. Thus any other—person, text, or event—is only a catalyst to a *jouissance* already fixed in the familiar, a known consistency of alternating pleasure/displeasure.

Lacan's development of the concept of *jouissance* teaches that the primordial *effects* of separation and alienation that underlie any later imagined symmetry of the sexes (as in myths of harmonious love or group oneness) first established *jouissance* as the libidinal glue of being, knowing, and feeling—none of which is One. And since the ego leads the chase in the love drama, most poignantly exemplified in sexual relations, the French term *jouissance* is well chosen, for it conveys the *dual* meaning of orgasm as pleasure in union, as well as a lethal side, the loss experienced in coming to the end of a moment of bliss. In *Séminaire* XX Lacan shows that no visible partner is needed to induce the psycho-physiological state of orgasm. Bernini's statue of Saint Theresa is meant to emphasize this idea (cf. the cover of *Sém.* XX). Put another way in "Science and Truth," Lacan describes "the subject [as being] in internal exclusion to its object."[16] What sustains sexual desire in love is the *illusion* that the subject and its object are reciprocal and in a state of mutual causation. But the myth of a fusionary oneness—"Il y a de l'Un" There is a One—is continually exploded by the unconscious Other, making the reality of love an "Un-en-moins" (a One-minus) (*Encore*, "Ronds de Ficelle," 107–23; 116).

What is subtracted from the mythical dream of union with another person is the fact that humans are divided into two sexes, each with a different mythic status. Moreover, the difference is asymmetrical, not oppositional. And this asymmetry arises out of a structural reality. The female sex represents the *union* of mother and infant as One in the unconscious. The male sex represents difference from Oneness. Out of these structural effects, women are id-ized and men logo-cized; women are identified primarily with the body and affects while men are identified with culture, or the social.

The enigma of sexual *jouissance* lies in the revelation that the body *qua* imaginary signifier "speaks." Because the "self" is cut up in its pretense at wholeness or autonomy, the body seeks a grounding in *jouissance*, i.e., in consistencies of meaning, drive, or affect. In this sense, *jouissance* is the equivalent of Lévi-Strauss's mana, a concept not dissimilar from Marx's surplus value. Or in Lacan's terms, desire adds up to more than the sum of its parts because the partner of each sex remains the Other sex, not the other person. But only in failing to maintain consistency in plea- sure, meaning, or body does one confront the negative effects of *jouissance* that bespeak the need to produce new desire. When our bodies "speak" the language of desire, an intrinsic lack, the Other makes its presence felt (Sém. XX, 109). But *jouissance*—unlike the lacking Other—obeys the law of psychic constancy, showing that excess is always subsumed by the Other. Thus a person's excess *jouissance* is either repressed within a socially acceptable ecology of conventions, or the person is excluded from the social. For *jouiss- ance* has a negative social value when it is given free rein. Excess makes others shrink in envy, fear, or disgust. This is one more "normal" social response, showing that any idea of a wholeness of identity is an illusion, an onanistic narcissism. And, indeed, the *jouissance* that reigns supreme in psychosis shows too little psychic individuation away from the mother. The resultant suffering of ma- nic madness (and attendant orgasmic infinity) shows that even *jouissance* has a limit, marked by the boundary confusions one might call a limit to the law of selfhood.

Jouissance is intrinsically bound to the fictions that link uncon- scious structures of desire to the ego. "What writes itself [in the unconscious] are the conditions of *jouissance*" (*Sém.* XX, 118). In "De la jouissance" Lacan talks about Don Juan as a character who incarnates the social myth of masculine virility. This myth is made manifest in his seductions of scores of women, one by one. As a career seducer, a man who does not hide his desires from public view, Don Juan refuses to be stopped by any social morality pro- scribed by the Other. When Don Juan finally meets his death at the hands of the Stone Guest, one may view this as a metaphorical display of the fact that sexual *jouissance* is "socially" regulated, if not determined, by the law of convention: the Other.

But what creates such law? In Lacan's teaching social law is not created by external censorship or by an impersonal superego. It is derived in the particular. One by one, each person internalizes a structure of "law" based on the necessity of turning away from the mother as the sole source of satisfaction. Such a *père-version* gives rise to a specificity of desire whose logic is internal to itself. Moreover, the effects of early separation from maternal partial objects, and the learning of individuality (or difference) in reference to a lineage of the Name-of-the-Father, place *jouissance* within the confines of law. Since *jouissance* exceeds desire, is a surplus value, Lacan calls it non-utilitarian, or that which is in excess of the necessary. *Jouissance* is the demand for love as a pure leftover extracted from desire and need. At this level, *jouissance* is the greed, pure and simple, to get what one values. But it finds *its* limits in the laws that impose various possible alliances between desire and love on individuals and groups.[17] While love and desire emanate from different psychic poles, love coming from narcissism and from imaginary dialectics, and desire eddying up from the unconscious to infer lack into love, *jouissance* plays between the two. Although *jouissance* is the name Lacan gives to the supposed consistency of being, body, or meaning that individuals seek to attain and maintain, desire takes on the garb of enigma, shrouding its passions in shadows.

But why should desire be so chameleonic? Lacan's picture of desire makes better sense when linked to his theory of *castration*; the learning of limits and boundaries—the child's acquisition of a sense of being as being separate—is so painful that the impact of "no" is a literal cut, akin to a slicing off: "No" your mother is "Not All." Although there is no terminological inadequacy in translating the word "castration" directly from Freud's *Kastrationskomplex* and from Lacan's *castration*, one must remember that Lacan might well have chosen a less evocative term. But the term "castration" dramatizes the fact that being is constructed in reference to the learning of difference as sexual difference: That is, the limits in identity and desire that constitute perception in the name of social order, family fictions, and so on, are derived from each person's experience of the phallic signifier whose signified is "No." Indeed, Lacan meant to emend the literalist (biological) meaning still resonant in the concept of castration as understood by post-Freudians. It is plausible that Lacan kept this word to insist upon the inseparability of the body responding to the cut (separation) and to the representational (alienation) imposed on human animals. In Lacan's teaching the body resides within the metonymical field of *jouissance*, while representation elaborates the metaphorical field of substitutive meanings (the Other). At the same time, no reading of Lacan's text could lead one to imagine his imputing a biological first cause to human being or motivation. His retention of an already tendentious word—in this case *castration*—stresses the fact that the play of the symbolic and imaginary upon the physical organism creates a real order of impasses—repressed traumatic meanings—in the body itself. By using such terms, Lacan tried to forestall any reduction of his major concepts to a sheer mentalism.

Jouissance glitters with the brilliance of a new and prismatic term which must be viewed in light of the full range of sexual response: The unconscious is the reality of sexuality. *Jouissance* also opens onto any joy linked to the Other's desire, while the concomitant loss of joy shows a severing of one's ties to the Other's desire. Unlike *jouissance*, the term *castration*, on the contrary, requires us to re-conceptualize a word whose meaning is already established. Such terms, fossilized as if in amber, must literally be freed from their imprisoning stone, and forced out into the light for re-examination. While Lacan extended the meaning of castration to the many levels on which loss/alienation/division occur, on a grander scale, he unveiled it as the causal event in creating an unconscious. Whereas *jouissance* is an equivalent of its German predecessor, *Lustbefrie-digung*, it offers greater scope for invention than does castration, whose already established meanings can only be emended at the cost of confusing interlocutors.

In any event, coining everyday words anew cannot but challenge listeners and readers to feel the discomfort caused when words and concepts are set askew. Indeed, such discomfort manifests the *jouissance* of willed consistency implicit in the way we use words—thoughtlessly and carelessly—as Lacan does not.

Notes

1. Sigmund Freud, *The Standard Edition of the Complete Works of Sigmund Freud*, trans. James Strachey, in collaboration with Anna Freud et al. (London: Hogarth Press, 1953).

2. Jacques Lacan, "The function and field of speech and language in psycho-analysis" (1953), in *Ecrits: A Selection*, trans. Alan Sheridan (New York: W. W. Norton, 1977), 30–113.

3. Judith Miller (interviewer), "Les Oeuvres complètes de Freud en français: Fin d'une aventure interminable—Entretien avec Michel Prigent," *L'Ane* 34 (April–June 1988): 28–30.

4. Marie Balmary, *Psychoanalyzing Psychoanalysis: Freud and the Hidden Fault of the Father*, trans. Ned Lukacher (Baltimore: Johns Hopkins University Press, 1982).

5. Janet Malcom, *In the Freud Archives* (New York: Knopf, 1984).

6. Ibid.

7. Bruno Bettleheim, *Freud and Man's Soul* (New York: Knopf, 1983).

8. Walter Kendrick, "Review of *Freud and Man's Soul* by Bruno Bettleheim," *Village Voice Literary Supplement* (Fall 1983), 16.

9. Helena Schulz-Keil, "Review of *Freud and Man's Soul* by Bruno Bettleheim," *Lacan Study Notes*, Special issue, *Hystoria* 6–9 (1988): 262–66.

10. Jacques Lacan, *The Four Fundamental Concepts of Psychoanalysis*, ed. Jacques-Alain Miller, trans. Alan Sheridan (New York: W. W. Norton, 1977).

11. Jacques Lacan, *Le séminaire XX (1972–1973): Encore*, text established by Jacques-Alain Miller (Paris: Editions du Seuil, 1975), 73–82; 76. See also "A Love Letter," in *Feminine Sexuality*, ed. Juliet Mitchell and Jacqueline Rose, trans. Jacqueline Rose (New York: W. W. Norton, 1982), 149–61.

12. Samuel Weber, *The Legend of Freud* (Minneapolis: University of Minnesota Press, 1982).

13. Catherine Clément, *The Lives and Legends of Jacques Lacan*, trans. Arthur Goldhammer (New York: Columbia University Press, 1983), 169.

14. Cf. Alan Sheridan's translation of *Ecrits: A Selection by Jacques Lacan* (New York: W. W. Norton, 1977).

1
Lacan's Theories on Narcissism and the Ego

In Lacan's long exegesis of Freud's texts, he developed a logic of psychoanalysis intended to clarify unfinished or contradictory thoughts in Freud's *oeuvre*. One result of Lacan's return to Freud's work was a scathing critique of ego psychology as it has developed since the death of the founder of psychoanalysis. Even though Freud himself gave increasing scope to the powers of the ego, changing his ideas depending on the psychic system in which it participated, Lacan argued that contemporary concepts of ego, self, and object owe little to the goals to which Freud aspired for the theory and practice of psychoanalysis.[1]

Lacan's teaching evolved, in part, as an effort to correct what he considered to be inadequacies in concepts of the ego as they have evolved since Freud's death. He maintained that psychoanalysis has become conflated with psychology at the level of ego (self, other, object), rather than explaining how the unconscious and its laws actually work. Attributing the growth of ego psychology to a dynamic repression of Freud's structural unconscious (conscious, preconscious systems), Lacan says post-Freudians have substantified the Freudian unconscious into a conscious ego *supposedly* aware of itself. Lacan argued, rather, that one *can* only acquire distance from the "ego" through the transference. Through a relation of love or hate for the analyst a patient *can* become aware of ego fictions to which he or she is otherwise blind.

Since post-Freudian analysts have for the most part dismissed Freud's early discoveries of a concrete unconscious that governs conscious thought from a repressed memory bank of knowledge, Lacan argued that they would also be unaware that the ego is concretely constituted. Moreover, because they view the unconscious as fiction, myth, or metaphor, post-Freudians believe the object of psychoanalytic focus should be the ego, or some related concept of the ego as made up of self/other relations. And given that the empirical method of research has been equated with "science" in the contemporary Western world, post-Freudian psychologists or analysts think they have emended or transcended Freud merely by evincing empirical data. Lacan argued that contemporary analysts who base their theoretical arguments on Freud's own concept of the development of his thought have turned psychoanalysis into a study of behavior, a quasi-biological theory of cognition, a developmental concept of object relations, or a medical therapy that views psychic life in terms of symptoms diagnosed as disease caused by physiology.

Lacan's "return" to Freud evolved in an opposite direction from such chronologically based, developmentally oriented readings of Freud. Through an unflagging fidelity to the unanswered questions in Freud's texts, Lacan saw Freud's method of mind as a "thinking against oneself." That is, Freud continually returned to the problems in his essays which remained unsolved. Disagreeing with his own conclusions, even years later, Freud constantly suggested alternative solutions (often contradictory one to the other) to the same problem. In his own solutions to the impasses left by Freud, Lacan reversed Freud's picture of "first causes." While Freud generally saw individuality as caused by the biological organism itself (with its neurological, hormonal, and genetic attributes), Lacan proposed that individual subjectivity is dialectically organized in unconscious formations operated by the associative synchrony of three constituted categories he equates with structure: the real, the symbolic, and the imaginary (or the Borromean knot).[2] Indeed, Lacan's picture gives us a new model of mind wherein contradictory functions constitute a new logic, a psychoanalytic one. While ego, thought, and consciousness have been generally equated one with another by contemporary psychology (some linguists and philosophers collapsing these into the system of language itself), Lacan argued that consciousness and language cannot "think" themselves. Rather, reasoning abilities, perception, and memory are first constituted from the outside world and return in the words (the symbolic) people use to talk about their lives, in the images with which people identify (the imaginary), and in the effects of loss that construct the real as an order of traumas. These orders organize language in a topological signifying chain of Borromean knots.

Lacan argued that perception and intentionality (*qua* desire) begin to be structured between birth and around eighteen months of age in a conjunction of primary identifications and "calling" to the other for satisfaction. The response given by others to the signifier of *the call* begins to structure the way an ego will be formed from the start of life. Lacan's explanation of how an individual first acquires and then uses the highly personal system of representations by which he or she later encodes reality points to a substratum of enigmatic or abstract figures of the unconscious. Yet, paradoxically, these can be decoded in later life (at the conscious level) to reveal fragments and details from the concrete realm of language and event, memorable from the moment language first serves as a way to describe one's experience of reality.

Lacan's Freud is dynamic and dialectical, then, and the topological unconscious from which one draws a sense of being an ego or "self" is symbolic and relational. Crisis, conflict, misunderstanding and reversals mark human subjectivity, not information, communication, understanding and reason. Because the real intervenes constantly, cutting into seemingly consistent thought, language is permanently split between any person's efforts to remain *fixed* within familiar (*Heimat*), albeit unconscious, repetitions, and its own inadequacy in guaranteeing constancy, permanence, or ongoing stability.

The Freudian Ego

Post-Freudian psychoanalysis has tended to think of the unconscious, conscious, and preconscious schemas of Freud's first topology as taking a back seat to the ego. Lacan's stunning explanation of how the ego is composed picks up threads Freud left dangling in this early model, and in the other models as well. Lacan maintained that Freud's ever-changing picture of the ego proved that his search to define it was incomplete. What Freud failed to grasp is that the ego itself is *split* or divided between ego ideals (others) and an ideal ego (*moi*). Because the ego is formed from the outside world, individuals depend on one another for "self" validation throughout life (which I shall explain further in the section on the mirror stage). This means that no person's ego is ever whole or autonomous. Rather, a continual constituting and re-constituting of the ego—composed of images, words, and libidinal effects—is *performed in* the eyes of others. The mere fact of this on-going human "show" suggests that the ego can never be static or whole, nor innately or instinctually determined.

Lacan's theory of the ego is of a piece with his rejection of models of mind that persist in the Freud one generally knows: the Cartesian Freud who split mind between rational (realistic) and irrational (fantastic) processes; the pre-Wittgensteinian Freud who rooted knowledge in sense data; the neo-Darwinian Freud whose biological psychoanalysis of innate forces modeled psychic development along evolutionary lines of linear stages and adaptive functions. This latter Freud reflected partisan theories of the competitive struggle for existence which appear in his idea that ego (self-pre-servative) instincts are opposed to sexual ones (continuity of the species). And contemporary versions of Freud have translated these nineteenth-century positivistic theories of rationalism, sensory knowledge, and biological sequence into modern theories where brain function, hormonal drive, and genetic mapping are said to be causative of behavior and being.

Lacan, like Freud, worked from the premise that psychoanalysis is definable and teachable as a science. But his own clinical ex-perience led him to describe the object of scientific inquiry—the unconscious—by logical and topological formalizations rather than in the Freudian terms of evolutionary biology. Thus, it is often erroneously claimed that Lacan viewed Freud's most innovative and creative period as prior to 1920. Perhaps Lacan has been seen in this light because his "return to Freud" took seriously the literal and concrete unconscious Freud first discovered in dreams, in the parapraxes of everyday life, in humor, in the Oedipal structure, in family myths, and in art, to name a few. But in fact, Lacan found evidence of the concrete nature of the unconscious throughout all of Freud's writings, not just his early ones.

In keeping with those historians of psychoanalysis who describe its development as an effort to uncover ever more primitive sources of psychic cause, Lacan located the sources of narcissism and iden-tification in earlier stages and more concrete places than did Freud. As early as his 1932 dissertation Lacan argued that Freud's failure to understand the concrete tendencies of the ego, including its concrete genesis, meant that its individual specificity could only elude him throughout the whole of his life.[3] But this does not make of Lacan a Kleinian. Nor is he a surrealist—painting an ego collage—as certain critics have recently claimed.[4] By reconceptualizing nar-cissism and identification, Lacan arrived at a new understanding of how the ego is formed, thereby validating Freud's conviction that the ego is a late development by comparison with narcissism. Lacan dispensed with the empiricist, positivistic, developmental theories wherein knowledge is acquired through observation and experience, theories by which psychology even today retains the concept of a self-sustaining consciousness of self. By realigning Freud's various concepts of narcissism, identification, drive, and ego, Lacan could argue that the *ego is not a synthesizing agent*. In so doing, he demonstrated that neonate identification with the objects of the world produces the narcissistic constellation we call the ego. But he maintained that such identification does not come about in a linear (two-person) operation. Rather, co-simultaneous identification with three different kinds of material organizes the ego: with the drives (the real), with images (the imaginary), and with language itself in its representation of objects (the symbolic). "There are not," however, "three dimensions in language," Lacan points out. "Language is always flattened out."[15] Moreover, one does not identify with "objects"—images, words, persons, bodily organs—because they are full and present to themselves. One identifies with "objects" because one lacks innate being.

But Lacan does not equate objects with persons or parts of persons (such as the breast representing the mother). Rather, he shows that no person can have a relation to an object except insofar as something is lacking, thereby giving rise to the *desire* to identify with objects. When an object lacks at the level of the image (such as in the little boy's fantasy attribution of a penis to little girls, for example), the resulting contradiction between the little boy's fantasy and the reality of organs being equated with images is what Lacan called separation: the experience of a cut between fantasy and visual reality gives rise to the *symbolic* order. Thus, another name of castration, as reconceptualized by Lacan, would be the repression of certain traits retained from the traumas of separation.

When an organic object (such as the breast in weaning) is removed, the *frustration* caused by the loss or the cut produces an *imaginary* lack (not the fantasy of an imaginary organ). One might argue that object-relations theories err in equating fantasy with imaginary lack, supposing some "good enough mother" (or analyst) to fulfill a fantasy lack. At the level of *privation* of a valued object in the symbolic (such as a child or a loved one), the lack is, however, *real* and opens up onto the void of loss and anxiety.[6] Thus, Lacan rereads Freud's theory of the object as functioning differently in the three categories: symbolic (castration), imaginary (frustration), and real (privation).[7] These give rise to the fourth order Lacan called the paternal metaphor or the order of the symptom that knots the three orders in a Borromean signifying chain of interlinked associations.

Furthermore, whether an ego (self-symbol or "object") is con-stituted as normative, neurotic, perverse, or psychotic—Lacan's four differential diagnostic categories that rename Freud's path-ologies—depends on its fate in the Oedipal structure: that is in ref-erence to the phallus and castration.[8] Put another way, an ego evolves as neurotic, psychotic, perverse, or normative depending on how gender, anatomy, and sexuality are aligned in the so-called Oedipal experience.

Narcissism

In his early efforts to deduce how the ego was constituted, Freud turned to Havelock Ellis's notion that narcissism derived from erot-icism.[9] In 1898 Ellis had added the idea of a concrete psychological aspect to the concept of narcissism, thereby linking narcissism to actual life, not to myth. Borrowing Ellis's use of the word "narcis-sism," Freud was able to denote an intermediary stage between auto-eroticism and object love—love for another person—a notion he then applied to the Schreber case (1911) in an effort to learn why Judge Daniel Paul Schreber had become psychotic.[10] He used the term again in 1913 in "Totem and Taboo."[11]

In "On Narcissism: An Introduction" (1914) and in "Mourning and Melancholia" (1916) Freud came up with several possible explanations of how eroticism could shift between ego and object, how one could love the self via another person. He suggested that a certain quantity of libidinal *energy* could shift from "self-love" to "object love."[12] But Freud quickly considered "On Narcissism" to be incomplete, perhaps because he could not define this energy, nor how it was constituted, and thus how it could shift from one place to another. Although he could not determine how narcissism functioned, Freud's essay still remains a nodal point in his thought precisely because the concepts of topography and drive theory intersect here for the first time. But because he lacked an explan-atory theory of energy, Freud's models of drive energy, derived from nineteenth-century theories of physics and biology, are no more descriptive of the human psyche than are the biodynamic descriptions of animal behavior still used today to explain human behavior.[13]

Freud's essay on narcissism is easily disregarded, standing as it does in opposition to other metapsychological essays he wrote at the same time. And Freud did not arrive at a satisfactory answer to what causes drive in any of these writings. Indeed, his other 1915 metapsychological writings point toward his 1920 theoretical turning point when the id-ego-superego model of mind would prevail over earlier models. In the other essays written in 1915, either Freud did not mention the concept of narcissism at all, or he said he had already surpassed that idea.[14] It was 1920 when Freud picked up his concept of narcissism once again. Still concerned to explain how libidinal energy could shift from one person to another, Freud proposed something new: a distinction between primary and secondary narcissism.[15]

By conflating narcissism and identification he created *primary narcissism* as a state of indifference between the ego and id, characteristic of newborns, psychotics, and those depressed or in mourning. While this mental state is specifically marked by an absence of object relations (i.e., social relationships with others), in *secondary narcissism* the id and ego maintain a distance one from the other. Depicting the id as a blind greedy force that strives only for its own pleasure, Freud says the ego differentiates itself from the id by its adaptive function of identifying with others. But Lacan found a problem in the logic of Freud's primary narcissism. If prototypes of primary narcissism are to be found in the state of sleep or in intrauterine life, Lacan asks, how can energy shift between one person and another? Although Melanie Klein pushed psychoanalytic theory of a fantasmatic basis for primary narcissism all the way back to fetal life, Lacan viewed such Kleinian theories as imaginary allegories.[16]

What perceptual opening would allow some "mysterious" energy to be withdrawn from an incipient ego (that one might also describe as a narcissistic investment in others) that would, in turn, allow this ego to be cathected (invested in or identified with) another object? That is, what holds the Freudian id, ego, and object (other) together in some supposed primary narcissistic bond? Throughout his teaching, Lacan maintained that primary narcissism was impossible as a state of being precisely because there is no perceptual opening to the world in the concept. The idea of a psyche enclosed on itself, imprisoned within elemental hallucinations or fantasies, describes a state of "death," not a stage in development.

But Lacan evolved an answer to the question of how one comes to love oneself as an ego via another. Insofar as the ego is made up of identifications whose purpose is to replace lost *jouissance*, the question is how this takes place. In *Ce qui fait insigne* Jacques-Alain Miller demonstrates a clear trajectory in Lacan's teaching. In the 1930s and 1940s Lacan took the *imago* as the operator of identifications. Yet, insofar as it is not just any image in play, but an image encircled by the signifier, at this early date Lacan had already advanced the idea of an insignia (named imago) at the base of psychic causality.[17] Miller's thesis is stunning: "What Lacan called imago is what we find again under the name *sinthome* at the end of his teaching. It is what I called an elegant arc" (course of March 18, 1987). In its particularity, the ego might be described as a constellation that seeks itself. Since individuals are not cognizant of their unconscious identificatory traits—unary traits which Miler describes as insignia or images already significantized—they must verify their own ideal ego images, projected from a closed substratum of fantasy, via others. This is quite a different theory from the poststructuralist notion that the ego is merely a fiction—one's life story as a narrative. Lacan argued that fiction has *structure*. And in the third period of his teaching, when he equated structure with topology—with the Borromean interlacing of real, symbolic, and imaginary chains of meaning—Lacan made it clear that structure itself produces the disjunctions of inconsistencies.

Although Lacan rejected Freud's idea of a primary narcissism, his theory of a primary or primordial *jouissance* retains a conceptual link to Freud's primary narcissism. Agreeing that elemental hallucinations (Freud's *Wunschvorstellungen*) may, indeed, provide a kind of pleasure (a primary *jouissance*), Lacan points out this paradox: Infants first seek pleasure because of the displeasure of losing the *jouissance* of a sense of consistency between body and the world. Primary *jouissance* is not only "content" specific, then, but also depends on the desire for consistency. Lacan explained that although pleasure (*Lust*) is first experienced as a consistency between being and body, it can only *ex-sist* by remaining unconscious. That is, if primary *jouissance* becomes conscious, in the shape of primordial hallucinations, a psychotic language of the real comes to the fore. And this language of privation and loss "speaks" the body at the edge of anxiety, in words of isolation, destitution, helplessness, despair, insult, and blasphemy.[18]

Although Freud concentrated on the primary and secondary differences of narcissism in 1920, he had not abandoned his 1914 notion of a narcissism contemporaneous with the formation of the ego through identification with others—a theory that hearkened back to the "Three Essays on the Theory of Sexuality" (1905), where love was either narcissistic (auto-erotic) or anaclitic (for another).[19] And even after proposing the id-ego-superego topology in 1923, Freud sometimes maintained that narcissistic identifications governed mental functions. But Freud's idea is far from Lacan's discovery that the fantasy—as the matrice of all meaning in psychoanalysis—has as its basis the imaginary function of castration, based as it is on the sexual non-rapport.[20] Viewing even the simplest idea of a contiguity between the ego and narcissistic investment as a borrowing from Melanie Klein, or as a regression to Freud's 1895 "Project for a Scientific Psychology," many critics have clearly not assimilated Lacan's rethinking of subject, object, ego, and drive.[21] Nor have they taken account of Jacques-Alain Miller's on-going distinction of the ego from the subject. Belonging to the imaginary order of images, insignia and *sinthomes*, the ego relates to the imaginary other through the fantasy. But the fantasy is cojoined with the symbolic via the subject's lack ($) or castration.

In the "Project" Freud posited the ego as a specific formation within unconscious memory systems, rather than as an essential subject of *being* in the sense of classical philosophy. By taking the Freudian ego of unconscious memory as an *innate* object, Laplanche marked his own departure from Lacan's teaching in 1968, a fact Lacan commented upon in Anika Lemaire's book.[22] But as early as the 1950s Lacan had already pointed out that even if the Freudian ego of the "Project" were invested with unconscious energy, one could only wonder why Freud failed to connect the primary-process unconscious of this same study to the ego.[23] Rather, Lacan suggested, Freud discovered the *truth of the unconscious* in the "Project" precisely *because* he repudiated the idea that the reality of the brain (sublimated in his concept of the neurone) was the same as the unconscious.[24] And not only did Freud not pursue the idea that the unconscious might have some connection to the ego described in that study, Lacan pointed out that the primary-process unconscious of the "Project" has nothing to do with the ego because Freud's mnemic systems had nothing *qualitative*—such as an ego—inscribed in them. Rather, Freud's neuronic systems were *quantities* of energy, reminiscent of Helmholtz's concepts of "mass" and "energy."[25] Nor is the Freudian "engram" of the "Project" assimilable to realities or concepts such as image, symbol, or any other analogy one might make to a perceived object (*Sem.* II 108). Although Freud evolved a theory of psychic energy in which a death force opposed a life force, many years later than 1895, his idea of energy was that of a tensionless state of inertia at the base of any functioning organism. It was clear to Lacan that no organism can be energized by inertia, any more than an ego can be constructed out of a solipsistic auto-eroticism. Moreover, Freud's explanation in "Beyond the Pleasure Principle" (1920) of why people pursue Eros runs into a similar logical impasse. By linking the concept of a biological inertia at the heart of the drive to the idea of an innate pleasure principle, Freud ended up in this dead-end proposition: that the repetition of fixations—the death drive—causes people to pursue pleasure.[26]

Whenever Freud arrived at a cul-de-sac in this thinking, he cited biology as the *cause* of the given effect. Those post-Freudians who try to base *direct perception* in biology, must argue that representations are images and thoughts derived from the *biological* experience of hallucinated satisfaction. In *Seminar* II Lacan had already shown that no pleasure principle—i.e., a hallucinated satisfaction— could exist without being connected to an outer reality. For if the hallucination of a satisfaction disposes of an energy, one must be able to demonstrate where this energy comes from.

Lacan's careful attentiveness to the dialectical give and take of Freud's own thinking takes us away from post-Freudian disciples who repeat Freud's arguments at the level of content, missing the structural issues at stake. How can there be an *experience* of satisfaction, Lacan asked, if it is not linked to something real? Lacan found the real aspect of Freud's primary hallucinations in elementary fantasies that serve as a first layer of reality. These are constituted in three different orders made out of concrete experiences of the world. While Freud considered hallucinations to be false— indications of fantasy, pleasure seeking, and pathology—Lacan understood that primary fantasies shape individual representations of reality—i.e. subjective perception—out of images, language, the partial drives, and the effects of trauma.

Neither Freud nor Lacan dropped the concept of an ego agent. And although Lacan followed Freud in thinking that no unity comparable to the ego exists at the start of life, he disagreed profoundly with post-Freudians who impute an innate causality to the ego, be it theological, biological, or mythological. Freud argued that the ego is developed by auto-erotic drives that are biologically present in the infant at the start of life, drives unified by a narcissism that arises from primal fantasies he called pleasurable hallucinations.

Lacan asked *what psychic action* would enable an infant to pass from a state of identification with disunified "drives" to a unifying narcissism capable of taking the ego as its own love object. Given that the drives are disunified and the primal fantasies have no perceptual opening to the world, *how* then can narcissism serve as the agent that develops the ego into an object able, in turn, to love itself? Moreover, how can an ego serve as a libidinal reservoir of quantitative energy even before that ego exists? And further, what have ego drives—whose aim is to preserve the biologic individual (according to Freud's Darwinian idea of a perpetuation of the species)—to do with the eroticism of sexual drives?

Lacan depicted an ego constellation that grounds body and thought in a *fiction* of being. Given its function of holding together language, body, and images *as if* they were grounded in something real, the ego *seems* to have always already been *there*, internal to the body. But Lacan's picture of how introjection and projection function to constitute an ego culminates in *new* theories of fantasy, representation, the symbol, transference and incorporation to name a few. Furthermore, the differential categories by which he reinterprets Freud's pathologies—neurosis, psychosis, perversion—show the ego functioning differently in each of these clinical categories. For example, one might speak of an autistic or psychotic narcissism. Colette Soler and Eric Laurent, among others, have demonstrated how negativism itself can be incorporated by an autistic infant as one mode of libidinal investment.[27]

One of Lacan's discoveries reveals the ego as itself a defense, or means of resisting the truth of unconscious desire. Indeed, the ego is constructed *for the purpose* of minimizing the anxiety produced by losses that constitute a void place within being and body—not outside being in heaven, hell, or *in* Heidegger's vase. The ego is driven to seek a different satisfaction than the ones Freud imputed to it: satisfaction of the drives or fantasies. Rather, the ego is driven to annul the anxiety produced by the unbearable pain of lack and loss. In this context, it makes sense to argue that the infant's first corporal satisfactions or pleasurable sensations give rise to desire—not to static fantasy hallucinations—as a *dialectical* call to the other (such as an infant's cry). This "demand" is the desire for connection that Freud called Eros, that Lacan called libido or *jouissance*. Thus seen, drives are themselves constituted on a paradoxical basis, both initiating the cut and attempting to annul the effects of primordial losses that make the primary human goal that of retaining illusions of consistency.

Throughout life humans continue to seek satisfaction via others *because* they first experienced *partial* "objects-cause-of-desire"—the voice, the gaze, the breast, the feces, etc.—in relation to another who seemed to guarantee a continuity between being and body. Lacan gave the name primary *jouissance* to the *substance* that glues together an ego as a collage made of images, words, and libidinal associations. Primary *jouissance* is not, however, innate fantasy or biological energy. It is constituted from the outside world by libidinal or narcissistic investments one might call values or qualities, as opposed to the representational "realities" one might describe as quantities. But *jouissance* is cognizable as such only once it has been lost during nursing, listening, being touched, looking, or being looked at. What remains after the cut is a mark or a unary feature. Traces are left on the body. These compose the libidinal responses we call erogenous zones.

Such inscriptions map or cut up the body itself into imaginary signifiers imposed on the biological organism. These "pure signifiers" are what Lacan called unary traits.[28] They are the first concrete details or wisps of memory that link the infant body to the world in terms of castration that mark the sites where *jouissance* was lost. One can say, then, that *primary identifications* furnish the material that links the body to the world—that shows how matter becomes mind—via necessarily narcissistic effects.[29] Specific signifiers name images that gradually add up to an ego fiction. From the start of life, any family describes an infant as having "Uncle Gene's nose," "Aunt Millie's gift for gab," and so on.

Lacan returned to Freud's "The Ego and the Id" as the source of his theory that the ego is first and foremost a body ego.[30] But it is not merely the Freudian surface entity Lacan had in mind. Rather, the body itself is *the projection of a surface*, cut up into the Borromean signifying chain of real, symbolic, and imaginary categories. Even though it was not until the third period of his teaching (1974–1981) that Lacan portrayed the imaginary as the "mental" or perceptual ordering of the body one has, the roots of this theory lie in his earliest efforts to connect the ego to the libido or sexuality.[31] Although Lacan argued that primordial being is libidinized from the start of life, he rejected Freud's explanation of this phenomenon. Freud argued that sexual development occurs in *instinctual* stages, by way of impersonal biological drives that oppose one another. In contrast with the Freudian ego, the Lacanian ego is not necessarily in conflict with sexuality.

But what did Lacan clarify by portraying the ego and sexuality as connected, rather than as poles in conflict? Lacan argued that because Freud could only view narcissism as pathological, he failed to find a logical link between what he called the ego's narcissistic efforts to preserve the "biological" individual (a Darwinian argument) and the eroticism of the sex drives. Thus, he could not understand *the role of narcissism* in first constituting and then maintaining ego function via libidinal investment in others. But the Lacanian ego is not the libido. It is a semblance of its libidinal investments. As such it is a mask.[32] An object *a*.

Lacan's explanation of how the ego is constituted does not propose a simple introjection of the other *qua* person or parental figure as object-relations theorists have. Indeed, his notion of a mirror structure ought not be confused with its use by theorists like Donald Winnicott or Heinz Kohut who mistook Lacan's concept of a mirror-phase structure for the thing-in-itself: that is, the mother and baby as prototypes of self and other. Even though Winnicott and Kohut split the ego into a dyad that usually refers to a third thing such as a transitional object, a self object, or simply biological energy, this third thing does not itself cause the split as does the phallic signifier or the *point de capiton* of the Father's Name in Lacan's theory.[33]

The *Ichspaltung*

Lacan found the lineaments of Freud's intuition of a literal split in the ego in Freud's second topology. The superego (as a social censor) that Freud imposed between the ego and id is the structural configuration Lacan called the phallic signifier. But the phallic signifier is not a *cultural* agent of law. It is the *effect* of a doubling of the ego between ego ideal (others) and the ideal ego. Generally speaking, however, Freud's idea of the *Ichspaltung* comes from his theory that fetishism corresponds to the mechanisms characteristic of perversion, which he describes as a strange coexistence of contrary propositions concerning the reality of maternal "castration." This coexistence permits a person to *avoid* psychic conflict by removing the sanction against the mother, by repressing the sanction itself as castration. Lacan's proposition includes the *same structure*—but inverted—for neurosis insofar as the ego is concerned. The ego avoids the conflict caused by castration through denial. It also avoids conflict by doubling itself in the imaginary trajectory (other$'\!\diagup$other).

Lacan reformulated Freud's concept of the *Ichspaltung* to explain the distinction between the denials of the speaking subject and the intentionality of *jouissance*. People generally mean something

"more" than is obvious in what they say (although this is not necessarily obvious to the person speaking). While Freud found evidence of splits in the ego only in fetishism and in what he called
the defense of psychosis, Lacan argued that a literal split in the
ego—between the *unconscious* ideal ego formation (o') and the ego
ideals (o) with which individuals identify, even if by only one trait
(Freud's *einziger Zug*)—is inherent in the elemental functions of all
imaginary relations.

In *Donc*, Jacques-Alain Miller is developing the split between
one's ego and one's being which marks individual beliefs with misrecognition and "self-delusion." Indeed, the Lacanian ego is not
defined by its access to reality in terms of conscious perception.
Rather, in its most archaic identifications, a subject is invited to
recognize this being in his ego *qua* devalorized object.[34]

In an opposite direction from Kernberg, Lacan argued that not
only is the conscious (speaking) subject not a unified perceiver nor
an agent of adaptability, synthesis, or integration, neither is the ego
the agency of a total person whose "autonomous" part can be correlated with some absolute and objective reality of good or bad
object relations. Rather, the ego is only one part of the subject
stretched over the four corners Lacan maps in the schema L as:
ego (*moi*), desiring subject (*je*), the other of imaginary relations,
and the Other as site of unconscious meaning production.[35] At the
lower left corner of the schema L, the ego is a narcissistic fiction
which papers over its own roots in the unconscious identifications
underlying its apparent unity. Since ego boundaries are limited to
a few narcissistic ideals and a set of myths acquired in childhood
and modified throughout life—except in psychosis, in which identifications are petrified—narcissism imposes a subjective intentionality on conscious speech which people erroneously try to reify and
verify in the name of objectivity.

Lacan argued here that the split between the speaking subject of
language and that of unconscious fantasies does not appear in ego
myths, however. Although an apparently whole ego is the conventional means by which language denies (*Verneinung*) that the ego
is rooted in anything other than itself, the split between language
and ego fictions gives the individual a way to believe in misrecognized truths about his or her being. Although the split subject appears to function as a unit, Lacan followed Freud's argument regarding the unconscious to show proof of the split between
conscious and unconscious meaning systems in dreams, jokes, slips
of the tongue and pen, psychosis, repetitions, and so on. Although

the ego is generally sure of itself, an agent of certainty whose doubts prove its convictions, a purveyor of the "self" as an ideology or system of set beliefs, Lacan gives us this stunning insight: what we call the ego is a knotting of the real (*a*), the symbolic *je*, and the imaginary ideal that keep people blind, thus protecting them from the real. Encounters with the real—be it the loss of a beloved, of a cherished myth, or of the place in which one lives—bring one face to face with the void, shattering, or at least shaking, illusions of unity and oneness in one's ego universe.

Lacan's ego is closer to the subject in "Beyond the Pleasure Principle" (1920) that blocks "death" from view by its repetitive function of papering over a real hole in being, than to Freud's various designs of the ego. Lacan's ego is certainly not a reality principle contrasted to a pleasure principle. Nor is it the surface of the Freudian id—unless one wants to name it a talking id (an *Es* or *ça*). At that level it resembles the "talking unconscious" described in Freud's first theory of the symbol in "The Interpretation of Dreams" (1901). The ego's function is not, however, to "fulfill wishes" within the privacy of sleep and in the absence of a censor, but rather to compensate for an eighteen-month period of relative helplessness via the images and words that constitute the ego as a *semblance* of an identity that protects one from the stark horror of the real (that societies have mythologized as hell, purgatory, etc.).

In his 1957–1958 seminar Lacan taught that the earliest experiences of biological need begin to constitute a desiring subject by aiming not at some fantasized satisfaction, but at real satisfaction.[36] In a similar fashion, dream desire aims at real satisfaction, not a fantasy (pretend) solution. Freud erred in his understanding of dreams, Lacan argued, by confusing the narcissistic ego with the unconscious and then placing both on the side of fantasy. Lacan portrayed dream desire as the home of the ego which sends messages to and from the Other, thereby attesting to the dialectical separation between ego and the Other. When the dream fades, the ego, dwelling somewhere between consciousness and the unconscious, shows a point beyond where consciousness cannot go: the place of the Other.

Lacan's theory of a split in the ego itself finds a shadow in Freud's dynamic system where the ego defends against the unconscious, equated with the repressed. Although the Lacanian ego is constructed as a defense against pre-mirror fragmentations and losses (death effects), it later defends against a primary-process scandal: it was formed in relation to others and is reconstituted within imaginary relations, making "alienation" the truth of being. This re-pressed knowledge is uncanny, haunting. The primary-process scandal is not sexual knowledge, then, but the real of human in-consistency and the fear of the real Otherness that inhabits us like an underwater emitting station. Like the ego in Freud's dynamic system, Lacan's ego experiences anxiety, but it also defends against anxiety. One might think of Melanie Klein's concept of object cleav-age here, but it is Freud's *Ichspaltung* which finally convinces.

Unlike Freud's ego of the dynamic system, however, the Lacanian Other is in dialectical conflict with its own ego through a dynamic form of repression, giving a certain ongoing malaise to conscious life which thus, retains the marks of its unconscious formation. Although the ideal ego is formed by the symbolic in the mirror phase, it only surfaces in the language employed in transference—that is, insofar as it projects a set of "self" myths constituted around the four principal unconscious signifiers Lacan recognized as re-lation, procreation, love, and death. Both ordinary discourse and ego narcissism serve as ways to resist the knowledge of the uncon-scious, to protect the ego's illusion of objectivity and its identifi-cation with "reality." Clearly the ego's inherent narcissism keeps it from recognizing in its very *Urbild* an identification with a neg-ative satisfaction, a death-like *jouissance* (Miller, *Donc*, course of February 2, 1994). But this picture of the ego itself as a principle of resistance makes more sense if one understands how Lacan rein-terpreted Freud on the issue of drive energy.

Drive and the Ego

The first pulsions that drive the ego are imagistic and verbal rep-resentations—Freud's *Niederschriften* (inscriptions) or his *Wahr-nehmungszeichen* (perception marks)—whose energy comes from purely physical need, but quickly becomes "psychic;" i.e., attached to desire. The primordial fantasies that structure libidinal energy do not, however, derive from innate infantile sexual feelings as Freud thought, or from pre-birth fantasies as Melanie Klein argued, but from the *jouissance* invested in images and objects.

Lacan translated Freud's *Besetzung* (occupation) as *investisse-ment*. One is "occupied" by things, busy with them, in the sense that desire is "invested" in objects. Such investment (or cathexis) is narcissistic and "thing" oriented. And it gives rise to the sec-ondary identifications Freud called secondary narcissism. Insofar as unconscious investments infiltrate consciousness in a dynamic and temporal unveiling of historical material throughout life, one begins to see how Lacan could attach the primary-process unconscious to secondary-process thought by reconceptualizing drive as a montage whose energy bases lie in *jouissance*.

Lacan answered Freud's question about the source of energy that serves reality. Narcissistic passion replaces the instinctual id. The goal of drive energy, in Lacan's recasting, is the desire to be loved which comes into conflict with the *demand* that one be loved as the ego one is. The libidinal object is not desire itself, then, but the joining of aim and object in the *desire* to be desired. Though Lacan retained the four terms by which Freud qualified *Trieb*—pressure, source, object, goal or aim—he located the *source* of drive in Eros and Thanatos, not in the body *qua* biological organism.

Although the ideal ego is an agent of constancy that aims at a tensionless state of oneness or *jouissance*, i.e., the imaginary illusion that loving another (Eros) can make one whole, its repetitions produce negative *jouissance* (Thanatos). Primary drive, thus, aims at an illusory mirror-stage consistency, while "secondary" *jouissance* is linked to narcissistic self-verification through identification with one's *own* requisites for satisfaction. But such verification requires one to cross the threshold of constancy imposed by Freud's pleasure principle because of its dependency on external—thus inconstant—sources. Drive is, thus, greater than the sum of its parts.

The term "death drive" appeared in Freud's *Beyond the Pleasure Principle* in 1920, and resulted in a reversal of his whole theory of drives, moving from drive to ego, and making of *Trieb* "somatic demands upon mental life." Its purpose was to reaffirm the fundamental economic theory of psychoanalysis—the tendency to zero constancy—and to give metapsychological status to its numerous discoveries regarding aggressiveness and destructiveness. In 1961 Heinz Lichtenstein proposed that an identity principle replaces the death instinct. In 1936 Lacan had proposed the ego as a strategy of defense for blocking the apprehension which comes from *situating* the infant body in the world. In the 1950s Lacan described the beyond in the pleasure principle as the principle of repetition whose modes are a few ego signifieds by which individuals try to guarantee their being at the level of their *position* in a social signifying chain.

By reinterpreting Freud's ego ideals as alter egos of the ideal ego, Lacan made more and more explicit statements. He praised the work of Melanie Klein who showed the centrality of the body as the real and fantasmatic origin of identification and symbolization. But Lacan's pre-specular infant, unlike Klein's, has no sense of boundaries yet, and thus cannot make moral judgments about what to "take in" or "expel" from the body. Rather, a prematuration at birth gives rise to the flux of "perceptual" experience that creates the dynamic conditions underlying introjection, projection and incorporation! Because primordial being is corporal, being itself is libidinized or eroticized from the start of life.

But Lacan rejected Freud's explanations of this phenomenon as caused by instinctual sexual evolutionary stages, impersonal drives, or sexual response to an originary parental sexual scene. In Lacan's redefinition of Freud's concepts, primary narcissism becomes corporal sensations that evolve into the meanings Lacan called "letters" that connect the body to the outside world via the drives. In the same pre-specular period, aggressiveness evolves as the coefficient of narcissism. The earliest imagos of the body—those of disintegration, dismemberment, and bursting—point to aggressive intentions that are, in fact, real frustrations that arise as responses to the losses Lacan calls the experience of the cut. Such aggressiveness later reappears in child's play, dreams, painting, sado-masochistic crimes, perversions, psychotic hallucinations, and so on.

The aggressiveness that characterizes life is not an animal drive, then, but a response to the loss of continuity triggered by any cut into ego fictions which causes humiliation or the loss of prestige. Aggressiveness is not just a part of the libido, then, but is a companion to the narcissism one finds at the base of the paranoiac structure of the human ego. In this picture, narcissism, "self"-worth, and identification with others are continually at war. Not only does one ego fail to impose its own ideal on the other, it also fails to mirror the other as the other wants to be. Yet narcissism holds the personality together by its negative effects of alienation, rivalry, grandiosity, and aggressiveness that are continually mediated in the symbolic. In psychoanalytic treatment, the analyst's role is to bring the subject who is trapped in a unary logic of narcissism and aggressiveness to an encounter with his or her fictions and alienations and to a realization that the answers to this suffering lie, not in the analyst, but in unraveling ego fictions in order to see the underlying desire that resides in the Other. The tragic lesson psychoanalysis dramatizes is that wanting transcends being, and that the two are enemies "within the same house."

Even though the ideal ego is reflected through others, it is not a psychological reality that others can finalize. Nor can validating it resolve the quest for being which is based on a dissymetry between the little one knows consciously and the mass of knowledge that remains a dark unconscious continent. The idea of "ego mastery" attainable through developmental stages, genital maturity, or object love, is a fiction based on the hope of an impossible wholeness of self. In summary, one can say that the ego builds libidinal relations, conforms to the register of a person's own experience, governs narcissistic and aggressive intentions, overdetermines discourse, and purveys subjective views of reality. But when it is recognized, unconscious truth hidden in ego narcissism is always revealed in a person's relationship to a specific signifier. Thus, the perceptual-imaginary system, whose subject is the ego, resides in a fantasmatic network of meanings made up of concrete images and events, symbolic words and conventions and the real of lethal *jouissance.*

But since the unconscious thinks imaginarily, perception floats between consciousness and the unconscious, unaware of the repressed parts governing it. And even though the ego is unified as a seeming ensemble of relational meanings, it functions to disunify the speaking subject through narcissistic resistance, dogmatism, love, jealousy, ambition, shame, etc.—the "stuff" of everyday life. In human relations, the ego offers itself as a symbol of exchange in the social meaning chain, but sadly, constitutes others by imaginary reduplication of its own narcissistic/aggressive structure— that is, by laws of idealization and hostile exclusion. The ego is not pliable or synthesizing, then, but formal, limited, and irreducible.

Lacan's concept of the ego is difficult to assess or grasp, partly because he made no behavioral separation between conscious and unconscious surfaces. Although the two systems are separate and closed within themselves, the ego connects them because it is both fixed and in play. Although the ego's narcissistic fixations seem substantive and permanent, its cracks and splits turn up in the ups and downs of everyday life. Clearly, the ego is *not an agency* whose ("supposed") defense mechanisms can be analyzed to reveal unconscious truth. Both language and narcissistic identifications *are* defenses that protect humans from the fear of castration, and from the knowledge that an Other speaks them.

Three *Phases of the Mirror-Stage Theory*

Lacan's mirror-stage theory of how the ego is constituted by identifications is germane to his rethinking of narcissism. But one must take account of all three theories of the mirror stage he elaborated between 1950 and 1980. In the 1950s Lacan argued that the body *qua* organism puts on the image of its species. In keeping with Henri Wallon's theory wherein the social and biological intersect, Lacan's mirror-phase neonate bridges the gap that appears at birth between a deficiency in motor skills and neurophysiological development by identifying with images.[37] Lacan called this process of identification (*usually taken to be perception itself*) the constitution of an imaginary order. Identification with others is the means by which an infant satisfies its primary drive to anchor itself against its fragmented experiences of the world. The mechanisms by which identification works—projection, introjection, and incorporation—create an order(ing) of the forms of the world that gradually constitutes an ego. Lacan taught that this ego—or self symbol—is constructed quite *literally*, however, not only from the objects of its attachments, but also from the precise details of touch, images, sounds, and words which embed themselves in the infant's flesh. Subsequently, identifications excite the nervous system, not the reverse.[38]

In the 1950s, therefore, Lacan considered the ego to be an imaginary constellation of identifications.[39] In his lecture given to the London Society (1951) he described the ego as "very close to a systematic misrecognition of reality."[40] But he put forth a second theory in the 1960s, according to which the symbolic dimension imposes language on the body.[41] We take on identities just as we put on body images, each seeking to incarnate ourselves as some ideal in the eyes of others. The mirror is an impasse—not a reflection—because each person wants to be verified as the ideal he or she imagines him- or herself to be. But this ideal is an unconscious formation already inscribed, not in the other person, but in the Otherness of what one does not know about oneself.

Lacan's theories in the 1950's and 1960's were based on Henri Wallon's work on imprinting behavior and social relativity in the constitution of human emotions, the research of Lorenz and Tinbergen on animal imprinting, the phenomenon of transitivism by which eighteen-month-old children impute their actions to each other, and studies of eight-month-old infants who mirror each other's gestures. But Lacan's originality lay in his grasping that the infant's identification with the human *Gestalt*, between six and eighteen months, is a *dialectical* instance which permanently situates any individual in a line of fiction and alienation. Although various commentators have found no *evidence* in Lacan's writings to prove that human mentality is developed through a mirror phase, his own teaching is replete with evidence: his study of paranoia in relation to narcissism and aggressiveness and the role of the double; his early theories of ethnology in *Les complexes familiaux*; the influence of object-relations theories and of Hegel's dialectic; the internal logic of his own work on narcissism; and the successes he accumulated in his work theorizing the cause and treatment of the psychoses.

These first two theories go a long way toward explaining how "mind" and "emotion" are constituted. And they contradict materialist (biological and economic) theories of cause. Although the newborn has sophisticated capacities for response to the world around it, the Lacanian ego does not come from any innate perception system. Rather, perception itself is formed out of the infant's experience of identifying with images of things, *jouissance*, unary traits and ego ideals. Later, however, the speaking subject will not be able to think of these unconscious aspects in any unified fashion, for there is no consistent point of contact between conscious and unconscious meaning systems except in the interdependence of humans on each other (the transference) and in repeating fantasies and dreams. The composite ego which results from its asynchronic composition is a bric-à-brac *fiction of identity* that gives the lie to theories portraying a "true" self to be unearthed.[42]

Although current studies in child development research unwittingly support Lacan's theories on the concrete development of the ego, post-Freudian psychoanalytic theory has tended to equate perception with consciousness. Such theory sees memory, cognition, and ego development as late occurrences, while the unconscious is equated with impersonal developmental stages and the biologically instinctual, if it is considered at all. Lacan, on the contrary, portrayed infants as passing from a state of nearly complete dependence on others to degrees of independence by way of primary (spatial) identifications. But later, individuals always anticipate being made whole via others, envisioned as orthopedic forms of totality because the visual seems complete within itself. These are the *secondary identifications* Freud called *secondary narcissism* (or the investment of self in other). But Freud's divisions into primary and secondary did not clarify the problem. This lot fell to Lacan who points to a terrible paradox: the human hope of finding satisfaction via others evolves as a desire for wholeness in which two persons *seem* adequate to fill each other's lacks. Yet the terms of fulfillment for each were constituted in childhood in the highly

specific criteria of the Other, and so can only be momentarily fulfilled by another.

Although Freud described the ego as "a precipitate of abandoned
object-cathexes" in "The Ego and the Id" (1923), he later argued
that a healthy ego will fend off those influences. It is the contrary,
Lacan said. Individuals cannot fend off the alien objects that constitute their being at the level of ideal ego out of identifications with
ego ideals. Nor can one *have* the distance from the ego that constitutes the "awareness" that would enable one to fend off unhealthy
parts. Thus, analysis is painful—if it is curative—precisely because
examination of ego identifications requires one to destroy pieces
of the ideal ego that already constitute one's illusions of *being* a
fixed self. Moreover, the ego—made up of bric-à-brac pieces—cannot be cured by being integrated into an already pre-existing whole
or true self, for such does not exist.

It is not surprising that throughout life individuals are confused
about what each can give to the other. One might call confusion a
signifier for blurred lines between sameness and difference. A mirror-stage identification with a *Gestalt* is an unnatural phenomenon
that constitutes an alienation between outer form (big and symmetrical)—an ideal unity because it seems whole—and inner feelings of affective chaos. Forever after, a person's sense of being will
vacillate because humans must anticipate their own images/ideals
in the *opaque* mirrors of the other's gaze. All successive separations,
or identificatory mergers, replay the original drama of taking on a
being from the outside, and then repressing it. Moreover, speech
can only try to represent it, not *be* it. In other words, the mirror-
stage drama moves from a sense of insufficiency to one of anticipation, but it does not finally lead to unity or a wholeness in being.

Consequently, human relations always entail a replay of discord,
not a realization of harmony. Having challenged Freud's idea that
the ego evolves from biological or developmental first causes, Lacan
offered his theory of a second exigency; i.e., the primacy of the
symbolic order or the outside world on being and body. In this
purview, identity might be described as the behaviors and knowledge individuals build up around a few master signifiers derived
from key identifications. Yet clearly the highly idiosyncratic conjunction of images, words, losses, and desires imposed on a child,
and the subsequent variability of their interplay, make of any so-
called identity a uniquely dynamic constellation. This constellation
is not reducible to gender or a unified agency of any kind—ego or
other.

But Lacan's mirror-stage *concept* only takes on its fuller meaning insofar as one deduces a prior phase during which symbolization of the infant body begins in pleasure and displeasure. But because an infant first experiences the world in the absence of any means to judge it, pleasure or displeasure are measured in relation to the infant's *jouissance* or bodily experience of the primary object. Contrary to Melanie Klein, however, Lacan argued that pre-specular material is *incorporated* by effect, insinuation, and associational relation, not by intrauterine fantasy, realistic recording, imprinting, or by reparation of loss.

Pointing to the fulfilling power of visual images that Freud discussed, Lacan added the castrating force of the gaze. Furthermore, he evolved a different theory of incorporation than Freud's idea of it as a purely corporal experience characteristic of the oral stage. While Lacan's idea is closer to Melanie Klein's view that partial objects are incorporated, he stresses that the objects are *partial* and fragmentary (not whole). Extending his concept of incorporation to the global effects of an environment and to the mysterious power of words as well, Lacan says one can see the *oral drive* as manifest in words like "eating up a book."

Much has been made of Lacan's early mirror-stage idea concerning human prematuration (or fetalization) as that which creates the necessary condition for humans to form a libidinal/identificatory relationship to the world. But Lacan's point was, rather, that the resultant ego that represents itself as "being itself" is not itself. It is, rather, a representation or mask covering over an actual split in knowledge. But the ego serves as a defense against anxiety caused by the affective decentering one encounters when confronted with loss. Yet, precisely because the ego is split from the start, people must seek themselves *outside* themselves. It is not surprising that identificatory (transference) relations with others seem to fill up the lack in being, even when the engagement with others takes a negative form.

One might think, upon first encountering Lacan's first and second mirror-stage theories, that he is merely repeating Freud's 1905 theory, wherein ego instincts aim at the maternal object only because she provides food.[43] Rather, Lacan stressed the *effects* of losing (or not losing) primary partial objects of which the breast is only one. His point is this: Actual biological events—experiences such as feeding or contact with an organ like the breast—do not constitute a self or an ego.[44] Nor does the fact that children want to possess their mothers arise out of any innate incest wish. Children are possessive, first of the mother (and later of others), *because* the mother (or some other primary caretaker) served as their first anchor of constancy, protecting them against the castration or lack that brings anxiety in the wake of any loss, even a momentary one.

In Lacan's *third* elaboration of the mirror stage, he returned to Freud's emphasis on repetition in his theory of *Trieb* or the drives. And Lacan surprises us by arguing that repetition is the *libidinal* glue that gives consistency to being and body.[45] Thus, the ego is not a subject of free will, but paradoxically, an object of drive. Because individuals value consistency—i.e., the absence of anxiety—above all else, they remain attached to repetitions that are consonant with the *jouissance* of the familiar. Sadly, people hold on to the fixity of symptoms as a guarantee of consistency, often at the cost of life, freedom, and joy. In Lacan's third theory, the mirror-stage ego is pared down to its libidinal reality as the object of alien desire and *jouissance*. Given that its limits are anchored in the corporal experiences of pleasure or displeasure, the ego remains stable by staying fixated to the already known. But because the ego is both a principle of resistance to radical change and always in flux, any person's narcissism is susceptible of deception and despair in the world of identificatory trade relations and within its economy of desire.

One could say that Lacan's pre-specular hallucinatory "ego" is akin to the object *a* as cause-of-desire, resembling Freud's ego from the economic system which aims at the pleasurable constancy of physical survival, taken as libidinal comfort. But in Lacanian theory, the incipient form of the ego takes on the added burden of defining a consistency in body by reference to *outside* imagoes, thereby ensuring that the ego will later contain the seeds of inconstancy within itself. By building on pre-specular identificatory fusions (one might call them primary unities or moments of *jouissance*), an infant shows its joy at "self"-recognition as a manifestation of the link between love, familiarity, and narcissistic response. But since the primordial ego is composed of identifications from, by, and for others, it is, by definition, subjugated to external desires and judgmental gazes. This dialectical interplay between self and other *in* the ego itself—o⁄°—makes the quest for recognition paramount in life.

Freud described conflict as arising from the libidinal push for pleasure, up against the demands of reality. Lacan blurred Freud's positivistic division by placing a divided, frustrated, semi-paranoid ego at the surface of language. And he defined this "subject" as frustrated by an object—the *petit a*—which is not antithetical to it, but in which its desire is alienated. The ego, thus seen, is not the agent of strength Freud assumed it to be, but rather a slave to the *illusion* of freedom and autonomy. Lacan reoriented analysts toward helping analysands to de-objectify their fixations in their own ideal ego. Freud's *wo Es war, soll Ich werden*, suggested that psychic well-being lay in replacing the pleasure principle (or id) by the reality principle (or ego). Lacan recast Freud here to say: where the ego (Es) was, there shall "I" (*Ich*) become. Cure becomes synonymous with the gain in freedom won from a de-being of what we take for being. Thus, although Lacan's ego is the subject of narcissistic individuality, it is not the ego or subject in the psychological sense. It is, rather, an unbridgeable gap between perception and experience that we try to "translate" in the *forms* of our communicating.

Narcissism and Identification

By now it should be clear that narcissism is the love of self learned via other persons by means of identification.[46] Lacan found, furthermore, that the problems of identification Freud tried to solve in various ways are finally resolvable only from the vantage point of understanding what causes psychosis, an issue which we shall take up in greater detail further on. What is clear is that Lacan's reconceptualization of identification and narcissism was heavily indebted to Freud's 1921 essay "Group Psychology and the Analysis of the Ego." In forming his theory of how the ego is constituted by identifications, he was particularly influenced by the distinction Freud made between an ideal ego and an ego ideal.[27] Freud himself never pursued the implications of his own distinction wherein the ego is split between a primarily narcissistic, auto-erotic, infantile *ideal ego*, and his idea that love arises out of investments in *ego ideals* who are meant to validate the ideal ego. By pursuing the idea of a difference between primary and secondary identifications here, Lacan developed Freud's own distinction. And Lacan showed Freud's concepts of primary and secondary identification to be as problematic as his concepts of primary and secondary narcissism. For example, Freud described identification as functioning intermittently at pre-Oedipal and Oedipal stages, and as alternately active, passive, or reciprocal; as primarily attached to the mother, or sometimes to the father; and as a problem in paranoia.[48]

Object-relations theorists have picked up threads of the various

Freudian ideas just mentioned, stressing the process of identification and differentiation in self-other relations. And some innovators,
such as Heinz Kohut, have not shied away from rethinking narcissism as well as identification.[49] But like Freud, Kohut remained
convinced that narcissism is fundamentally a pathology, a failure
to develop an *independent* or autonomous sense of self-love. Furthermore, by collapsing narcissism and identification into one entity, Kohut did not see what Freud was pursuing by keeping the
concepts separate. Since Lacan retained Freud's insight that the
narcissistic investment of objects and the process of identification
were different phenomena, he was able to figure out how each
functioned. By distinguishing between the *ego ideals* that first constitute one's narcissistic sense of being in the imaginary (i[o]), and
the *ideal ego* (I[O]), he discovered that the ideal is identified with
the point in the Other (a *symbolic* order construct) where one finds
oneself worthy of love. Lacan therefore deduced that identification
is what separates narcissism from the superego, which carries no
element of identification. Rather, the superego comes from the
real.[50] It is what Lacan called the real father or the death drive.
That is, the principle of interdiction contradicts itself by obscenely
enjoying its very power to forbid, prohibit, and deprive. Indeed one
might call this the "normative" position of morality.

Unlike Freud, Lacan did not, however, see narcissism as pathological *per se*, but as the irreducible, atemporal cornerstone of the
ego. In his 1932 dissertation Lacan proposed that narcissistic pathology was caused by the process of identification rather than by
sociological defects or biological development.[51] Thus, narcissism
as such is inseparable from its mode of functioning by identificatory
relations with others. Its difficulties do not derive from the *fact* of
self-love (which some have labeled a "descriptive narcissism") at
the base of the ego. Narcissistic problems come, rather, from a
person's relation to the primary object Lacan first called the primordial mother. He also described this "primary object" as the
only Good, thereby reconceptualizing Aristotle's efforts to define
the Sovereign Good.[52] But by incorporation of the primary object
Lacan did not mean that one actually "takes in" another person as
a kind of whole object. Rather, an infant incorporates specific traits
of persons and things associated with pleasure or displeasure at the
same time he or she responds to the Ur-objects that cause desire:
the mamilla, the feces, the (imaginary) phallus, the urinary flow,
the gaze, the voice, the phoneme, the nothing (Lacan, *Ecrits*, 314–

15). And matrices of nonsense meaning and *jouissance* meaning build up around these objects.

Jacques-Alain Miller attributes these primary sensations to a primary *jouissance*.[53] At this level the ego becomes an object *a*, the fundamental and real kernel of a person's being which is neither container nor contained, inside nor outside. It is both inside and outside: an extimate object.[54] The object *a*, as used here, refers to that which is precious to one because it is composed of residual details incorporated in the wake of losses first attached to the mother. These "objects" that cause desire—and that one subsequently desires in substitute forms—can be described as giving rise to desire as the desire for annulling loss. Desire is not for objects in and of themselves, then, but for the fulfillment one equates with constancy, consistency, oneness, unity, and stability—a guarantee or grounding to one's life.

The "romanticized" dyad of mother/child is the paradigmatic couple on which illusions of oneness and goodness are built. Lacan's genius was to show the obvious here: there is no symbiosis between the mother and child *qua* persons. Symbiosis occurs, rather, between signifiers, between objects, and within the order of signifiers Lacan calls the Other. But no object *a* is ever a signifier. It is absolute in the sense of not being dialectical or dialectizable.[55] In 1988 Jacques-Alain Miller clarified Lacan's solution to Freud's quandary concerning how ideas can be linked to drives (*Triebreprasentanzen*); i.e., Lacan's theory of the object *a*.[56] Freud remained perplexed as to how a *quota* of affect (the pleasure principle that cannot be suppressed) can be divided from the *Reprasentanz* (Lacan's reality principle or the positivized phallus [Φ]) and yet *remain* as an excess of feeling. Lacan symbolized this surplus value or excess in *jouissance* by the *petit a* which denotes a nonutilitarian residue between the libido and language: $\frac{O}{J}$ (*a*). The object *a* joins the pleasure principle to the reality principle by the narcissism of identification, then, at the point where the subject *is* itself a libidinal object that language tries to re-present (Miller, "To Interpret the Cause," 49–50).

It is not surprising that mourning and melancholia have long given poets material for writing about human suffering, or that Freud tried to describe the energy that fuels the ego by trying to account for the ego's depletion. But it is Lacan's theory of the object—not Freud's—that is an innovation in psychoanalytic thought here. The object *a*, as Lacan defined it, denotes a palpable something one seeks to replace loss itself, thereby seeking to fill up a positivized void *in* being and body. One can study the function of this object in psychosis where the mother *qua* primary object is not lost. The logical operation of separation as conceptualized by Lacan describes a relation to the primary object in neurosis, perversion, and normativity. The failure to lose the imagined primary object constitutes a psychotic subject, structurally incapable of understanding the reality principle. Lacan renamed the reality principle as a signifier for the incorporation of law at the level of "no" (the Name [or non/*nom*] -of-the-Father that gives rise to the Oedipal structure).[57]

Thus, Lacan isolated four structures in which narcissism functions differently, yet according to a precise logic: the phobic, the neurotic, the perverse, and the psychotic. But the variations in function all arise from one structure: the psychic separation (or not) from the mother at the level of imaginary castration ($-\varphi$).

Psychosis and the Ideal Ego

The four paths narcissism can take do not define health versus pathology—all of which are inscribed *within* the realm of phallic signification (the law of no), except for psychosis. That is, an infant inscribes his or her desire in an ideal ego/I(O) whose point of reference is the sexual difference itself. The difference between males and females becomes a third term or signifier to be repressed, denied, repudiated, or foreclosed. In the coming together of identification and libido (or narcissistic investment in the other), an infant's biological anatomy is imaginarily built upon myths about gender. The consequent result is a confusion between *having* and *being*, adjudged in relation to the imaginary phallic organ (its presence, absence, lack, or potential loss), that comes to define the phallus as a construct concerning reality, rather than as the biological organ it sometimes represents.[58]

At the social level, individuals usually arrange their lives within the conventions of the accepted sexual masquerade. Neurotics, for example, suffer at the level of *being* by identifying unconsciously with the split between the masculine and the feminine. While the obsessional is troubled in language, figures of loss plague the hysteric. Perversion, in Lacanian theory, does not concern homosexual or heterosexual libidinal object choice *per se*, but an effort to incarnate the mother's fantasy of what the phallus should be (or should have been) as an instrument of *jouissance*. In psychosis there is no inscription for the phallus as a signifier for the child is already the mother's phallus, the *object* of her *jouissance*. Psychotic suffering comes precisely from not having been *signified* in identification by a "law" of difference powerful enough to separate him or her from the excesses of the mother's *jouissance*. Consequently, the psychotic subject's body exists in a unary conjunction between the imaginary and the real ɤ, as the *real* object of the mother's desire (diCiaccia, "Quelques notes," 187–88).

Neurotics—hysterics and obsessionals—suffering from a frozen narcissism, a denial of castration, a refusal to accept that anything was lacking in the family novel, *fail to repress childhood*. This keeps them from entering the social order of debt and exchange as easily as does the "master" who seems happy and in control of his or her destiny.[59] The neurotic pays a painful price for staying fixed in archaic *jouissance*, for trying to relive a flawed childhood. Repeating painful scenes in present life, these eternal sons and daughters replay particular failures, remaining enchained to dead letters of the past in preference to the vital pleasures of the present.

In perversion, castration is repudiated or disavowed in the unconscious, making this subject the instrument of his mother's lacking *jouissance*. His principal goal is to ensure that the Other enjoys. Although fetish objects sometimes play a large role in perversion, ensuring *jouissance* by some replaced attachment to the mother taken as a "forbidden" object of desire (black stockings, blue velvet, etc.), *perverse* fantasies or fetish objects are essential to any sexual *jouissance*. In psychosis the image of an omnipotent mother who lacks nothing is maintained to the point of the child's *foreclosing* the importance of difference or Otherness. Thus, the psychotic subject experiences the realm of distinctions—the symbolic—as intrusive. Indeed, so powerful is the reign of *jouissance* in psychosis that identification with the ideal ego actually substitutes for the phallic signifier which normally inscribes law at the level where language and "no" coalesce, splitting knowledge into conscious and unconscious parts. Faced with the lack of the father's "Name," the psychotic puts himself in this place in order to supplement the lack. Although his eternal quest is for a father—not a mother, lover, or child—at the level of ego he incarnates himself as that which guarantees the order of the universe.[60] Since the ideal ego formation regulates the psychotic's mental activity, rigidity and petrification rule the day.[61]

That psychoanalysts have pinpointed narcissism as a particular problem means only this: that neurotics, perverts, and psychotics who are suffering seem "self"-absorbed by contrast with the relatively untroubled (anaclitic) souls. But there is clearly no structure untroubled by narcissism. This is another way of saying that we are all subjects of our pathologies. In Lacanian terms, being absorbed with "self" means being proximate to the object a: the remaining kernel of the image that first caused desire. In Lacan's reconceptualization of the relation of the ego to narcissism, there are two possible paths within these four structures: identification with social law (the Other) or identification with *jouissance* (the drives). While neurotics are captive to the past, often having given up altogether on personal *jouissance*, perverse and psychotic subjects are captivated by *jouissance* such that they live out their "Oedipal" dramas at the level of sexuality and the body.

Lacan reversed Freud's theory of narcissism by showing that identification with objects outside the organism forms a narcissistic structure one might just as well call the ego. Einstein's "relativity principle" applies to the universe of egos as well as to the physical universe; the ego coheres—paradoxically—as a seemingly autonomous unity, but only in reference to others. We depend on others to acquire a primary narcissism—an ideal ego—in the first place which we in turn verify and reify in a secondary narcissism of transferential interaction with others (or ego ideals). Moreover, identification with others serves as a buffer between the imaginary and the real, thereby regulating narcissistic being.

Narcissism and Psychosis

Lacan said he had to take up the Freudian problem of narcissism again because the clinic of paranoia made it necessary. Indeed, anyone who adheres to a literal mirror-relation concept of Lacan's early work will not see how he advances beyond object-relations theories in clarifying how the ego is constituted. If, however, one considers his early work on the ego and the imaginary in light of his work on psychosis in the seminar on the *Sinthome* (1975–1976), it becomes clear that narcissism cannot be reduced to the ego, to the imaginary, or to identification. Indeed, Lacan's work on psychosis is crucial to an understanding of how the ego is constituted as a dialectical principle—in light of the failure of this dialectic in psychosis.

Where Anglophone analysts have stressed the idea of the strong paranoid ego, Lacan studied the *structure* of paranoia. As early as his doctoral thesis in 1932 Lacan had proposed that narcissistic disorders were caused by something other then heredity or poverty. If another person is seen as a persecutor, an *effect* of paranoia—as in the Aimée case or the Papin sister case—Lacan suggested that the *other* may also be the *cause* of paranoia. But Lacan did nothing more to advance his theory of psychosis until his third seminar on the psychoses (1955–1956). And toward the end of his first period of teaching (1953–1964), Lacan made a resumé of that particular seminar in "On a question preliminary to any possible treatment of psychosis."[62] In this *écrit* he tried to develop a logic of the psychoses. To that end he elaborated the schema L, the schema R, and the schema I, three schemas that elaborate a theory in which the Father's Name is foreclosed as a phallic signifier or reality principle of social law (S_1).

In his second theory of the psychoses, articulated twenty years later, Lacan's focus had changed radically. He had discovered that something other than the Father's Name could function to knot the orders together, thus giving a kind of stability to the psychotic's suffering. This something is the object *a* which functions like a kind of ego, as a supplement to the imaginary order.[43] From this one can deduce that the formation of the ego is not concomitant with the installation of narcissism. One might even speak of narcissism— a clinging to certain identifications—as the lack of any self agency one could call an ego. While the ego is an imaginary structure that relates itself to others via ideals (i[o]), the ideal ego is a narcissistic formation, contiguous with the symbolic order (I[O]). Agnes Aflalo explains that since individual narcissism is the result of any person's experiences of identification, its imaginary formation is strictly correlative with the *symbolic* coming into being of the ideal ego.[64]

Lacan pointed out in his seminar on James Joyce (*Le sinthome* [1975–1976]) that while the ego usually functions by adding and subtracting identifications throughout life, the psychotic ego is non-changing, non-dialectical.[65] Supported by the single identifications given by the mother, the psychotic clings to these primordial identifications—a great name in the symbolic, a symbiotic identification with a well-fed and protected animal, etc.—as an "imaginary security blanket." Such identifications function to knot the three orders together as a pseudo Name-of-the-Father (Liart, p. 114). Thus, the *name* of a great person or precise images (superman, the wife of God, a kitten who drinks only milk, animal protection agencies) constitute a supplemental imaginary, the imaginary order of representational distance being the order that lacks in psychosis. Although the psychotic is *in* language—in the symbolic—and speaks a pseudo-academic discourse, he does not have the distance from the symbiotic mirror illusion of a Oneness of two that other subjects have, allowing them to constitute the imaginary as an ordering of distance from the primary object.[66]

This insight—that the psychotic's narcissism is built upon a single identification that replicates itself in myriad forms—enabled Lacan to understand how narcissism and identification both differ *and* interact. Both processes function to constitute and maintain the ego agent and its objects by introjection, projection, and incorporation. In schizophrenia, on the contrary, the ego is always at risk of fragmenting, thereby dramatizing the mirror-stage experience of the *corps morcelé*. Indeed, in schizophrenia the ego functions as a body surface always being taken apart and put together, *without* the cushioning help of a Father's Name to anchor imaginary identifications that enables most people to keep the unbearable real at a distance. Yet, in a sense, paranoia seems more mysterious than schizophrenia because the paranoid ego is unified to the body. That is, the paranoid seems *almost* normal. But insofar as paranoia is the condition of never having separated from the mother's *jouissance*, bodily *jouissance* itself—not social law—establishes the rules by which he or she will live in the symbolic.

Lacan asked what role the ego plays in constituting the complete self-absorption of the paranoid subject. He arrived at the following answer. Paranoid narcissism compensates for the foreclosure of the signifier for sexual difference—that is, for lack of a mirror image of oneself as separate from the mother. Not only does this subject not lose the mother as primary object, he or she must embody the *lost* object of the mother's desire at the level of *jouissance*. The cause of paranoia is not, as is usually thought, a problem of perception, lost reality, brain dysfunction, or primitive mentality. Rather, the problem lies at the level of the Other; the language to which the child was first soldered by *jouissance* without the aid of the key differential signifier by which others position themselves in the social dialectic of lack and exchange. The psychotic subject tries to avoid the intrusion of the outside world. He shuns the voice, the gaze, even affectionate touching from others. These are all signs of a presence of Otherness that disturb this subject's *jouissance* because they infer difference, as opposed to the simple, static illusion that things are as they are.[66]

In paranoid narcissism one is confronted with a person whose speech communicates with his or her own ego, not with the spoken desires of other people. The meaning or desire expressed by others is not taken into account, except as a superego command to be slavishly followed or repudiated. "For the psychotic," Liart writes, "there is incessant communication between the emitter and the receiver, without any further relation to the A(*utre*)" (Liart, "Joyce," 115). He is *in* language, but not *in* the social network. One can say that in matters of identification the psychotic deals with the real Other, not the Other of imaginary relations.

In other words, the psychotic has narcissistic being, but no split between the ideal ego and ego ideals. In consequence, such subjects constitute their ego ideals (imaginary relations with others) on the model of their own ideal ego. Not surprisingly, they try to merge with others at the level of a shared *being*. And even though others may serve them as a *medium* of address, or as *witness* to the artic- ulation of their thoughts, these others are never accepted as subjects of demand or desire.[68] Never having exited from the mirror illusion of oneness with the mother's *jouissance*, the psychotic lacks nothing in his or her mentality. The signifier One (the phallic signifier or S_1) for difference has not been inscribed, thus carving lack into the narcissistic ideal image. While lack sends most beings in search of another person to complement them, the psychotic seeks a literal image of him or herself in others, not a supplement to lack. When the psychotic subject is threatened by another person's difference (distance), he treats that other as a persecutor, as the superego Lacan described as an agent of ferocious *jouissance*. When the par- anoid experiences a particular other as an outsider, that person becomes a gaze to flee, a voice to obey, or someone to attack, but never a being of lack with whom one negotiates desire.

Like every person, the psychotic child is only a subject insofar as he or she is plugged into the Other. But unlike other persons, his or her connection to, or awareness of, a dependency on others— that Zenoni calls the imaginary knot—is not symbolized or repre- sented (Zenoni, "Le corps de l'être," 49). Thus, the psychotic child quite literally *carries* the Other who lives from him parasitically. This makes the psychotic subject "inhuman" insofar as he or she lives by *jouissance* alone, excluding the human zone of lack that makes us creatures of the flaw: wanting and desiring.

In his second theory of psychosis, Lacan worked from the idea that the real, symbolic, and imaginary orders are knotted by a symp- tom (Σ) that contains the properties of all three orders in the knot itself. When the *supplemental* imaginary knot ceases to compensate for the lack of an inscription for sexual difference, a psychotic break or episode may ensue. A physical symptom may suddenly appear, or the paranoid's language is suddenly given over to delirious metaphor or fiction that constitutes an effort to reknot the orders, to re-establish "mental" stability. But the delirious system that comes to the fore in the moment of a psychotic break is not absent from the apparently normal life of this subject. The delirious symptom may reside in the subject's writing(s) and subtends all affective modes of his or her being.[69] Finally, it is logical that psychotic language not be dialectically aimed at another person, for the psychotic concretizes words out of a certain knowledge. In this structure one sees a mentality functioning in which the signifier does not vacillate, does not represent a lack in the subject that seeks its response in another person's validation of the signifiers in his or her own unconscious chain of meanings.[70]

Notes

1. Jacques Lacan, "The mirror stage as formative to the function of the I" (1949), *Ecrits: A Selection*, trans. Alan Sheridan (New York: W. W. Norton, 1977), 1–7.

2. Jacques Lacan, *Le séminaire XX (1972–1973): Encore*, ed. Jacques-Alain Miller (Paris: Editions du Seuil, 1975).

3. Jacques Lacan, *De la psychose paranoïaque dans ses rapports avec la personnalité*, Thèse de Doctorat en Médecine, Faculté de Médecine de Paris (Paris: Le François, 1932).

4. David Macey, *Lacan in Context* (London: Verso, 1988). See chap. 3, "Baltimore in Early Morning."

5. Jacques Lacan, *Le séminaire XXII (1974–1975) R.S.I.*, (unpublished seminar); "Session April 15, 1975," *Ornicar?* 5 (1975): 15–66; M. Dewez, "La Topologie dans le Séminaire R.S.I.," *Cahiers du Lycée Logique: Revue de psychanalyse* 4, 1990 7–10: 7.

6. Jacques Lacan, *Le séminaire IV (1956–1957): La relation d'objet*, text established by Jacques-Alain Miller (Paris: Seuil, 1994).

7. Russell, Grigg, "Lacan on Object Relations," *Analysis* 2 (1990): 39–50.

8. Marie-Hélène Brousse, "Feminism with Lacan," *Newsletter of the Freudian Field* 5, 1–2 (1991): 113–28.

9. Havelock Ellis, "Autoeroticism: A Psychological Study" (1898) *Alienist and Neurologist* 19 (1898), 260.

10. Sigmund Freud, "Psycho-Analytic Notes on an Autobiographical Account of a Case of Paranoia (Dementia Paranoides)" (1911), *SE*, 12: 9–82.

11. Sigmund Freud, "Totem and Taboo" (1912–1913), *SE*, 13: 1–161.

12. Sigmund Freud, "On Narcissism: An Introduction" (1914), *SE*, 14: 67–102; "Mourning and Melancholia" (1917 [1915]), *SE* 14, 237–58.

13. See discussion of Jules Masserman in Jacques Lacan, "The function and field of speech and language in psychoanalysis" (1953), in *Ecrits: A Selection*, trans. Alan Sheridan (New York: W. W. Norton, 1977), 30–113.

14. Sigmund Freud, "Papers on Metapsychology" (1915), *SE*, 14: 105–215.

15. Sigmund Freud, "Beyond the Pleasure Principle" (1920), *SE*, 18: 3–64.

16. Melanie Klein, *The Psychoanalysis of Children*, trans. Alex Strachey (London: Hogarth Press, 1937).

17. Jacques-Alain Miller, *Ce qui fait insigne* (unpublished course in the Department of Psychoanalysis, Paris VIII, 1986–1987).

18. Sylvia Tendlarz, "Le savoir entre dévotion et blasphème," *La lettre mensuelle* 96 (février 1991): 12–14.

19. Sigmund Freud, "Three Essays on the Theory of Sexuality" (1905), *SE*, 7: 125–245.

20. Jacques-Alain Miller, *Du symptôme au fantasme et retour* (unpublished course in the Department of Psychoanalysis, Paris VIII, 1982–1983), course of May 4, 1983.

21. Sigmund Freud, "Project for a Scientific Psychology" (1950 [1895]), *SE*, 1: 281–397.

22. See Lacan's comments on Laplanche's theoretical break in Anika Lemaire, *Jacques Lacan*, trans. David Macey (London: Routledge, 1977); xiii–xix.

23. Jacques Lacan, *The Seminar of Jacques Lacan*, Book II: *The Ego in Freud's Theory and in the Technique of Psychoanalysis, 1954–1955*, ed. Jacques-Alain Miller, trans. Sylvana Tomaselli (New York: Norton, 1988).

24. Ibid.

25. Freud, "Project for a Scientific Psychology."

26. Freud, "Beyond the Pleasure Principle."

27. See chapter 5 on the paternal metaphor for further discussion.

28. Jacques Lacan, "Subversion of the subject and the dialectic of desire" (1960), in *Ecrits: A Selection*, trans. Alan Sheridan (New York: W. W. Norton, 1977), 292–325; 314–15.

29. Ibid.

30. Sigmund Freud, "The Ego and the Id" (1923), *SE*, 19: 3–66.

31. Ellie Ragland-Sullivan, "The Imaginary," in *Feminism and Psychoanalysis: A Critical Dictionary*, ed. Elizabeth Wright (Oxford: Blackwell, 1992), 173–76.

32. Jacques-Alain Miller, *De la nature des semblants* (unpublished course in the Department of Psychoanalysis of Paris VIII, 1992–1993).

33. Donald Winnicott, *Playing and Reality* (New York: Basic Books, 1971).

34. Jacques-Alain Miller, *Donc*, (unpublished course in the Department of Psychoanalysis, Paris VIII, 1993–1994), courses of January 26 and February 2, 1994.

35. Jacques Lacan, *Seminar II*, ibid, 109.

36. Jacques Lacan, *Le séminaire V (1957–1958): Les formations de l'inconscient* (unpublished seminar).

37. Henri Wallon, *The World of Henri Wallon*, ed. Gilberg Voyat (New York: Jason Aronson, 1984).

38. Ragland-Sullivan, "The Imaginary," 173.

39. Jacques Lacan, *Le séminaire IX (1960–1961): L'identification* (unpublished seminar), 128.

40. Jacques Lacan, "Some Reflections on the Ego," *International Journal of Psychoanalysis* XXXIV (1953): 1–17; 4–5.

41. Jacques Lacan, *The Four Fundamental Concepts of Psychoanalysis*, ed. Jacques-Alain Miller, trans. Alan Sheridan (New York: W. W. Norton, 1977); 17–28.

42. Jacques Lacan, *The Seminar of Jacques Lacan*, Book VII: *The Ethics of Psychoanalysis 1959–1960*, ed. Jacques-Alain Miller, trans. Dennis Porter (New York: W. W. Norton, 1992).

43. Freud, "Three Essays on the Theory of Sexuality."

44. Lacan, "The Mirror Stage."

45. Ragland-Sullivan, "The Imaginary."

46. Ellie Ragland-Sullivan, "Narcissism," in *Feminism and Psychoanalysis: A Critical Dictionary*, ed. Elizabeth Wright (Oxford: Blackwell, 1992), 271–74.

47. Sigmund Freud, "Group Psychology and the Analysis of the Ego" (1921), *SE* 18, 67–143.

48. Freud, "Psycho-Analytic Notes."

49. Heinz Kohut, *The Analysis of Self* (New York: International University Press, 1971).

50. Slavoj Zizek, "With an Eye to Our Gaze—How to do a Totality With Failures," *Newsletter of the Freudian Field*, vol. 4 nos. 1/2 (Spring/Fall 1990), 51.

51. Jacques Lacan, *De la psychose paranoïaque dans ses rapports avec la personnalité* (Paris: Seuil, 1975).

52. Jacques Lacan, *The Seminar of Jacques Lacan*; Book VII: *The Ethics of Psychoanalysis 1959–1960*.

53. Jacques-Alain Miller, *Les divins détails*, (unpublished course in the Department of Psychoanalysis, Paris VIII, 1989).

54. Jacques-Alain Miller, "Extimacy," *Prose Studies* 11, 3 (1988): 121–31.

55. Antonio diCiaccia, "Quelques notes sur la psychose chez l'enfant dans l'enseignement de Lacan," in *Clinique différentielle des psychoses* (Paris: Navarin, 1988), 184–89; 187.

56. Sigmund Freud, "Papers on Metapsychology: Repression" (1915), *SE*, 14: 141–58.

57. Bruce Fink, "Alienation and Separation: Logical Moments of Lacan's Dialectic of Desire," *Newsletter of the Freudian Field* 4, 1–2 (1990): 78–119.

58. Jacques Lacan, "Desire and the Interpretation of Desire in *Hamlet*," trans. James Hulbert, *Yale French Studies* 55/56 (1977): 11–52.

59. Jacques Lacan, "A Jakobson," *Le séminaire XX (1972–1973: Encore*, text established by Jacques-Alain Miller (Paris: Editions du Seuil, 1975), 19–27; 21.

60. Jacques-Alain Miller, "Sept remarques de Jacques-Alain Miller sur la Création," *La lettre mensuelle* 68 (April 1988): 9-13.

61. Alexandre Stevens, "Two Destinies for the Subject: Neurotic Identifications and Psychotic Petrification," *Newsletter of the Freudian Field* 5, 1-2 (1991): 96-112.

62. Jacques Lacan, "On a question preliminary to any possible treatment of psychosis" (1955-1956), *Ecrits: A Selection* (New York: W. W. Norton, 1977), 179-225; 193, 197, 212.

63. See Monique Liart, "Joyce et la psychose," *Quarto* 28-29 (October 1987): 114-25; 122-23.

64. Agnes Aflalo-Lebovits, "Place et function de l'identification idéale dans la dépersonnalisation," *Quarto* 29-29 (October 1987): 35-36; 36.

65. Jacques Lacan, *Le séminaire III (1955-1956): Les psychoses*, text established by Jacques-Alain Miller (Paris: Editions du Seuil, 1981); *Seminar III: The Psychoses*, ed. Jacques-Alain Miller, trans. Russell Grigg, *et al*, (New York: W. W. Norton, 1993). *Le séminaire XXIII (1975-1976): Le sinthome* (unpublished seminar).

66. Jean-Jacques Bouquier, "Pour un mathème du hors-discours de la psychose," *La lettre mensuelle* 92 (September-October 1990): 20-24.

67. Alfred Zenoni, *Le corps de l'être parlant: De l'évolutionnisme à la psychanalyse* (Bruxelles: Editions Universitaires, 1991): 52.

68. C. Delcourt et. al., "Stratégie de l'amour, stratégie du transfert en psychanalyse," *Les stratégies du transfert en psychanalyse*, ed. L'Association de la Fondation du Champ Freudian (Paris: Navarin, 1992), 53-74; 54.

69. François Sauvagnat, "Histoire des phénomènes élémentaires: A propos de la 'signification personnelle,'" *Ornicar?* 44 (1988): 19-27.

70. Antonio diCiaccia, "Quelques notes sur la psychose chez l'enfant dans l'enseignement de Lacan," 185.

2
"Foreclosure," or the Origin of the Psychoses

In the first chapter I referred to Lacan's two theories of psychosis. In this chapter I shall only address his first theory. In chapter five ("The Paternal Metaphor") I shall work with the implications of his second theory of psychosis. Lacan taught that narcissism and the Oedipal structure elaborate themselves through the defiles of the signifier which functions in the imaginary, symbolic, and real orders, elaborating ego fictions, scenarios of desire, and impasses of impossibilities. But Lacan found something more. He uncovered the logic of a limit to language in psychosis. Moreover, he discovered that psychosis is not *caused* by organic disturbances or social deprivation. Lacan's departure from theories of biophysiological first causes of psychosis is perhaps most startling in this: He puts into question the post-Freudian hypotheses implying that good and constant care of infants is the source of later adult (i.e., "ego") health.

I argued in chapter one that Lacan's clinical findings show reductionistic biologism as too mechanical to explain the ego's development; and current child development research supports Lacan here. "The child is father of the man" for reasons other than missing out on the breast, or too early acquaintance with the potty.[1] But Lacan's work gives answers to questions child-development researchers are still researching and pondering. Society—made up of desiring subjects—is the outcome of the experience of alienation into language as it organizes *the way* language "means" through the signifier for sexual difference. This *phallic* signifier is not, however, as Freud thought, the superego: the sublimated result of the repression of sexuality which produces an inhibition of the pleasure principle in the service of the reality principle. Nor is the phallic signifier the male sexual organ. While the penis—the real organ—takes on symbolic attributes insofar as it shows desire (or its lack), it is not the phallus. And the paternal metaphor or Name-of-the-Father by which Lacan replaces Freud's theory of the Oedipus complex describes the limits of a person's knowledge as a relation to the Other, which means that the "laws" of language are stronger than one thinks. Normally, people repress the link between their being and their childhood. And such repression subjectivizes any person's speech by splitting it into conscious and unconscious parts, enabling most subjects who have repressed the primary tie to the mother to move in the language of the social moment by the "law" of *lack*. Unlike most subjects, the psychotic speaks a superego language of ego narcissism wherein one may encounter disassociation of word and affect, word salad, or simply the seemingly recorded words of the symbolic spoken by him or her as if they were real.[2]

In the 1940s and 1950s Lacan thought the neuroses dwelt in the realm of the search for an ideal father whose unconscious image was, however, split. He saw psychosis, on the contrary, as a foreclosure or rejection of the mark (or signifier) that inscribes a Father's Name, such an inscription being necessary to the creation of the unconscious by a splitting in conscious thought processes. In that the father acts as the agent who represents a subject's social tie to the symbolic, provides an image of identification in the imaginary, and marks an empty place in the real, Lacan called the *agent* of division the phallic signifier; i.e., the signifier that inscribes difference as *sexual difference*. In psychosis, no matter how much the person tries to live as a subject, he reveals, instead, a robotized position of object enslavement to an Other's *jouissance*. Put another way, a psychotic has not been split by the phallic signifier. No master signifier marks lack in his being or knowledge. No inscription for a Father's Name prohibits the totalized identificatory merger of mother and child that eschews symbolic law.

Freud's second topology—id, ego, superego—offered Lacan a theoretical basis for rethinking the normative splitting of the subject along the following lines: The phallic signifier is an effect of the experiences surrounding Oedipal division—that is, the assumption of sexual difference through language, identification, and drive. While the Freudian id might be roughly equated to the libidinal energy (or *Es*) that reveals itself as *jouissance*, the Freudian ego would itself be split between the *je*'s vague awareness of Other knowledge—a kind of *savoir naturel*—existing somewhere beyond speech, and the ideal ego's narcissistic efforts to verify certain fantasies about itself in relation to others (ego ideals).

The superego is another name for a "law" of language if one takes the Freudian superego as akin to the narcissism of the paranoid ego. Lacan's work on psychosis revealed that there is no innate inscription for law, no signifier for a third term of governance beyond the ego, no subjectivized meta-language. But what does the superego have to do with psychosis? The Freudian superego was first mentioned in later editions of the "Interpretation of Dreams" (1900) in relation to dreams of punishment. Later works of Freud describe the superego in reference to the censor in dreams whose mission is to deceive the ego by cutting off forbidden parts from consciousness. The more the "drives" (*Trieben*) are repressed, Freud said, the more demanding and severe the superego becomes. Or, as Lacan has shown, the failure to separate from the mother at the level of a primary *jouissance*—i.e., a refusal of castration or loss of the primary object—produces a subject whose demands for satisfaction are unmediated by the phallic third term. Demand bypasses the lack in desire, allying itself directly with *jouissance*, trying to skirt the temporal tension implicit in wanting (or waiting). In psychosis, then, certainty goes hand in hand with superego speech that can *only* demand. Indeed, the ego is the lawgiver. In psychotic speech, collected words or paragraphs are strung together without any clear direction or dialectical tension.

Insofar as psychoanalytic clinical practice, as documented in the United States, has not validated the Freudian notion of the superego, interest in the superego (and in the death drive) have waned. The American clinic has opted, rather, to help analysands strengthen their egos by adapting to "reality" and strangely enough, no serious question is asked about the multiple definitions of reality that are given. By contrast, Lacan placed the ego in great proximity to the superego. Indeed, one source of human drive is the narcissistic passion closely allied to the ego's idealizing and judgmental functions.

Lacan and the Kleinian Superego

In November of 1969 in *Séminaire* XVII (*L'envers de la psychanalyse*), Lacan said that language inscribes a certain number of stable relations as primordial unconscious enunciations concerning desire. But these do not suddenly appear in consciousness as "self "-

knowledge, although they do serve as a basis for the speaking subject's illusion that it "knows" what it is talking about. One only finds out later, through clinical experience, that there are also elemental aspects of the superego which are primordial.[3] Although Lacan sees the superego as formed earlier than Freud did, Lacan does not find, as did Melanie Klein, a superego functioning as early as three to six months. Because she viewed the infant as fused with the mother in fantasy, Klein believed that any threat of separation from her provoked the infant to imagine sadistic and vengeful destruction of this primary caretaker. Klein supposed that a subsequent tendency toward alternating guilt and reparation provided the kernel of a superego at this early stage. Lacan praised Melanie Klein's investigation of the imaginary relationships of the child and her consequent understanding of aggressiveness, rivalry, envy, and so on. But Lacan stated the obvious. No neonate is innately able to discriminate between good and bad "objects." Such affirmation (*Bejahung*) of good or bad objects occurs in an imaginarisation of the symbolic order where traits of rejection (*Ausstossung*) are incorporated (or not) in response to the drives which make all of us creatures of *jouissance*, long before we are alienated by language.

In "Des modalités du rejet," Jacques-Alain Miller notes the difference between the two different kinds of affirmation and negation developed by Lacan, in the wake of Freud. In neurosis one still finds a fundamental *Bejahung* or yes to life because the Father's Name is taken as a limit or law beyond which *jouissance* cannot go. While neurotic denial (*Verneinung*) occurs at the level of the word, in psychosis denial is foreclosed. Instead, there is a fundamental no to life—a "no" to the limits which permit subjects to negotiate in the social realm of language and judgmental gazes. Rejecting the signifier of the Father's Name, the psychotic's foreclosure (*Ausstossung*) is a refusal of the limits placed on the drive by language itself. The myth that "at least one" is an exception to castration that introduces lack into the universe of language—that set of signifiers—is expelled in psychosis. Rather, a "negativity" is forged on the radical absence of a representation for "no."[4]

Lacan dispensed with Klein's moralistic view of infant sadism as a rote response of consume or be consumed by showing that drive is structured for meaning, even prior to judgment. That is, drives are primordially structured not only in relation to the need for food, but also in relation to the objects Lacan calls the gaze and the voice. Unlike Klein, Lacan found no fantasized destruction of the mother followed by guilt or reparation. Instead, he theorized the kernel of a superego formed by the voice and the gaze as they mark language and transference with the positivity of *jouissance*.

Lacan and the Superego

At first Freud thought the superego was formed at around five years of age as a correlative of the decline of the Oedipus complex. Freud supposed that children are suddenly startled by their forbidden sexual feelings toward their parents. Consequently, they renounce Oedipal desires and transform their *narcissistic* investments in their parents into an *identification* with them. Children, thereby, interiorize the incest taboo as the superego. Forever after, this agency supposedly judges or censors the ego. In his essay "On Narcissism" (1915) Freud connected ego ideals to censorship, the *ego ideal* being an intra-psychic formation that projects an ideal as a substitute for the lost narcissism of childhood. But in "Group Psychology and the Analysis of the Ego" (1921), he attributed the model of infantile narcissistic omnipotence to a new formation: the *ideal ego*. In "The New Introductory Lectures" (1932) Freud assigned three functions to the superego: self-observation, moral conscience, and a function of the ideal.

By capitalizing on the nascent distinction Freud made in "Group Psychology" between an ego ideal and an ideal ego, Lacan explained why Freud had difficulty linking the ideal ego to the superego. Instead of being superego functions, both functions of the "ideal"—ego ideal and ideal ego—are actually narcissistic manifestations of the ego. While the ideal ego refers to primordial narcissistic fixations (primary identifications), the ego ideal corresponds to secondary identifications with others, its function being to command the imaginary play of relationships. But Freud had already suspected a convergence between the primordial *moi* (the ideal ego) and ego ideals (others or alter egos) in dreams and hypnosis, Lacan argued, although he took both to be objects of desire. Going in the opposite direction—viz. to maintain a distance between ideal ego and ego ideal, and to separate both from the mechanism of desiring—Lacan taught analysts to help patients *not to disappear* into the identificatory merger and closure of "apparent sameness" that characterize imaginary relations wherein the ideal ego cannot distinguish itself from ego ideals, based as it is in fundamental fantasies.

At eighteen months of age, more or less, the identificatory images that form an infant's incipient ego undergo a transition from imaginary presence to repression. Since the primordial ego is not innate, however, but a *structure* gradually built up out of infantile experiences and erected on "natural" consciousness, so to speak, the agent effecting this repression is quite simply and concretely language itself. Language makes a split between the imaginary immediacy of identificatory response and its deferred translation via the only possible route: words. But the way language is later deployed is determined by the Oepidal context—Mother ◊ Father, Man ◊ Woman—where the experience of castration determines the way desire will (or will not) function: as phobic, neurotic, perverse, or psychotic. In mathematical terms, some masculine agent breaks the child's mirror-stage illusion of a dyad of mother and infant. This agent can be the father, the mother's lover, and so on, a signifier for the Father that appears to the child as a barrier to a psychic union of mother/child. A male presence, desiring the mother, teaches a child that it is not one with its mother, but has its own psychic boundaries and individual body integrity. To be *in* the symbolic order means, quite simply, to have the distance from the imaginary primary object that allows one to *symbolize* or represent the real.

At around eighteen months of age an infant begins to use language to *represent* experience by substituting one thing for another; words are used in an attempt to represent an image or a drive. Such metaphorical movement occurs via the *effect* of the mother's desire, as well as the father's desire, in whose name or by whose "law" the child will differentiate from her identificatorily. The effect of this genesis of the "law" of culture (an awareness of the wishes of others)—a prohibition of Oneness with the mother that creates the "law" of language—constitutes "dialectical" thought. That is, the repressed effect of the Father's "no" instills the structure of order Lacan attributed to the phallic signifier—away from the mother *qua* primordial object, in the Name of a Father.

Freud defined the castration complex as a literal fear of loss of the penis (for boys), and a sense of something already lost (for girls). Lacan gave a new meaning to the castration complex: It derives from a child's attempts to decipher the enigma of the difference between the sexes. But since the mother/father couple does not translate into boy/girl in any one-to-one way, the enigma facing every child is how to align his or her gender, anatomy, and sexuality.[5] Whether the solution is masculine or feminine does not depend on gender, but on identification which Lacan redefines as sexuation. The social norm is the heterosexual, defined by the difference itself taken as *sexual* difference, which is played out in the register of the masquerade. "Heterosexual" myths generally pretend that the difference is natural and harmonious. In *Encore*, Lacan argued that there is no "sexual relation" of harmony and oneness between men and women.[6] While neurotics deny that the difference makes a difference, perverts disavow the difference between the sexes. In psychosis, the signifier for sexual difference has been foreclosed.

Thus, Lacanian castration refers to an interpretation of the phallus where organs are interpreted in terms of *having* or *being* at the levels of narcissism and identification. By castration Lacan does not mean biological emasculation of the male testicles or penis, then. Although the *organ* first in question in deciphering the difference between the sexes is the penis, Lacan dismissed the biological argument in which an organ *causes* its own meaning. Rather, the penis takes on attributes of the symbolic, not because of any natural superiority or inferiority, but because any person's "interpretation" of this organ concerns a certain confusion around issues of *having* and *being*. Lacan "translated" this meaning to that of the desired or desirable "object" he called the phallus. For Freud the penis, breast, and feces were equivalent—albeit diverse— partial objects. Within a Lacanian context, these organs or body matter only take on meaning at the level of loss or the cut whose effects are then *incorporated* into language. Moreover, partial objects enter language at the level of meaning only in terms of loss. While Lacan would have argued that his concept of an Ur-castration anxiety was fundamentally Freud's idea that *castration anxiety* arises in a series of traumatic experiences of loss (or weaning—loss of the breast, and so on), Lacan makes the radical move of showing that these losses create real effects that enter meaning as drive signifiers.

Subsequent confusion about whether sex organs impose a meaning on language or whether language dictates their functions to them arises from the fact that in identification we interpret the imaginary effects of the mirror-stage and Oedipal dramas as sexual. We use language in various ways in our attempts to describe the ineffable in reductionist terms of theology, biology, myth, and so on. From a Lacanian viewpoint, the father possesses no innate or biological supremacy, not even in some literalist overvaluation of the penis.[7] Lacan departed from Freud's phenomenological rendering of the penis as a literal image of the male organ to stress, rather, the imaginary dimension surrounding an image that will always be described in terms of loss or gain. But it is not organ turgidity that is at stake. Rather, male castration anxiety is in question, and female prestige. Insofar as the masculine is defined precisely as identification *away* from the mother, males who take the masculine position in subjective identification experience anxiety upon re-encountering the early identifications they have sacrificed: the feminine.

Thus, the penis only takes on its meaning for a given man, metonymically. Unlike Freud, Lacan saw that the importance accorded the penis is not owed to its organ reality. It takes on meaning from effects of the symbolic, imaginary, and real—meanings Lacan sought to characterize by the word phallus whose role in structuring psychic reality is veiled.[8] In pointing to the (phallic) effects of division between the masculine and feminine, Lacan spoke of the ancient phallus as a simulacrum or a function. Using the term "function" in the mathematical sense, he meant that which has laws and governs an ordering or structure which arises out of a series of associations.

For Lacan, the superego gives proof of a *split* in the subject made by the linguistic and imagistic imposition of cultural (Other) values on a speaking being. The verbal capacity to *represent* experience is a mechanism for surviving the pain of a division in knowledge necessary to psychic stability. But unlike psychoanalyst Margaret Mahler or more recent child-development researchers who have found the universal and first profound trauma in human life to be dread of the loss of the mother, Lacan stressed the effects of separation in constituting the subject of desire. In this sense, there is no mirror-stage duality in being. The only symbiosis is within the signifying process itself, a process that does not occur in linear fashion but is marked by the movement of anticipatory fantasies and the retroaction of Oedipal experience.

When an infant is cut off from the partial objects that represent the mother, he or she loses *jouissance*. Such loss gives rise to desire as the desire to replace lost "objects." If such losses do not occur— that is, if the mother does not push her child towards representing itself as an effect of the difference between herself and the symbolic order—the child may well foreclose the signifier for lack in being, a lack which unconsciously opposes phallic division to the elemental mother such that a dual perspective co-exists in the interior of the ego.[9] That is, a child learns its position in society by submitting to the myths, roles, and rules of its social order, and by internalizing them, thereby acquiring the superego Lacan described in *Seminar* II as a secondary introjection in relation to the function of the ego ideal (Sem. I, 102). In contrast to the ego ideal, the superego is essentially created from the symbolic plane of speech, then, as an imperative consonant with the register of law. But its tyrannical, blind character makes it more than mere language (Sem. I, 98). Indeed, the voice and the gaze function as pure drive in psychosis. In his later teaching Lacan attributes the tyrannical aspect of the superego to the real, to the absoluteness of *jouissance* whose law is a non-dialectical will to power. But in *Seminar* I, he depicts the superego only as "the law and its destruction" (102).

At the level of law, the superego dictates the sociocultural refusal of omnipotence to the "miraculous infant" of narcissistic primordiality. As an effect of phallic division, what we call the superego pushes infants to learn differences and accept the alienation of language itself. But in a more global sense, the very foundations of society derive from superego structure insofar as phallic division creates the unconscious as a demand for an interpretation of the difference between the sexes. Cultural myths arise as efforts to explain the unrepresentable: relation, procreation, birth, and death. The superego is a *paradoxical* agent of social adaptation and pathological morality, then. Indeed, we know only too well the superego's power to induce guilt and anxiety. In stressing the pathological function of the superego, Lacan insisted on its paradigmatic command: the paradoxical *"Jouis!"* (You *must* enjoy!)[10] This moralistic character of social law led Lacan to portray the superego as obscene and ferocious.

Given that a child begins to represent the world of differences and the value of otherness at about eighteen months, the origins of culture are located much earlier than Lévi-Strauss's marriage exchange would place them. But even prior to the onset of a coherent representation of one's "inner" world by language, the superego begins to be constituted from the castrating power of the gaze and voice. While it may seem that Lacan's concept of identification (with language, the gaze, etc.) is commensurate with Freud's idea of fixation, it is not. Lacan discovered a split in identification itself, between the imaginary register of transference effects and the symbolic register of language differentials.[11] Lacan, thereby, shed light on the mistake Freud made in his early notion of fixation.

Fixation

Freud spoke of fixation as an attachment to infantile modes of satisfaction and to archaic objects or traumas. While Lacan agreed that the descriptive potential of this notion for pinning down the origin of a *neurosis* is incontestable, he taught that the concept in and of itself cannot explain neurosis. But Lacan added this insight. If the fixation itself is repressed—even found at the origin—this can tell us something about psychosis, as well as something about neurosis. Arguing that the fixation of repression depends upon two kinds of conditions—those provoked by historical factors, and those favored by constitutional factors—Freud never really clarified the nature or meaning of fixation although he used this concept to describe regression and perversion as well as biological and ontophylogentic phenomena. But the similarities between originary mechanisms and between the conflicts in neurosis and perversion actually raise a question regarding a simplistic notion of fixation.

In "Beyond the Pleasure Principle" (1920) Freud wrote that a mode of libidinal satisfaction does not completely explain the notion of fixation to a trauma,[12] adding the idea of repetition compulsion partly to compensate for this theoretical gap.[13] Lacan looked to Freud's first notion of fixation, where fixation of a memory or symptom were presented in a realist manner. Noting that real inscriptions (the *Niederschriften*) of traces deposited in memory systems could be translated from the unconscious to the conscious system, Lacan explained that a fixation of representation is correlative to the idea that excitation is affixed to the traces. And the best expression of this Freudian idea is to be found in his most complete theory of repression.[14] Laplanche and Pontalis have followed Lacan's argument concerning Freud's 1915 metapsychological writings. An originary repression (*refoulement/Urverdrängung*) attaches itself to a signifier (*Vorstellungsrepräsentanz*), thereby constituting the unconscious. But Freud never found the link between representations, repression, and drive that Lacan found. Citing Freud's first objects of desire as the bodily extensions of an infant's own physical being-in-the-world, Lacan added to the breast, the feces, and the urinary flow stressed by Freud, the (imaginary) phallus, the gaze (the *regard*), the phoneme, the voice, and the "unthinkable"— nothing ("Signification of the Phallus," 315). If the voice is itself an "object" that causes desire, leaving in its wake phonemic traces in the unconscious that Lacan called *la lalangue* (or the primordial maternal discourse), then representation, regression, and drive *can* be linked to language itself via identification.[15] *Representation* starts as the effort to depict the ineffable of the object itself—*das Ding*, the primary Good that is the mother—in images and words, while *regression* is the return into language of images and words inscribed (or fixed) at an earlier time. And *drive* is a montage of inscriptions and bodily effects that aims at realizing its own *jouissance* at the level of oral, anal, scopic, or invocatory material.

Freud did not think representations were accessible to conscious life, except insofar as they produced a fixation. Indeed, this idea can be found even earlier than 1915 in his letters to Fliess and in the concept of *Niederschriften* invoked in "The Interpretation of Dreams" (1900). In that text the representation that corresponds to a fixation is said to subsist in the unconscious, with the drive remaining attached to it (Laplanche and Pontalis, *Language of Psychoanalysis*, 413–14). Freud elaborated this concept in his metapsychological texts by the distinctions he made between visual and verbal representations. In certain of these writings the representations of words are linked to the growth of consciousness. But even earlier, in the *Project* (1895), Freud had already associated a verbal image to the memory image. Although one must note that Freud always retained a distinction between visual and verbal representations, he never resolved the problem of how to attach verbal representations to what he called preverbal ones that already represent things (Laplanche and Pontalis, *Language of Psychoanalysis*, 417–18). That verbal representations—or signifiers as Lacan called them—give rise to images in an enigmatic associative coding is not a theory Freud would have supported. Assuming that images have a privileged and prior language of their own, Freud did not understand that they only have a life insofar as words describe them.

From Fixation to Structure

Lacan proposed early in his teaching that "structure" is a primary group of elements that form a covariant ensemble whose rudiments of knowledge are serial parts ordering the subjective material inscribed in relation to objects. Language will later refer to the resonance of this primordial material, the "pure symbols" found at the base of any person's psychic graph. That is, primary effects travel in language, parasitically hearkening back to the genesis of perception in unary traits that dwell outside the conceptual memories of consciousness. Insisting that Freud intuited these "letters" or traces in his early work on dreams and jokes and in his attention to philology, Lacan linked them, instead, to mirror-stage and Oedipal experiences whose vital power derives from their formative impact. Having rendered the concept of *structure* itself dynamic, Lacan showed how it is transformed—i.e., functions—via the unconscious, repetition, drive, and transference. These "four fundamental concepts of psychoanalysis" play out a person's history in the present of language and relationships. In other words, elements that are unconsciously fixed in relational categories of meaning— the imaginary, the symbolic, and the real—take on differing faces in the actual movement of conscious life where they are submitted to the variabilities of specular politics, semiotic codes, and symbolic customs. The representations or signifiers that constitute the elementary "cells of desire" that make the unconscious dynamic might be described, in general terms, as fixations attached to drives.[16]

Lacan's Theory of Repression

Lacan sought to link Freud's idea of fixation to verbal and visual representations and to explain them by repression. He was thus obliged to reinterpret the manner in which past history affects temporal life. He did so by distinguishing between primary and secondary repression. Originary or primary repression (Freud's *Urverdrängung*) is the basis on which secondary or dynamic repression (Freud's *Verdrängung*) is built. Here Lacan used Freud's concept of *Unterdruckung*, or suppression. With these distinctions, Lacan explained how verbal and visual representations can exist side by side unconsciously, yet still function contradictorily in signifying chains fixed by *jouissance*—to anchor and unsettle conscious speech.

Lacan's return to Freud's idea of fixation via the concept of *structure* may well be one source of Jean Piaget's ideas on epistemology. In 1970 Piaget argued that structure is dynamic; therefore, knowledge should be studied as a process instead of as a state of mind or a place of essences. But Piaget viewed the learning "process" as aiming at an evolutionary adaptation to reality, while Lacan blurred the distinction between individuals and reality by portraying humans as biological creatures of contingency on whom images and language impose a body of meanings.

The conscious subject flees those "truths" that operate it from the unconscious. That is, people do not perceive by contemplating objects—i.e., objectively—but through a subjective filter of representations that allows them to perceive at all. Paradoxically these representations which were created in the first place by concrete processes reappear literally in the realm of experience, proving that language represses something. Indeed, language is itself a kind of "transitional object" for mastering loss, the referent of all being.[17] Consciousness, then, is not consciousness of something. It is a mode of perception—a scotoma—that negotiates repression and desire via substitutions, finding its own origins in desire and identifications. From this viewpoint, consciousness is not commensurable with reality or perception, but is merely a reflection of a fundamentally subjective network of associations, a reflection each person takes on from the point of view of others.

Lacan made it clear that consciousness is quite observably an irremediably limited principle of "self"-idealization and misrecognition. When he spoke of consciousness as a *scotoma* (Greek: obscuration of part of the field of vision), he reconceptualized it as the dialectical mark of the speaking subject, oppressed by inner gazes and voices. By contrast, the realism of the *unconscious* resides in desire and sexuality. Negation becomes epistemologically important then, because it is indicative of a split between consciousness and the unconscious—a sign that something is repressed. While Freud thought denial (*Verneinung/dénégation*) pointed to the memory of unconscious desire and was perhaps a guidepost to "cure," Lacan saw *Verneinung* as indicative of the subject of speech denying its own truth *cum* desire. By showing thought and being as both derivative of the effects of language, and the true subject as the subject of unconscious desire, Lacan both libidinized philosophy and gave a philosophy of psychoanalysis to the language of the body.

Although Lacan adhered to many Freudian conceptions of the unconscious—the unconscious knows neither contradiction, doubt, or negation; its processes belong to the past; primary process is inhibited by secondary process; there is greater mobility of "investment" intensity in the unconscious than in consciousness—he went further than Freud by arguing that the unconscious leaves no human action outside its domain: Lacan's conception of the unconscious viewed any discourse or behavior as intermittently marked by unconscious desire. Although most post-Freudian psychoanalytic thought shares Freud's 1920 view of the unconscious as the seat of the id (instinctual drive) attached to fantasies, Lacan claimed in 1957 that there is no instinctual unconscious.[18] By developing Freud's representational models in conjunction with his dynamic and economic systems, Lacan departed from the familiar Freud, showing how conscious and unconscious systems overlap. The unconscious makes its presence felt in language in the literal ways Freud discovered: jokes, slips of the tongue, dreams, lapses of memory, and so on. Since conscious and unconscious laws work differently, the unconscious will be decoded not only in terms of desire and *jouissance,* but also via the word which reveals the conscious use of language as itself an effort to translate the unconscious. Psychotic subjects, by contrast, tend to speak in monologues, or to remain silent. Their goal is not to translate the unconscious so that the other will understand something, but to keep the outside world at bay.

Even though unconscious language is abstract and already constructed in the Other, it is the basis of conscious speech for most speaking subjects. Precise words or homophonic resonances are fixed to the partial objects that cause the desire that gives body to fantasies and memories. Unconscious signifiers coalesce into signifieds elaborated around transference and Oedipal effects, unveiling the uniqueness of each infant as the object of the Other's desire. Lacan shows us that Freud's *Vorstellungersreprasentanzen* are not static, then, but are catalyzed into activity by the outside world, which finds its *particular* vibrations in each person.

Freud's hypothesis of representability developed his economic model wherein bodily and psychic energies are quantifiable. He wrote in "The Unconscious" (1915) that when certain ideas (*Vorstellungen*) are made unconscious, repression or defense occurs. Affects, unlike ideas, are attached to consciousness and are ultimately discharged or manifested as feelings, which, unlike ideas, are not repressed. The logical impasse here is obvious. In such a scenario the body would fall on the side of the represented or repressed—on the side of ideas. Repression would supposedly occur without affect. The body would be experienced in silence. In the opinion of psychoanalytic critic Jim Swan, psychoanalysts abandoned the economic model precisely because "quantified and objective" scientific concepts could not describe the experience of the body.[19]

Lacan agreed with Freud that affects are not repressed. When one takes the measure of Lacan's innovation here, one sees that he equated *Vorstellungen* (ideas) with his own concept of the signifier, but held, along with Freud, that *Vorstellungen* are repressed. One begins to grasp how Lacan could logically situate Freud's perception marks (*Wahrnehumungszeichen*) in the unconscious system.

Insofar as perception marks are signifiers that represent unconscious ideas, man is a representational animal at every level of being. Images and identifications first present forms to an infant. These forms, first named by language, are *incorporated* into the language that subsequently serves as the mode or material by which individuals re-present themselves in the world. So this discourse of the Other that Lacan called the unconscious "thinks" actively by representational marks derived from the outer world of concrete language, which become associationally attached to visual images (*perceptum*) and to the drives long before they enter a grammar system (*Sem.* I, 102).

Repetition, Repression, and the Death Drive

Lacan differed from Freud by teaching that repetition—not memory—leads to unconscious truths. Not only do repetitions reveal the specificities of a neurosis, they also show the insistence of the unconscious in conscious life. Indeed, Lacan's idea of repetition goes much further than Freud's theory of repetition compulsion in "Beyond the Pleasure Principle" (1920) taken as a manifestation of the death instinct. Lacan "translated" this into the desire to maintain *jouissance* as a constant. The ego coheres in mythic forms by repeating a few fictions that continually reconstitute it in the eyes of others. In a psychotic structure, ego repetition eschews substitutions since the ego does not reconstitute itself for others. This failure to *exchange* with others indicates a foreclosure of the social order wherein the ego has been swallowed by the primary Other and become equal to itself. Put another way, the psychotic does not reconstitute his ego dialectically. The desire to be recognized does not "drive" him or her. Rather, the psychotic is *perplexed* if he does not receive the recognition he believes he merits. Thus, any deconstruction of his or her ego partakes of "death work." By this Lacan did not mean conscious death anxiety, but death mimicked in the very kernel of the "drive" itself.

Psychosis Rethought

It is of capital importance that Lacan returned to Freud's ideas on repression before finding a mechanism proper to psychosis. Freud first conceptualized fixations as attachments to persons or to *imagos*, interpreting them as modes that produce satisfaction. By this

Freud meant the satisfactions obtained in evolutionary sexual stages. Thus, Freud generally meant a genetic progress commanded by the libido when he spoke of fixations (Laplanche and Pontalis, *Language of Psychoanalysis*, 160). But Freud himself left the door open to another way of conceptualizing fixations, as Lacan demonstrates. Freud first thought an original repression of sexual desires—caused by castration anxiety—created neurosis and showed up as the refusal of sexual drive representations. But by 1930 when the Freud of *Civilization and Its Discontents* related repression to sublimation—the pleasure principle (constancy) sacrificed to the reality principle (compromise) in the interest of civilization and economic survival—he had unknowingly opened the way for an inversion of the Puritan ethic which equates "reality" with hard work.

Ineptly extrapolating Freud's principles, Herbert Marcuse, Norman Brown, and others, equated the pleasure principle with sexual freedom. Indeed, sexual freedom, equated with the best reality, became the 1960s panacea for civilization's discontents. While North American gurus of sexual rehabilitation worked in laboratories (Kinsey, Masters and Johnson) or in sensory group-touch settings, Lacan explored the engima Freud had not resolved: Why does repression occur at all.[20] By valorizing Freud's early concept of a primary repression, Lacan equated *Urverdrängung* with the fixing of a signifying chain in pre-specular and mirror-stage moments. Although this early material is repressed, paradoxically it remains suspended in conscious life, acting to shape human choice without our ever knowing that an *a priori* conditions the future.

Lacan taught that individuals do not repeat repressed material in order to master neurosis, nor to recreate pleasurable id states, but in order to place something unified and familiar—an ego—between the real of traumata and the exigencies of the symbolic and imaginary. Although language erects an ever growing alienation between conscious and unconscious knowledge, this barrier does not prohibit the play of repressed knowledge on conscious thought as long as such knowledge is denied or misrecognized. Yet, both the subject's denial and the ego's misrecognition are forms of resistance to the "return of the repressed."

Signifiers constitute a kind of secondary repression that resides on the side of language—what one says and what one might say—where ego repetitions are operated by the substitutive mechanisms of desire. Primary repression would be a coefficient of *lalangue*—the primordial material of unknown maternal desire $\left(\dfrac{\text{DM}}{\text{x}}\right)$—while secondary repression means that conscious and unconscious ideas coexist simultaneously (Freud's *Niederschriften*). More surprising still, Lacan argues that secondary repression *engenders* the unconscious as an interpretation of castration—that is, as an interpretation of one's biological gender in reference to parental relations. In "To Interpret the Cause," Jacques-Alain Miller explains that the interplay of language (O) with *jouissance* (J) governs the quota of affect one finds in representations (or signifiers). The particular structuring of desire (as neurotic, psychotic, or perverse) derives from a child's effort to translate the parental formula—Mother ◇ Father—into a comprehensible sexual formula for a relationship between boys and girls, a formula that will make the relationship of man to woman clear. But the relation of mother to father does not provide the formula for a sexual identity, nor give the key to what a cohesive or harmonious relation of man to woman would be. Thus, repression is repression of the sexual impasse created by the loss of identification with one's "other half." This loss shows up in a displaced manner. Repressed signifiers re-enter consciousness *dynamically*, carrying their energy to the heterogeneous terms of language by the mechanisms of substitution, displacement, referentiality, similarity, and contiguity.

In his rereading of "Totem and Taboo" (1912) Lacan found a psychoanalytic truth in Freud's symbolic drama.[21] The idea of the sons murdering the father was Freud's effort to explain repression as something originally learned through guilt and retribution. Lacan explained that "something" as the human desire to retain a consistency of *jouissance*; i.e., a state of oneness or unity in being. The structural reality Freud sought to express in his narrative is this: Society is formed on the basis of the *belief* in an Ur-father—omnipotent and all powerful—who, paradoxically, serves as the referent of moral law. The effect of foreclosing the symbolic father in order to remain identificatorally united with the mother introduces what Lacan called the real father, or the stasis of the death drive. Another name for the real father is primary *jouissance* or the *jouissance une* which marks the initial failure to grapple with the question posed by sexual difference. One can always infer this in psychosis where a refusal of the limits of the social order (or the reality principle) means that *jouissance* reigns supreme. Such difficulties always have this feature: a primordial attachment to the mother which eschews the link between identity and sexual difference.

While the pervert repudiates the idea that the mother lacks the penis *qua* phallus, he does not unconsciously foreclose the sexual difference. Rather, he fetishizes desire itself. In this way he forestalls the anxiety that accompanies the threat of loss *qua* loss of the primary object. While the neurotic remains troubled by the object, the hysteric identifying away from the mother and the obsessional holding tight to this sacrosanct identification, the normative *père-version*—the sexual masquerade—centers on the sexual difference as the basis of social exchange. The psychotic's failure to differentiate from the mother by inscribing the father as the image and point of identificatory difference forecloses the castration by which individuals learn lack, but the libidinal link to the mother—such as taking her dead father's vocation (musician, for example) as a supplemental identification—can serve as a prosthetic knotting of the three orders, compensating for the inability to repress *jouissance*. Since the psychotic lacks a way to say "no," he dwells on the edges of reality, society, and compromise.

Lacanian Foreclosure

In his own search for a mechanism specific to psychosis, Lacan found traces of such an idea in Freud's concepts of *Verwerfung* and *Verleugnung*. By *Verwerfung* Freud meant alternately a refusal that operates like repression, or a conscious judgment or refusal. Lacan referred to "The Neuroses of Defense" (1896)[22] where Freud described psychosis as existing in a very energetic defense, stressing rather, that the subject repudiates an *unbearable* representation and the affect attached to it. In such foreclosure a subject acts as if the representation had never existed. Thus psychosis bespeaks the *failure* to repress a trauma. But Lacan's preferred text on psychosis was "der Wolfmann" where Freud described his patient as having rejected castration in a primordial period.[23] Although Freud used the term *Verwerfung* there and in various instances, Lacan introduced the term "foreclosure" (*forclusion*), which is not exactly equatable with Freud's *Verwerfung*. Lacan's concept is, nonetheless, an effort to respond to Freud's eternal quest to define a defense mechanism specific to psychosis. Freud finally opted for *Verleugnung*—meaning not "denial," as in *Verneinung*, but a disavowal (*déni*) or refusal to accept the reality of the mother's missing penis. He ascribed this unconscious denial of reality to the child, the fetishist, and the psychotic. The absence of the penis is denied; castration is rejected.

By looking at these various Freudian texts in conjunction with Freud's 1925 article "On Negation," Lacan reinterpreted the *cause* of foreclosure in its relation to the Oedipal structure.[24] Defining foreclosure in its relationship to primary process, Lacan stressed that two operations occur: primary symbolization (*Bejahung* or affirmation of introjected material) and *Ausstossung* or expulsion from the "I." For Lacan *Ausstossung* is synonymous with foreclosure, consisting in an original failure to symbolize the signifying mark or symbol for the reality confronting each sex: each one lacks something; each one differs from the other one. In foreclosing this fact, a delusory system develops in psychosis, such system revealing the psychotic's attempt to define himself as male or female since the signifier for that particular difference has been expunged from his unconscious. It is crucial to understand that a delusion is not a fantasy, but rather, a massive elaboration of thought around the idea that the psychotic subject is fundamentally a woman.

The psychotic's crazy thoughts or hallucinations may be described thus: "What has been expelled from the symbolic reappears in the real."[25] One can recognize delirious memory traces as *jouissance* meanings that lack symbolic ordering. These are symptoms—not signifiers—that appear in "pure" nonsense form when they are freed from the unifying interpretative scanning of a symbolic order ego.[26] The substitutive function of metaphor has failed: Lacan gives the example of James Joyce's nonsense words in *Finnegan's Wake*, supported only by the real of the voice.[27] Indeed, in *R.S.I.* and in *Le sinthome* Lacan changed his theoretical position on the structure of the symptom. Rather than depicting it as a metaphor, he portrayed it as a piece of the real. But when Lacan first developed the concept of foreclosure in his 1957–1958 seminar (*Les psychoses*)[28] and in the *écrit* treating the same material, "On a question preliminary to any possible treatment of psychosis," he explained that any infant or child is traumatized by the signifier for castration or difference insofar as no child wants to experience loss of imaginary plentitude.[29] At this date, Lacan considered the agent of psychosis to be the *unconscious* desire of the mother (or the primary caretaker). It is she who mediates the infant's relationship to the father's name. It is she who takes the infant as the object of her *jouissance* in the real. It is she who fails to introduce the child to its difference from her.

When no signifier for otherness is given, no question concerning identity arises at the level of the child's ego. Indeed, the form of the question itself arises from curiosity about difference *qua* sexual difference. But when the child confronts only his or her mother's desire in the real because no father—no different other—answers his or her call to the Other, *jouissance* governs "thought," organizing the psychotic's language around the mother's *jouissance.* Subsequently, the *raison d'être* of this subject's language will center on this question: what is a father? Insofar as the problem of sexual identity is primary for the psychotic because he or she remains one with the mother, this subject's primary identification will always be on the side of Woman. Judge Daniel Paul Schreber wrote in his *Mémoirs* that God is the father and that he—as a man named Daniel Schreber—is finally sure of his true sexual identity as the *wife* of God.[30] Their children are "divine rays."

Lacan always found the phallic signifier foreclosed in psychotic episodes. It follows logically that Lacan's reinterpretation of Freud's ideas on representation, fixation and regression would come to bear on his concept of foreclosure. In a psychotic structure, there is no repression of *jouissance.* And, although signifiers are repressed, they often function strangely in language: delusorily, nonsensically, or as word salad, and so on. And insofar as any *repressed* signifier is still active (i.e., re-represented) or susceptible of being represented in conscious life—triggered by relationships and desire—then Freud's idea of regression as a sliding into past instinctual stages of repressed history is incorrect. Freud would also be incorrect in thinking that ego frustration leads first to aggression and then to regression as correlated with developmental sexual stages. "Psychic" maturation—or the lack of it—occurs, instead, in a child's experience of the Other. So regression takes place at the temporal level of unconscious meanings which surface *in* language, in relation to others, and in the present. Regression is not an instinctual sliding backward into repressed fantasies arising from the pleasure principle.

Metaphor and Metonymy in Relation to Psychosis

Unconscious discourse functions in two ways to deploy memory: in a combinatory network that makes meaning within a differential opposition of signifiers and symbols, and through a spatial or topological aspect which contains the history of a person's life as elaborations of transference and Oedipal structures. These form the real, imaginary, and symbolic orders that make up the Borromean signifying chain, elaborating even the most abstract and metaphysical of material out of a few key signifiers of life: birth, love, procreation, and death. Lacan, in trying to show the complexity and perversity of human thought, operating as it does from denial and repression, subverted existing paradigms of mind to give a truer account than anyone before him had of how what we call "mind" functions.

By reformulating Saussure's concept of the linguistic sign and Roman Jakobson's concepts of metaphor and metonymy, Lacan hoped to correct, not only Freud who failed to problematize language, but also philosophers like Immanuel Kant who reduced nonsense to the simple absence of meaning and Martin Heidegger who dismissed the value of "small talk" (Gerede/Unsinn). In Seminar III (Les psychoses) Lacan analyzed Judge Schreber's delusion by giving a positive value to nonsense. Arguing that Schreber's articulations exhibit organization and a kind of rational thought, Lacan taught in this seminar that speech is a field of meaning where certain signifiers are organized, or not. The absence of normal grammatical language in Schreber's articulations indicates his inability to screen out the unconscious. His capacity to repress has ceased, which is typical of psychotic discourse where the ego ceases to serve as a screen between the Other and the speaking subject. The result is that the Other—a mechanical god of dead "letters" and decomposed phrases—speaks the subject at the surface of grammar.[31]

In interpreting Freud's "Loss of Reality in Neurosis and Psychosis" (1924) Lacan departed from the theory that psychosis is caused by a brain dysfunction that produces a supposed "loss of reality."[32] In psychosis the person continues some relationship to reality, Lacan said, but experiences the unconscious as real rather than imaginary. Indeed, for a psychotic subject everything carries a personal meaning, such that there is little distance between events in the world and the belief that they are meant for him or her. In other words, psychotic language is itself an organization of language that compensates for an organizing signifier never placed in the unconscious. Because the psychotic speaks directly out of unconscious savoir, he lacks the enabling distance to discern the "laws" or codes of the symbolic order out of the mass of knowledge he has.

This subject's tragedy is his inability to escape the onslaught of the speech imposed on him by the Other. Insofar as the psychotic cannot find the extension of a term (its definition or criterion), he or she cannot judge it as true or false. To say "I am as good as my word" represents a narcissistic belief for a psychotic, not an ethical relation to what the words themselves promise. Since metaphor does not function in psychosis as an unconscious mechanism to maintain repression via substitution, it does not offer the psychotic speaker a means to reconstitute the ego dialectically, that is, in relation to others. Insofar as the normative functioning of language by metaphor and metonymy is based on a lack in knowledge created by the signifier for sexual difference, the psychotic is at a loss. This lack normally causes the function of substitutions and referential displacements. But the psychotic subject cannot substitute or displace in language. Having never lost the primary object—the mother as real object of symbiotic oneness—he or she has nothing to replace.

In his seminar on psychosis, Lacan pointed to a curious phenomenon: psychotic language resembles the mechanisms of metaphor and metonymy. In schizophrenic episodes, the subject names things, but does not make meaning. Such agrammatical speech (or "word salad") resembles the *motor disorder* of *aphasia* in which Roman Jakobson located the linguistic slope of metonymy. The psychotic who "names" but without making meaning, alludes to the Other where words were originally recorded, creating new words—neologisms—by combining fragments of words and sounds. In other instances, psychotic language operates as a kind of metalanguage that makes propositions and paraphrases. It has been aptly described as a pseudo-academic discourse: a kind of speech that functions grammatically and offers great theories that seem to have profound meaning, although it does not really "mean" in a dialectical give and take. Lacan pointed out that this style of speaking or writing resembles the *sensory order aphasia* in which Jakobson first pinpointed the language mechanism of metaphor. In the paraphrastic speech of psychosis one can see (or "hear") the stitching that sews together the usually invisible two-dimensional or metaphorical structure of the ego. In such speech the Other behind "identity" is revealed in a use of language divorced from exchange with others. Thus, psychotic language reveals what lies beyond the ego fiction and what underlies the capacity to make meaning at all: images and words in the Other.

The Lacanian Signifier and the Ideal Ego

In emphasizing Saussure's discovery that there is no *natural* connection between objects and words, Lacan argued that Freud had already intuited this in his separation of word presentations and thing presentations. Lacan goes beyond Saussure and Freud to argue that the signifier is not present in the Other for the purpose of "meaning" something. And psychotic speech demonstrates this. Although a psychotic subject *can* function in society by imitating imaginary father/son, father/daughter, and other family models, psychotic episodes occur when the lack of an inscription—that is, the key signifier for differing from the mother—is put into question. That is, when this subject's tenuous identity as a man or woman is challenged within the symbolic order because he has no signifier for the Name of-the-Father, he is confronted by a great threat which Jean-Jacques Gorog has described thus: A hallucination appears in the psychotic's search within language for the place he or she loses when invaded by the pure real. At the moment when supplemental limits disappear, they are replaced by a violence without recourse to law.[33] When the psychotic's pseudo-imaginary relations with others collapse, they are often followed by aggressive attempts on the subject's part to keep his ideal ego intact. Indeed, striking out at others who threaten to destroy the tenuous base from which this subject makes the "world" cohere is a logical response.

The psychotic's ideal ego may also become the "victim" of attack in suicide attempts. In a pre-psychotic state this subject feels uncertain and besieged. His narcissism is impugned. In that a psychotic lives totally from narcissism, his "rational" response to the incursion of difference or Otherness lies in trying to save this narcissism by employing its correlative: aggressiveness. When a psychotic's legitimacy—his pseudo-authenticity—is put into question, a paranoid "defense" is not, for the subject in question, a matter of attack, but an effort to prevent the death of an ego that must shoulder the whole burden of being. After an initial period of confusion and perplexity, and before a psychotic *break*, the psychotic's ideal ego merges with his or her ego ideals. Speaking from a position of divine certainty, the psychotic's own proper name recedes. Daniel Paul Schreber "became" the wife of God. Others "become" Napoleon, Jesus Christ, and so on.

When ego fictions disappear, the name that accompanied these fictions disappears as well. The psychotic must reorganize whatever "knowledge" he possesses in order, quite literally, to stop up a hole in the universe of his being. Thus, the psychotic solution is mental. Ideal ego figures substitute for the "I" which takes on the names of grand and powerful figures; alter egos take over the Other's place as the "source of knowledge." Both hallucinatory voices and images appear in conscious language, and are experienced by the psychotic *as if* coming from the outside world. The return of the repressed from the real enters intrusively into the symbolic—split off. Insofar as auditory and visual hallucinations originated in the external world, they reveal not so much that the psychotic is "crazy," but the way ontology and representation were structured in the first place. As any semblance of transference relationships with others ebbs away, the psychotic reorders his or her associative sets of signifiers in the Other. Here, one can see the original impasse of the role of the signifier as it structures the speaking subject out of idiosyncratic meanings which must be rendered conventional in order that a person be able to communicate with them. Because identity has been built up at a distance from the Other's *jouissance*, a subject's speech tallies with the grammatical language we usually associate with social rationality or reality. In psychotic episodes, what we typically call "mind" unravels into the fragmented parts which previously functioned in a somewhat unified fashion, as long as they were anchored by a cohesive set of fictions.

Speaking rigidly and non-dialectically, the psychotic reveals the mental side of pre-castration eternity and immortality. When the supplemental signifiers that permitted this subject to imitate the imaginary order outside his own "inner" world disappear, he confronts the lack of a signifier for law; i.e., a law of limits. He or she *is spoken* like a robot. His flat, sterile, repetitive tones unveil the *fixed* signifiers that make up the Borromean chains of the Other, his discourse enunciated in the tones of a mechanical god of power and certainty. With the illusion of coherent being gone, psychosis shows that language quite literally "parasites" us, and quite literally, wounds. When the ego ceases repeating itself, the psychotic subject becomes an object of the real. He or she takes the place of the missing signifier by which Lacan defined the "subject"—but as an absolute object of *jouissance*, not as a dialectical subject of desire (lack). That is, signifiers become *objects* in communication, rather than its vehicle. Words actually become real living things for the psychotic who has become the victim of language, not the unsuspecting agent of desire and *jouissance*. Lacan created the word *parlêtre* in trying to convey the sense of a being *being* spoken by the Other in psychosis.

The Double and "Lalangue"

In the collection of essays, *Returning to Freud*, Jacques-Alain Miller presents "A Lacanian Psychosis: Interview by Jacques Lacan." In

"Teachings of the Case Presentation" Miller discusses Lacan's interview, pointing out that insofar as meaning is not inherent in the signifier itself, this is even implied in its name: "echo."[34] Stressing the fact that de Clerambault was the first to break away from the idea of psychology as the analysis of affect by pinpointing the order of structure, Miller indicates what Lacan found important in de Clerambault's work: his description of a *mental automatism* operative in psychosis. De Clerambault first spoke of a neutral automatism that he reduced to the first letter of the word "*Syndrome*." Miller argues that the structural basis of this "automatism" is constituted by the outside world, not by innate biological phenomena. He asks:

> What is the "echo of thought" which de Clerambault makes the original positive phenomenon of mental automatism, if not a disturbance between statement and enunciation that emancipates a parasitic source? The subject finds himself continually shadowed by a double that emancipates him, accompanies him, or follows him and cannot say anything. Fading, mute, empty, this double still has the power to suspend the subject in the position of receiver. . . . The terms that I substitute for those of de Clerambault indicate that it is not in some obscure "deviation of influx" that we can found the syndrome of mental automatism, but rather in the grasp of intersubjective communication. It follows that the sender of a message becomes its receiver and that the psychotic disturbance consists only in his experiencing himself as such (Miller, *Returning to Freud*, 47).

Perhaps the role of the double—which emanates from a mirror-stage effect experienced prior to the coalescing of an ideal ego—in psychosis does not situate the moment of trauma in the formation of paranoia (cf. object-relations theory on oral disturbance) so much as it reveals that the lack of a key signifier can turn the elemental origins of ego structuration back on a subject.[35] If one accepts that imaginary meaning (*connaissance*) is commensurate with perception and encompasses those layers of meaning built up in the confluence of the symbolic and the real, then one can understand what Lacanian analysts have deduced from their clinical work: that the psychoses are illnesses of mentality, in which being has become pure seeming or semblance (Miller, *Returning to Freud*, 51). Psychosis occurs, Miller continues, when the imaginary relationship is emancipated. The result is a reversal of ego and object (ibid.).

By the reversal of ego and object I understand Miller to mean that the ego collapses into its own metonymic shadow and becomes the real object, the object *a* cause-of-desire. At that point the subject is reduced to an object—a response of the real—that approximates the drive itself. There the psychotic subject is directly tied to the gaze or voice or the oral or fecal symbols, rather than to a fictional structure. This subject has passed from the substitutive—i.e., metaphorical—ego function, to the real of *jouissance* usually hidden in the symptom. In life as normally lived, Otherness keeps people from being One with themselves. Functioning by dynamic repression or castration, the unconscious produces the sense of lack that constitutes being as an *Un-en-moins* (One-minus) (*Sém.* XX, 116). The psychotic delusion of Oneness (Lacan's *Il y a de l'Un*) is reminiscent of the illusion that a mirror-stage oneness with the mother actually existed (*Sém.* XX, 63). Yet paradoxically, in psychotic episodes the subject becomes an object, broken down into images, phrase fragments, and partial objects that repeat nonsense, strange phrases, neologisms, and inanities. Observers speak of a loss of reality or a personality deterioration. Or, they argue that the brain has become dysfunctional.

Lacan's innovation was to have shown what is really at stake here: a structure of mentality that has never grasped the possibility of the impossible (the real). The psychotic has never been psychically castrated. When some key episode challenges the imaginary fictions of such a person—when the real will not bend to these fictions—the petrified ego unravels into the metonymic meanings it had previously been able to screen out by adhering to rigid signifying systems. One sees how psychosis, paradoxically, requires an effort to create a void where there is none. The empty, aloof quality of psychotic speech reveals someone who was shadowed in infancy by a too full mirror—a mirror which did not reflect the child's difference from the mother and whose consistency was never challenged by a father.

Lacan's discovery of the cause of psychosis, and its subsequent effects, offers a new explanation of how the matter of the world creates mind as a vast associative network, a materiality of language. We know that language is first acquired in relation to others, and that the other of primary transference usually refers an infant to a third thing—to the desire for being desired. Lacan named this early layer of enigmatic "knowledge" about the mother's desire *la lalangue*. In adult life, language will be "what we try to know about the functioning of *la lalangue*" (*Sém.* XX, 126). Primordial "object" language or *lalangue* will retain "effects which are already there [in the unconscious] as knowledge, [and] go far beyond what any speaking being can utter."[36] In psychosis, however, we glimpse the mysterious source of this knowledge in this skewed relation to truth.

Lacan made much of Saussure's discovery that *meaning* relations are created by diacritical oppositions. This law, Lacan said, is more elemental than any literal or substantive character generally imputed to objects. Freud, by opposing words to things, failed to see that liaisons persist within a context of oppositions. Insofar as psychotic language is itself *opposed* to the surface of normative discourse, such language "means" *per se*. The psychotic's efforts to solve the mystery of a missing signifier for the Name-of-the-Father produces the disembodied language which Lacan, following de Clerambault, described as mental automatism. Put another way, repressed material surfaces or is laid "bare" when ego unity comes unraveled. Thus, a psychotic episode attests to the possibility of a radical absence of symbolization, as well as to the necessary dependence of the human subject on the signifier. When imaginary relations cease, the unconscious representations that supported grammar float into view, but without animation—insipid, because the energy that generally infuses language via narcissism and desire has disappeared.

The language of psychosis also unveils the fuller meaning of metonymy: its libidinal structuration by *jouissance*. One can see the seemingly disassociated material as the concrete building blocks of identificatory fusions. The projections left in the wake (*dérive*) of *jouissance*, for example, are often hallucinations of symbiotic signifieds (*Sém.* XX, 102). This "double" language of "self" images—the underside of communicative language—may describe potential phallic saviors (spirit guides, ideal doctors, wives or husbands) or the gleeful thwarting of any figure of authority. The language of male psychosis may aim only at insulting and humiliating the Other sex. Or, psychotic language may depict a fantasmatic universe whose objects are "free" gifts.

Sol Aparicio points out in "La forclusion, préhistoire d'un concept" that since psychosis arises from the place of primordial Otherness, the basic structure of mentality is revealed when narcissism recedes and repression is lifted.[37] But even when coherent language disappears, "drive" attachment remains fixed to chains of introjects, making of this imaginary material the real phenomena of hallucination. Yet most people are not psychotic. Most subjects never experience the loss of a sense of identity cohesion around which the social exchange itself is organized. And although the psychotic lives tenuously and with difficulty in the world of social exchange, at best, many such subjects do live most of their lives *in* society, not in a "mental hospital" or prison. Perhaps we begin to see why Lacan located the *limits* of human freedom and rationality in psychosis.

Notes

1. Judy Dunn, "Distress and Comfort," in *The Developing Child,* ed. J. Bruner, M. Cole, et al. (Cambridge: Harvard University Press, 1977), 17–43.

2. Jacques Lacan, *De la psychose paranoïaque dans ses rapports avec la personnalité,* Thèse de Doctorat en Médecine, Faculté de Médecine de Paris (Paris: Le François, 1932).

3. Jacques Lacan, *Le séminaire XVII (1969–1970): L'envers de la psychanalyse,* November 26, 1969, text established by Jacques-Alain Miller (Paris: Editions du Seuil, 1991).

4. Marie-Jean Sauret, "De l'infantile à la structure: *Die Verneinung,*" *De l'infantile à la structure: Les séries* de la découverte freudienne (Toulouse: Presses Universitaires du Mirail, 1991), 193–227; 210–12.

5. Jacques-Alain Miller, "To Interpret the Cause: From Freud to Lacan," *Newsletter of the Freudian Field* 3, 1–2 (1989): 30–50.

6. Jacques Lacan, *Le séminaire XX (1972–1973): Encore,* text established by Jacques-Alain Miller (Paris: Seuil, 1975), 10.

7. Jacques Lacan, "The signification of the phallus" (1958), *Ecrits: A Selection,* trans. Alan Sheridan (New York: W. W. Norton, 1977), 281–91.

8. Ibid., 287–88.

9. Jacques Lacan, *The Seminar of Jacques Lacan,* Book I: *Freud's Papers on Technique 1953–1954,* ed. Jacques-Alain Miller, trans. John Forrester (New York: W. W. Norton, 1988), 97–98.

10. Jacques Lacan, *Le séminaire XX: Encore,* 10.

11. Jacques Lacan, *Le séminaire IX (1961–1962): L'identification,* (unpublished seminar).

12. Sigmund Freud, "Beyond the Pleasure Principle" (1920), *SE,* 18: 3–64.

13. Ibid.

14. Jean Laplanche and J. B. Pontalis, *The Language of Psychoanalysis,* trans. Donald Nicholson-Smith (New York: W. W. Norton, 1974).

15. Jacques Lacan, *The Four Fundamental Concepts of Psychoanalysis* (Seminar XI, 1964), ed. Jacques-Alain Miller, trans. Alan Sheridan (New York: W. W. Norton, 1978), 82.

16. Jacques Lacan, "The subversion of the subject and dialectic of desire in the Freudian unconscious" (1960), in *Ecrits: A Selection,* trans. Alan Sheridan (New York: W. W. Norton, 1977), 292–325.

17. Jacques-Alain Miller, "Language: Much Ado about What?" in *Lacan and the*

Subject of Language, ed. Ellie Ragland-Sullivan and Mark Bracher (New York: Routledge, 1991), 21–35.

18. Jacques Lacan, "The agency of the letter in the unconscious or reason since Freud" (1957), in *Ecrits: A Selection*, trans. Alan Sheridan (New York: W. W. Norton, 1977), 146–78.

19. James Swan, "*Mater* and Nannie: Freud's Two Mothers and the Discovery of the Oedipus Complex," *American Imago*, 31, no. 1 (Spring 1974): 1–64.

20. Herbert Marcuse, *Eros and Civilization: A Philosophical Inquiry into Freud* (New York: Vintage Books, 1959); Norman O. Brown, *Life against Death* (New York: Vintage Books, 1959); Alfred Kinsey et al., *Sexual Behavior in the Human Female* (Philadelphia: Saunders, 1953); William H. Masters and Virginia E. Johnson, *Human Sexual Response* (Boston: Little Brown, 1966).

21. Sigmund Freud, "Totem and Taboo" (1912), *SE*, 13: 1–161.

22. Sigmund Freud, "The Neuroses of Defense" (1896), *SE*, 1: 220–29.

23. Sigmund Freud, "From the History of an Infantile Neurosis" (1918), *SE*, 17: 3–123.

24. Sigmund Freud, "Negation" (1925), *SE*, 19: 235–39.

25. Jacques Lacan, *The Seminar of Jacques Lacan*, Book VII: *The Ethics of Psychoanalysis 1959–1960*, ed. Jacques-Alain Miller, trans. Dennis Porter (New York: W. W. Norton, 1992), 157.

26. Jacques Lacan, *Le séminaire XXII (1974–1975): R.S.I.* (unpublished seminar).

27. Jacques Lacan, *Le séminaire XXIII (1975–1976): Le sinthome,* (unpublished seminar).

28. Jacques Lacan, *Le séminaire III (1955–1956): Les psychoses,* text established by Jacques-Alain Miller (Paris: Editions du Seuil, 1981); *Seminar III: The Psychoses* (New York: W.W. Norton, 1993).

29. Jacques Lacan, "On a question preliminary to any possible treatment of psychosis" (1955–1956), in *Ecrits: A Selection*, trans. Alan Sheridan (New York: W. W. Norton, 1977), 226–80.

30. Daniel Paul Schreber, *Memoirs of My Nervous Illness* (1955), ed. and trans. by Ida Macalpine and Richard Hunter (Cambridge: Harvard University Press, 1988).

31. Lacan, *Le séminaire III (1955–1956): Les psychoses.*

32. Sigmund Freud, "The Loss of Reality in Neurosis and Psychosis" (1924), *SE*, 19: 183–87.

33. Jean-Jacques Gorog, "Actes Imposés," *La lettre mensuelle: Au-delà de l'Oedipe, Actes,* no. 103 (November 1991): 18–21; 20–21.

34. Jacques Lacan, "A Lacanian Psychosis: Interview by Jacques Lacan," in *Returning to Freud: Clinical Psychoanalysis in the School of Lacan*, ed. and trans. by Stuart Schneiderman (New Haven: Yale University Press, 1980), 19–41. For a discussion of this essay, see Jacques-Alain Miller, "Teachings of the Case Presentation," in *Returning to Freud*, 42–52; 48.

35. Jacques Lacan, *Les complexes familiaux dans la formation de l'individu* (Paris: Navarin Editeur, 1984), 107.

36. See the commentary on *lalangue* by Jacques-Alain Miller in *Ornicar?* 1 (1975): 16–34.

37. Sol Aparicio, "La forclusion, préhistoire d'un concept," *Ornicar?* 28 (Spring 1984): 83–105; 105. See Aparicio's discussion of Freud's use of the concepts *Verdrängung, Urverdrängung, Verleugnung, Bejahung,* and *Verwerfung,* in relation to Lacan's elaboration of these concepts.

3

Lacan's Concept of the Death Drive

Not only is Freud's theory of the death drive sketchy, many analysts maintain that he did not pursue his thoughts on Thanatos, but dropped the problem by opposing it to Eros as an opposite and equal force. Ernest Jones maintained that even though Freud spoke about Thanatos, it was Federn who introduced the idea into psychoanalytic writings.[1] But once Freud had discovered the automatism of repetition in *Beyond the Pleasure Principle*, he could no longer sustain the idea of an instinctual movement from pleasure to reality, insofar as life was actually submitted to death principles.[2] And in the seventh section of "Analysis Terminable and Interminable" Freud presented Eros and destruction as universals: the two principal drives governing human action.[3]

Ernest Jones, among others, criticized Freud's concept of the death drive in "Beyond the Pleasure Principle" (1920)—where repetition compulsion equals a death drive—arguing that the idea of a death drive contradicts the biological principles they describe as a thrust toward life. Lacan suggested that perhaps Freud dropped the idea of a death drive because his colleagues opposed such a theory. Or perhaps Freud himself found no reasonable answer to this concept. Indeed, Freud gave ever greater play to the idea of an equally strong life force. In this way, Lacan suggested, he calmed his colleagues who were offended by the idea of there being any "drive" toward death. But Lacan remained firm in maintaining that Freud's discovery of a death drive at the heart of mental functioning was embryonic even in Freud's earliest writings. Although thinkers from multiple disciplines continually try to ascertain the *causes* that motivate human behavior, no one except Freud throughout his career and Lacan throughout his fifty years of teaching claim that humans are actually driven by a death principle. Although Freud retained the problem of the death drive in his writings until the end of his life, Lacan submits the following stunning insight: that Freud's second topography (id, ego, superego) was a reworking of all his previous theory and practice. When he could not avoid seeing that the pleasure principle did not motivate humans, Freud's response was a frenzied effort to reconceptualize nearly three decades of constructing psychoanalysis. Seen in this light, Freud's second topography is an implicit admission of his failure to understand, or go further with, his own discovery of an unconscious function governing mental life.

Picking up where Freud left off, Lacan retained the death drive as an ongoing problem in his work. Given this premise, the two questions I shall try to answer here are: What is Lacan's concept of the death drive? and Why would humans be motivated by death, not life? But Lacan's concept of the death drive is neither Freud's repetition in "Beyond the pleasure principle," nor aggression à la Melanie Klein. It is, rather, the inertia of *jouissance* which makes a person's love of his or her symptoms greater than any desire to change them. But how does Lacan get to this?[4] Jacques-Alain Miller's categorization of Lacan's teaching into three different periods helps one to follow Lacan's evolving reinterpretation of Freud's thoughts on the death drive.[5] Lacan redefined the death drive in terms of meaning in the 1950s in "The function and field of speech and language in psychoanalysis." Basing his thoughts on Hegel's phenomenological idea that the word kills the thing, he argued that a sense of oneness in perceptual (imaginary) experience is lost in the human effort to *re*-present a thing.[6] Lacan developed this theory in his reinterpretation of "Beyond the Pleasure Principle" in *Seminar* II.[7] As soon as "reality" (the data of the word) is caught up in a symbolic network—that is, symbolized or given meaning—the thing becomes present in a word or concept rather than in any immediate experiential reality. Moreover, one cannot return to the unmediated joy of a given reality *qua* perceptual merger with the thing-in-itself once language names the thing. Forever after, one can only know the thing through recourse to words. And words imply the absence of the "thing" as a fullness or presence. That is, although words seek to re-present the thing-in-itself, they can never be one with what they seek to say or embody at the level of oneness, unity, correctness, saying it "all."[8]

In this first period of Lacan's teaching, visible or imaginary images mask the symbolic by repetitions that give rise to something other than pleasure. At this time, Lacan viewed clinical practice or treatment as engaging an inter-subjectivity of the word. He viewed the analysand as reaching out to the analyst for recognition of being *in the word itself*. Symptoms were seen as non-symbolized parts of a person's life story (*histoire*) that could be integrated into the symbolic by the telling of a narrative, or by recognition of the Other as desiring in one's stead. In the second period of Lacan's teaching, he shifted accent in his account of the death drive from the inter-subjectivity of speaking to language, taken as a synchronic structure. In that context, language was portrayed as a senseless, mechanistic automaton that produces nonsensical meaning. He had shifted from a phenomenological view of language to a linguistic structuralist one in which language was a differential system of inherently meaningless elements.[9] He equated the death drive with being alienated behind the mask of the symbolic order itself.

During this second period, Lacan also came up with the concept of the "second death" opposed to the "first" or animal "death" of the biological body. The concept of a "second death" is an attempt to describe castration as a function or structure of alienation wherein the symbolic order is taken on as a mortification (or castration) of the physical body. Language implicitly imposes a "no" (a limit, or "kind" of law) on the immediacy of satisfaction. In this way language serves as a structure of *alienation* from *jouissance*. As such, language introduces a certain division in the subject. And humans are forever after "thrown" by the experience of trying to recuperate forbidden *jouissance*.

But in the world of objects or things, the operative function is separation or loss. For example, the loss of "objects" with which one identifies—thus grounding oneself in things or ritual acts—disrupts the momentary sense of pleasurable oneness or consistency they offer (be it a warm bath, watching television, or smoking a quiet cigarette). Losses give rise to the use of metaphor (substitution) which functions to displace (metonymy) the effects of loss. Indeed any cut into a person's relationship to the things of the world disrupts a *sense* of well-being that one might define as a continuity between the body and the surrounding world. Thus, anything that imposes the momentary real of loss on one's sense of being whole (being one with oneself), *cuts* into perception itself. The cut dramatizes the fact that perception emanates from the body *qua* imaginarily constituted—in parts, not as a whole.[10]

In his third period of teaching, Lacan hypothesized that the Other—made up of Borromean signifying units enchaining the symbolic, the imaginary, and the real—has a traumatic element at its very center. He called this element the irreducibility of loss taken as a positive factor: [S($\emptyset$)]. A *palpable* void lies at the heart of language, being, and body. Thus, it is loss that drives life, making of the death drive a matter of clinging to known consistencies rather than encountering the unbearable real of loss *qua* anxiety.[11] The object *a* denotes any filler of this void.[12] As such, it quickly grounds being in repetitions—repeating relations to *objects* whose crucial function of semblance is that of filling up an actual void. Thus, human beings pursue objects that sustain fantasies, even though attaining an object of fantasy can never completely close the void. Even those "objects" (one might describe as familiar contexts) that give pleasure in a first moment, offer the fixity of "death" in a second moment. Repetitious rituals become habits, turning Eros into Thanatos.[13] Even though repetition is not inherently lethal, it attaches us to stasis by invisible bonds. In consequence, we defend whatever gives us fixity—a sense of *being* grounded—over the dialectic of movement where freedom, truth, and change lie.

What, then, is *jouissance*? Simply put, *jouissance* is Lacan's effort to translate Freud's concept of libido. Put another way, *jouissance* names that which makes human beings vacillate between the sublime and the ridiculous, pleasure and pain, being and nothingness: the value one assigns to one's being at the level of worth. *Jouissance* is the essence or quality that gives one's life its value. Primary *jouissance* is the libidinal energy that collects at points of loss in response to the cut and holds together the unconscious fantasy material that makes of humans inert, defensive, resisting creatures.

In Freud's efforts to understand what lay beyond the pleasure principle, he described *a quantity of pleasure* he called the id. Its demands exceed what reality actually offers in the way of pleasure, the imbalance giving rise to the death drive or the law of entropy whose aim is stability or constancy. In Freud's second topography (1923), the ego becomes the mediating reality principle that will strive for equilibrium between the cultural demands of reality (the superego) and the greedy demands of pleasure (the id). In Freud's view, the id—selfish and blind—drives psychic energy by seeking impossible totalities of pleasure. But the primary-process death instinct protests against the id's excessive demands for pleasure since the aim of the death drive is to lower the excitation level or pressure points in human life. "The aim of all life [is] death" (or entropy), Freud argued in "Beyond the Pleasure Principle" (38). But by aligning repetition with the quest for pleasure, Freud reached a logical impasse in which he was led to argue that repetitions—themselves mortifications—give pleasure by reducing tension or conflict.

Freud ended up in this double bind: stasis equals pleasure. As early as *Séminar VII: The Ethics of Psychoanalysis* (1959–1960), Lacan had begun to comment on this paradox or impasse in Freud's work.[14] Disagreeing with Freud about the nature of the death drive, Lacan said that humans are not driven toward death as entropy. Rather, we are driven by "death" in the form of excesses in *jouissance*. That is, we cling to fetish objects (the object *a*) which we identify as our Good. Humans remain locked in double binds for no apparent reason, unhappy *as if* on purpose. The reason is not mysterious in Lacan's teaching. We are controlled by traumatic events that have already constituted the real as an order of meanings that remain, nonetheless, in thought, memory, or the body, as blockages. Traumatic material is unsymbolized knowledge which is present as knots or suspended impasses in language (thought).

This is quite a different notion of primary bodily energy from Freud's. In Jean Guir's would-be Lacanian adaptation of Freud's theory of the death drive, the repetition compulsion that lies beyond the pleasure principle is a kind of bio-organic primordial masochism.[15] Guir calls this an erotogenic masochism that finds pleasure in pain. Typical of other post-Freudian misunderstandings of the death drive, Jean Guir's argument is that death is the good of life, and *jouissance* is a fundamental masochism ("Phénomenes", 64).

In Lacan's third period of teaching he developed the theory that *jouissance* is constituted as an order of meaning whose goal is to maintain consistency in an effort to screen out encounters with loss and lack, since the latter evoke anxiety. One cannot, however, equate Lacan's concept that the aim of the drives is consistency with Freud's aim of the drives toward entropy. In Freud's biological theory the physiological organism seeks the stasis of satisfaction, defined as the absence of conflict, or pleasure. In Lacan's theory, humans aim for a consistency of meaning that protects the imaginary body from encountering the holes where the pain of the real—*qua* impasse—enters thought. Nonetheless, the effect of a real order of unspeakable material produces enigmatic symptoms of the body.

But how is Lacan's theory a rethinking of the Freudian death drive? Lacan's concept of the death drive is diffuse, and plays on every level of his theoretical and clinical work. Lacan argues that Freud missed a major step. The pleasure principle is not opposed to the reality principle. Rather, that which produces pleasure or joy in a first moment turns into the displeasure Lacan calls the reality principle or the death drive in a second moment of repetition. Pleasure turns to displeasure because repetition, by definition, refers to a preceding moment—to the loss of a pleasure (or consistency). The pleasure remains, however, as a fixation, a trace (or "letter") in memory, and gives body to fantasy. Thus, pleasure is retrieved via repetitions that constitute fantasies of eradicating loss.

Although the goal of repetition is to re-experience a prior ("hallucinated") satisfaction, the effort to recapture such lost moments depends on the fixations put in place to compensate for the loss of the primary object: that is, the illusion of a primordial oneness between child and mother. Yet, the lost object stays lost. Lacan said in his seminar of January 14, 1970, that *jouissance* is lost even at the very moment of a repetition.[16] One tries to recuperate "it"— the id or libido—via actual objects, but retrieves only wisps of *jouissance* that were inscribed (or written) before in unary traits linking one's physical body to the world via the drives that constitute a primordial *jouissance*.[17] Thus, Lacan follows Freud in bringing together the death drive and the concept of repetition. But by finding repetition proximate to reality—and not pleasure—he argues that reality is not benign, but lethal.

In 1959–1960 Lacan sketched the framework of an argument he developed throughout his career. Language seeks to re-present the real. Subjects exist in the field of language—not in some pure reality, but—as narcissistic objects of the *jouissance* that first structured them by identifications. These, in turn, require the validation of recognition from others by which any person maintains the illusions he or she lives by. Thus, we experience ourselves as subjects of desire with*in* the field of language. In order to feel stable, whole, and at one with ourselves in the world, we repeat words and actions that once gave us pleasure—desiring not the constancy of some minimal entropy, as Freud argued, but the bodily satisfaction of consistency that protects us from the real of anxiety.

Because repetitions produce the familiar constellations of *jouissance* that first established a continuity between a person's particular narcissism and his or her "objects," *jouissance* marks the fact of its own conflictual relation with desire. While desire concerns the unconscious—the "I don't know"—it is *de facto* dialectical. But *jouissance*, on the contrary, is certain and absolute. Rituals or habits already predict the *jouissance* a person takes for granted. At the heart of fantasy ($\$ \lozenge a$) which seeks to satisfy unconscious lack, Lacan found a paradox that led him to call all drives death drives. We desire change in fantasy (to wit, the endless variations of fashion), but are driven to seek satisfaction via the already consti-tuted—the familiar. That is, the guarantee of a consistency in *jouiss-ance* cannot ever really satisfy desire which always rephrases the implicit question: What am I? What am I worth in the lane of the social gaze? That is, what do I lack? How can I reify myself as ideal? Yet one cannot satisfy desire for the new—for change—by repeating the known, for this grounds individuals in something they value above all else: the consistency of the expected. This is the death that drives us in all our daily acts.

In *Encore*, Lacan interpreted the primordial father in Freud's "Totem and Taboo" (1912–1913) as Freud's intuition of the power of the real embodied in a dead figural father—the signifying father taken to the second degree—at the base of human cognition.[18] But Freud's primal father—the one who lives beyond the law, an ex-ception to the rule of castration—was a *mythic* father for Lacan. And by myth, Lacan does not mean untrue or fictional. Rather, "myth gives epic form to that which works from structure."[19] In logical terms, there must be an exception to the rule for there to be a rule. Yet the myth that one omnipotent man—an Ur-father—is exempt from the law, from the incest taboo, serves as a paradoxical basis for group law. That is, the mythical father gives rise to a cul-tural superego by requiring his own murder. Freud suggested that group rule arises out of shared (Oedipal) guilt over murdering the father who kept all the *jouissance* for himself. This mythical Ur-father is subject to no law, then, but he founds the structural basis for law not only because he is a tyrannical figure, but also because he functions as a *principle* of prohibition. The further paradox is this: law is founded on the belief that there is a super figure whose right to full enjoyment makes the conditions of law necessary for others. Freud's myth of a primordial father beyond the law who takes all the women for himself, thus denying the pleasure of *jouiss-ance* to others, means this to Lacan: the law prohibits full *jouissance* to anyone as a matter of structure, not as a matter of morality.

The impossibility of living at the level of pure *jouissance* is shown in varying cultural scriptings of a superego that Lacan described as "ferocious and obscene." But what did Lacan mean? Insofar as the first form of the superego is created by the primordial castrating power of the gaze that judges, thereby promoting ideals, superego injunctions will forever after intersect in the projective optics of imaginary relations in Lacan's topological geometry. For example, when a *cold* stare from a stranger stops a person dead in his tracks as he walks down a crowded sidewalk, what has he done? or not done? Perhaps he has innocently cut into a *jouissance* bond—that is, the projective illusion of oneness held by a couple of lovers strolling along, unaware that their psychic proximity is not a *visible* bond in space itself. By inadvertently stepping between two people, not handcuffed or with arms locked, the bypasser serves as a reminder of the phallic law of castration or lack merely by breaking up their illusion of oneness.

Thus, Lacan interpreted the Freudian pleasure principle as a paradoxical model of death. What Freud called unconscious assumptions, Lacan called fundamental fantasies, which spawn lure images—i.e., things that seem to promise satisfaction. But satisfaction quickly becomes addictive. And it is paradoxically the enemy of desire. Although a cultural superego mocks human failures, showing up in constellations of words that infer a "morally" (politically) correct standard or paradigm by which to judge oneself in reference to the *jouissance* "norms" or social *ideals* of a moment, the deadlier side of *jouissance* appears in haunting gazes and voices. That is, since *jouissance* is tethered to the Other—not the other, as we think—individuals find themselves inexplicably burdened by death weights or inertias that do not really correspond to realities "outside." Although people project guilt and blame onto others, such projections are actually narcissistic identifications with unconscious ideals of "self." While developing his thinking on the order of the real (from 1974 on), Lacan elaborated his second theory of the symptom which he linked to *jouissance*. He argued that the symptom is not just a metaphor—a substitute formation—but depends on the death drive, the "more in us than us" that keeps us sick. Indeed *jouissance* itself is the very principle of symptom formation, insofar as symptoms are enigmas that circle around an irreducible residue of traumatic knowledge at the heart of every signifying chain. In this sense, *jouissance* produces in us the "drive not to know" that grounds denial and makes of desire itself the desire not to know. And even after the end of an analysis, Lacan found an excess in *jouissance* that remains and resists cure. Indeed, wherever suffering persists, one finds an overvalorization of *jouissance* which Lacan depicted, from 1975 on, as a constituted meaning system that wants no knowledge of itself. No one wants to be cured of his or her symptoms because the death drive—translated here as *jouissance*—lies beyond the pleasure principle and beyond the principle of repetition, on the side of the real impasses that organize our lives in the negative familiar we hold on to.

Freud found chaos in what one could not control and called it negative transference or unconscious masochism. Lacan viewed chaos as a symptom of fundamental displeasure, discontent, even perverse enjoyment in the breach of the pleasure principle that places a stubborn obstacle in each person's life and a *malaise* in civilization.[20] Yet the *malaise*—the lack in being or want to be— lingers because it is structural. Sad to say, the contents with which we try to close that gap become more valuable to us than any question about the horrors they produce. Such satisfaction is certainly distinct from instinct.[21]

We know that Lacan always returned to Freud for theoretical support, even though his own references were to philosophy, language study, anthropology, and topology, while Freud's references were to the "natural" sciences. In 1923 (in the second topography of id/ego/superego) Freud reaffirmed the primacy of the unconscious over the ego, and the primacy of the death drive over the other drives.[22] The Freudian ego of the 1923 model took on the burden of expressing the unconscious as an unknown force that acts without the subject's having knowledge of it.[23] Freud inscribed the ego in the id, the ego serving as the repressing agent. Lacan translated this Freudian idea thus: Just as language is unknowingly deployed to translate what lacks in one's conscious thought—but is known in the Other extrinsic to knowledge—*jouissance* adds an affective dimension to words. This recalls Freud's idea that the silence of the drives somehow speaks.

The fundamental reality on which the death drive is based is that human subjects do not have direct access to the meanings that govern their lives. People speak and behave in conscious life without knowing that their words and acts derive from a set of unconscious suppositions (S_2). These constitute a knowledge, made up of fictive and subjective interpretations of the world that are neither relative, haphazard, nor random, but are overdetermined by the concrete signifying material built up in the family of one's childhood.

"Self"-believed descriptions are anchored in identifications that verify the myths one lives from, based as they are in *jouissance*. Thus, the desire that drives human beings to seek freedom and change is stymied by one's clinging to the already known. At the level of human experience we fail to achieve the balance of "constancy" as defined, for example, in physics or in the "natural" sciences. That is, the human drive works more like a montage than by any natural causality. But because the archaic bank of unconscious knowledge is opaque and asymmetrical to conscious scrutiny, it is erased as "knowledge" at the moment it is borrowed as thought. Neither the linearity of speech and grammar nor the familiarity of "self"-repetition, will reveal the Otherness in language itself. Only unconscious desire will do that. Yet language gives the false impression that humans are synchronic, narrative, linear beings, fully present to themselves as subjects of "free will." Thus meaning, at any given moment, seems correct and believable.

And this seeming sufficiency of language to thought and of *jouissance* to being, blocks any person's vision of the permanent flaw in every human's engagement with the cultural order: the impossibility of representing oneself adequately in language. This flaw derives, on the one hand, from the *lack* that is the memory bank itself—the absent and opaque Other. On the other hand, the unconscious guides the actions of any conscious subject via desire. Commonsense wisdom errs, then, in believing that satisfaction inheres in objects, things, and people. Rather, words "act" as data or scar tissue, "speaking" a language of confused "knowledge" about being, desire, and *jouissance*. Lacan argued that being is painful because it depends on meaning derived from the effects of loss, organized as they are in an imaginary nexus of images and fantasies of plenitude. Although this early material is never directly retrievable, nor can it ever fill up the gap of loss itself, meaning still always chases "something" just out of grasp. This something, caused by a dependence on *jouissance* "objects" that glue a person together, manifests a death drive in being.

Lacan claimed that the most important questions about the object, for psychoanalysis that is, consider it from the point of view of its lack.[24] Russell Grigg clarifies Lacan's startling point.[25] Lacan discerned in Freud three different ways in which the object can lack: castration, frustration, and, he added, privation. Unlike object-relations theorists, Lacan was not concerned with the phenomenological concept of persons as objects in social relations—"objects" to whom one must adjust or readjust in terms of internalized parental images, good or bad. Rather, the primordial matrices of fundamental fantasies organize the body imaginarily around objects that cause desire. These so-called objects cause desire in ways that are opposed, not attuned, to the post-Freudian notion of a harmonious, regular, natural, and normal developmental sequence. Development, Grigg points out, occurs from the start of life in reference to objects—oral, anal, etc.—that are never what they seem to be. They are always taken for something other than what they are because they are endowed with meaning from the outset (Grigg, "Lacan on Object Relations," 42).

In 1953 Lacan wrote that "the anal [or any other stage] is no less purely historical when it is actually *experienced* than when it is reconstituted in thought, nor is it less purely grounded in inter-subjectivity."[26] In the 1960s Lacan described such "knowledge" as each subject's repressed truth or dialectical epic.[27] But in reinter-preting Freud's idea that the death drive brings the human subject back to an inorganic state of nature characterized by constancy or entropy, Lacan changed the meaning of "inorganic," dropping any sense of the physiological decomposition of biological matter.[28] In-stead, the death drive refers quite concretely to the detritus of mem-ories embedded in our flesh through family myths and archaic trau-mas. The identifications that form us leave slivers and splinters in the words that plague ego certainties in their myriad efforts to equate ego with thought and thought with conscious perception.

Lacan argued that just beyond clear meaning lies another kind of knowledge where people oscillate between the sense of being a Being (of free will and self-determination) and encounters with the void: The *jouissance* left over in the wake of losses gives both a positive and a negative aspect to the death drive. One literally iden-tifies oneself at the level of value as some*thing* or nothing. Thus, on the one hand, *jouissance* blocks the drive as it aims at consist-ency because we, paradoxically, create discontinuities in clinging to the past. This excess in *jouissance* holds the key to the meaning of one's symptoms, then, rooted as they are in fundamental fan-tasies. Yet, even though it is possible to learn something unknown about oneself within one's history of signifying chains, no one wants to "awaken" to a knowledge of the unconscious *savoir* that makes him or her a victim of Other desire, not a subject of his or her own free will. For if we admit we have been constituted as Other to ourselves, our ideals are attenuated. However, nothing less than the death of ego certainties can enable a person to reconstruct his or her being around new desire. For the alienations that anchor one in fixed identifications base *jouissance* on the fear of loss. Peo-ple settle for any known set of identifications, however painful, lest they fall out of the familiar symbolic order into the real of anxiety which opens onto a void of actual emptiness at the center of being.

Lacan credited Freud with being the first person to name the unconscious as *an existing place*. But post-Freudians have collapsed conscious and unconscious mental fantasies into some rough equa-tion with the brain. For Lacan "mind" is a metaphor for the orders that are built up from the start of life out of associational traits: sounds, smells, images, objects that *cause* desire. Such concrete effects constitute *jouissance* as a set of identifications in the three orders, yielding three different kinds of *jouissance*: that of the biological organism (the real); that of the body (the imaginary); and that of the subject (the symbolic). At the juncture between the symbolic and the imaginary, *jouissance* concerns the meaning that gives positive value to one's life (Φ). At the juncture between the real and the imaginary *jouissance* concerns one's engagement with lack that Lacan calls castration ($-\phi$). And at the intersection of the real and the symbolic one finds the Other *jouissance* where the void dwells at the level of the physical organism itself [$S(\emptyset)$].

Although the three orders function associationally in the making of meaning, they are split and overlapping at points of intersection. And in these spaces of "blindsight," elements are mapped onto one another in such a way that mental functions are contradictory within themselves. Freud described such impasses in thought as unconscious slips that occur within a supposedly correct and naturally smooth functioning of language. Although Freud hypothesized an unconscious part of the mind that causes the "errors" of forgetting, lapses, slip-ups, fadings, accidents, jokes, kidding around, silliness, surprise, irony, denial, and so on, he took them to be aberrations within a norm. Lacan argued, rather, that being is defective. It is that which language lacks and so cannot designate. In "The subversion of the subject," Lacan called the being of the subject its object *a*. This place beyond designation which is caused by the lack of a signifier and "makes being itself languish" is *jouissance* (316).

Lacan argued that the dedicated belief that language coheres in an unruffled surface that merely mirrors the objective accuracy of some scientific certainty or the subjective reality of some interpretive opinion is itself a testimonial to the fact that people use language in order to hide the very gaps and holes it tries to fill. But since language is the material thought is made of, the holes and gaps in it appear as contradictions, temporal discordances, and so on. Yet these point to a "beyond" *in* language itself that concerns desire and *jouissance*. Once a child can speak coherently—is able to present himself or herself as a subject represented by one signifier (S_1) for another one (S_2)—speech erases the knowledge base from which memory derives. Thus, even though consciousness and memory are co-extensive, they cancel each other out in a lightning-flash movement or instant of usage.[29]

Lacan's discovery—that meaning is dialectical only insofar as it re-presents a "subject" for some other meaning or signifier—shows the dependence of seemingly "natural" meanings on the invisible and unconscious references we endow with certainty and conviction in conscious life. Yet we are only certain because we are lethally fixed in the *jouissance* of familiarity that grounds our belief in meaning, fixed fantasies, and organic realities. Language speaks one message: the word kills the "thing" of immediate fusion or satisfaction, introducing deferral—which is actually the temporality of the unconscious—as a function of language that places active memory in all acts of language. This temporal movement in language itself reveals the gaps between words and images. Neither words nor images are adequate to cover over loss and, thus, annul the fragmentations or discontinuities produced by unconscious thought.

Yet we try to cover over the basic instability of reference with imaginary consistencies. But not only is the locus of meaning hidden in the Other, and thus opaque to conscious interpretation ($), there is also a void right in the center of every person's knowledge [S(∅)]. Thus, the most intimate knowledge any person has is built around the unsymbolized, impossible, and radically lost "thing" which no one can articulate, but whose sheer density drives most of us (who are not autistic, psychotic, or physically unable to speak) to deny, repress, and sublimate, while insisting that nothing is a-miss. For dependency on meaning starts at the beginning of life when infants register the sounds and gestures of the primordial Other in order to elicit a response from the other on whom they depend. Even a tiny baby's cry is a *parole*, a "word" encoded for the meaning which speaks the desire for a response to his or her cry, lest he fall prey to the anxiety produced by loss or lack.

Lacan's concept of the death drive does not reduce human "drive" to animal "instincts." Rather, precise meanings structure the human biological organism, making of it an imaginary signifier. In that the body is "cut up" by signifiers, human animals are ensured of acquiring a sense of "being" (an *esse*) that represents itself in the myths and fictions that tie body and meaning to the world. Thus "meaning" is always already alien because it is imposed from the outside. In other words, there is no *a priori*, innate, true "self" meaning. "Alienation" means foreign, "Other," strange. Unlike the animals who simply want the *jouissance* or satisfaction derived from being fed, being stroked, etc., most human animals want to know what they must do to be loved. Love, they hope, will enable them to shut out loss and satiate the lack implicit in desire.

One can see parallels between Lacan's idea that the drive to maintain *jouissance* is auto-erotic and his description of all drives as death drives. Because meaning is never adequate to satisfy the demands of desire, the imaginary takes up the slack, taking appearance for truth or reality, making perceptual consistencies out of the visible. But in the life game where no one wins finally or completely, real pieces of words and images coat meaning with the only "essence" Lacan admits: *jouissance*. Indeed, anxiety links the death drive to fantasy (and thus to the desire for *jouissance*) precisely around the fear of losing the identifications that constitute the libido as a real, yet invisible, organ *in* the body.

But these fixations of death—of petrified *jouissance*—have nothing to do with Heidegger's "being-for-death" which concerns the human preoccupation with worry. For worry and anxiety (which encounter "death" as positivized loss) have nothing to do with each other.[30] Heidegger, like other thinkers across the centuries, asked why human suffering persists despite all we know, all we can do. Lacan gave a different answer than the philosopher. We cannot avoid human suffering because the symbolic is governed by the death drive and we cannot do much to change this. Indeed, the function of repetition enters human relations at the level of the symptom as Thanatos. And Thanatos manifests itself in three different *jouissance* responses to the sexual *non-rapport* [S($\emptyset$)] at the heart of desire and drive: either social norms or conventions compensate for the absence of a sexual rapport (country club life, sports, television, etc.); or, perversion gives enough access to *jouissance* to satisfy the sexual nonrapport; or, neurosis maintains itself as a dissatisfaction with norms and with *jouissance*.[31] However, no one of these symptoms is a remedy for the fundamental lack—or *malaise*—for which humans seek to compensate: a lack-in-being.

In this context, Lacan taught that transference does not, as Freud thought, repeat childhood relationships. Nor does mirror-stage interdependency provide an adequate explanation of how the function of repetition is constructed. Lacan stressed Freud's idea that for something to be repeated, it must have already been grounded, foreshadowed, laid down *a priori*. Repetition only makes (logical) sense after the fact, then, in reference to a before. And the "before" concerns the grounding of one's knowledge and desire in *jouissance*. Thus, whether repetition marks the normative patterning of an "ego's" everyday life by the rigid rituals characteristic of obsession, the mimetic parrot songs chanted by psychotics, or the useless sacrifices cherished by hysterics, the repetition of "acts" brings about the *jouissance* of "self"-recognition within the confines of the pleasure of the known.

Because people reject the unconscious as a "knowledge" about desire, they remain blind to the identificatory power of *jouissance* which blocks access to knowledge about desire.

Yet, people cannot block out the real that returns in *jouissance* effects, mocking ego efforts at wholeness and certainty. While unconscious signifiers persist in language, but are easy to dismiss, *jouissance* repeats lethal tunes of forced illusions. While signifiers belong to the language of knowledge, *jouissance* is constituted even prior to coherent language, as consistency organized around objects. The point is not that the objects are lost, but that *jouissance* is. Jacques-Alain Miller has described the real which returns in language and *jouissance* as *non-sens*. This non-utilitarian nonsense perforates the unity in things and explodes into our words. The lacks, fadings, and equivocations of the *symbolic* subject make up the lapses of everyday life, while fictions, myths, and ideologies justify belief in *imaginary* self-idealizations. But the *real* returns in palpable impasses which "drive" us to validate an ideal image of the "self" in the eyes of others. "Ego" exchange comes down to a matter of the lethal weight of narcissistic power, then. One seeks "self"-reification—i.e., the perpetuation of *jouissance*.

Not surprisingly, most people have these things in common: susceptibility to doubt, anxiety, humiliation, despair, as well as moments (or periods) of happiness, fulfillment, delight, and contentment. Since neither positive nor negative *jouissance* is a temporal constant or a state of being, individuals vacillate between an absolute sense of being somebody—being "there" (*Da-Sein*)—or being nobody, being "gone" (*Fort-Sein*). *Jouissance* gives rise to predictably correlative postures of narcissism and aggressivity that mark all human dealings one with the other. Is one "here" or "there"? somebody or nobody? Since normative narcissism is essentially a principle of resistance to true knowledge about one's "self," aggressivity serves as a compensatory response to narcissistic wounds, running the gamut from a deprecatory joke or ironic aside to a crime of passion or national war.

Lacan followed Freud's idea that the repressed parts in (unconscious) thought return in slips of the tongue, dreams, laughter, jokes, and so on. But Lacan goes beyond Freud in telling us precisely what is repressed (*Urverdrängt*). It is unsymbolized meanings (the real of unassimilated traumata) that make empty places resonate with meaning in the biological body, meanings that have not yet been translated into language.[32] It is also *la lalangue* or the primordial tongue which can never be translated, although its effects are determining. The re-pressed—what presses back, pressing against language and identifications—is the *jouissance* substance in the biological (real) and imaginary bodies. Its meaning is that of excitement or dread. Quickly veering from excitation to *malaise*, *jouissance* goes from discontinuities that are omnipresent in enigmatic affects, to mysterious symptoms or suddenly erotic moments—in all those instants that make us less unified than we think we are.

The space of the real constitutes the limits of the Lacanian symbolic (or cultural) order. There where the symbolic is no longer ordered, the real carries the *jouissance* weight of inertia in archaic signifying chains. The death zone in each of us is demarcated by the limit of the symbolic, then, at the point where it fails to stretch over the real. Given the god-like power of the real, Lacan mocked concepts of free will, good intentions, temporary "cures," pep talks, behavioral rewards, or any other psychological vitamin pill. He spoke, rather, of the individual pain of fading in and out of a hole in the Other [S($\emptyset$)] that marks human consciousness with something devastating. *Jouissance* effects bespeak a knowledge of loss so fundamental in the grounding of one's illusion of being a being, that people never quit trying to recapture or maintain a sense of Oneness in all things.

Freud explained the death drive as seeking entropy or constancy, basing this on the idea that the pleasure principle dominates psychic processes. In his economic model, Freud argued that "unpleasurable tension" spurs one to seek pleasure. That is, the psychic processes aim at the pleasure of lowering tension in order to avoid the displeasure caused by external prohibitions requiring the repression of id instincts.[33] This theory, recast by Lacan, takes on a darker meaning when pleasure is seen as the lethal *cause*—the pleasure in displeasure or shock—that one seeks as the *jouissance* of his or her life because (and only because) it gives consistency.

Freud connected repetition to biological instincts by defining the "drive" as "an urge, inherent in an animate organism, to restore an earlier state" (i.e., an inherent inertia as in situations of preperceptual awareness).[34] The death drive was, in his view, the push toward an absolute state of objective, affective well-being. Such a state was defined by equating the constancy of a pleasure with the absence of tension. Just as Lacan wondered how a state of primordial narcissism could be enclosed on itself (cf. chap. one), he asked what would constitute a primary state of inertia. Lacan derived an answer where Freud found none. The early fixations of primary *jouissance* (inertia) are made up of the residue left in the wake of the traumata of loss (separations, cuts, weanings). The absurd aspect to the death drive is this: that original or first pleasures—having become libidinal fixations—do not ground humans in genuine *pleasures*, but in the pain of repetition Lacan called the reality principle. In our attempts to keep the ground from shifting, we idealize our objects, clothe people and thoughts with the ideological garments of the good, the true, and the beautiful. But, the unconscious moves as desire tracking evacuated *jouissance*, as desire and sexuality dancing in an endless vacillation around a void.[35]

Lacan argued in the third period of his teaching that the real drives us to decide, choose, act. Emptying continually into conscious life and language, the real gives a positive value to seemingly impenetrable mysteries. We are used to the real, Lacan says. It is truth we repress.[36] The real ex-sists as a kind of "extimate" object at a point where subjects are objects—the gaze, the voice, the void, and so on, not masters of the word.[37] Indeed, one can say that the ego is itself an object *a*. In this capacity it bolsters the death drive by trying to maintain an imaginary consistency of oneness over and above truth.

The marriage between the ego and the death drive becomes all the clearer in the psychoanalytic clinic where the symptom defines itself as a symptom precisely by refusing to recognize its attachment to *jouissance*. A familiar example is of a husband who abuses his wife who justifies his maltreatment in any number of ways: he was tired; his mother was mean to him; he didn't do it on purpose. But the truth of the symptom in the couple lies in such a woman's refusal (that of the hysteric) to expose her substitute "Daddy" as less than ideal. Indeed, the symptom claims that nothing outside the visible can cause it.[38] In this purview, desire-as-cause is sublimated in its relation to *jouissance*, leaving the fields of language and the body vulnerable to the death components that a person's superego brings via the obscenity of guilt (Cottet, *Freud et le desir*, 134). In his later teachings, Lacan's early ethical imperative—"First, the only thing one can be guilty of is giving ground relative to one's desire" (*Sém.* VII, 321)—becomes: "The only guilt lies in giving up on one's *jouissance*."

Insofar as speech and fantasies are organized in reference to the real which appears in fragments, one cannot view Lacanian psychoanalysis as a science of meaning or interpretation—that is, as a hermeneutics. Rather, the ungraspable elements in speaking, being, and wanting—the *a* part—inhere in the Borromean structure (or topology) of any person. Thus, all impasses are of the real and, as such, have the structure of paradox which is itself a constituent of language, not merely a genre, figure, trope, or philosophical problem.

Within Lacan's context, analytic patients are innocent. They come to analysis for one reason. Their suffering has led them there. But the change that will free them from a particular suffering is hard to attain. The inertia of unconscious *jouissance*—the unconscious masochism attached to superego gazes or voices—that resonates with the sense of some punisher-to-come or some ideal-to-reach is so pervasive within being that no simple equating of health with "better behavior," or even with the disappearance of symptoms, can be labeled a cure. Thus, Lacan considered post-Freudian analysts—who see the patient as guilty or childlike, but easily curable, or who relegate man to the Cartesian slope of rationalism that equates reason with the norm in most Western thought today—as unethical: Dale Carnegie rewriting Freud and Descartes to the "power of positive thinking."

If it were easy to relinquish suffering, every person would do so. One must wonder why people cling to their misery in some metaphorical analogy to Voltaire's serpent: the asp one fondles and calls hope, even as it eats away at one's breast.[39] Lacan maintained that the power of the death drive is impossible to conceive because it is welded to the *jouissance* of being that makes of desire a lost cause. Individuals fake cure, play any game they imagine an analyst wishes, endure any miserable life, rather than break up cherished illusions based on unconscious identifications and fantasies. Based on this theory, Lacan saw the *analyst's desire* as crucial to any treatment. For the analyst is enjoined to simulate the suffering underlying the analysand's unstated, even unconstituted, desire. The analyst takes the position of semblant, simulating sorrows too deep for the patient to speak, revealing a place of empty despair and the silence of *jouissance* behind any question of desire. At this level of despair, the analysand as subject is a response of the real, an "object" of alien *jouissance* he or she defends by myth, fantasy, and fiction. The analyst is enjoined to push the analysand's desire beyond his or her closed ego system, for encloistered desire comes from the destitute repetitions of the Other's desires that continue to enslave. Thus, the analysand's pathetic cause surges forth as someone else's life issue.

That the analyst is enjoined to act so as to embody the analysand's alienated desire does not, however, mean enacting empathy—a vacuous, fatuous ego function. Rather, the analyst is enjoined to mime the whine of forlorn desire, blocked as it is by a lethal *jouissance* that acts even on the body's immune defense system. In this way *jouissance* points to knotted meanings whose effects control a life, even though they are too painful to remember or to say. Such unsymbolized material is organized anyway. And it acts noxiously. But since the real is absent to memory, *yet present in effect*, it is not a lost cause. Indeed, blockages in language provide the entry point to aid analysts in using the symbolic to work on the real. The power of our own lethal garbage—the leftovers—whose *cause* we support, lies in the fact that *jouissance* is literally backed up in the body. And it hurts us. The pain of the "not said" works quite concretely to encumber a life even from beyond the grave, by haunting gazes one might describe as an "inner" evil eye or as the superego of moralizing judgments.

In his 1915 essay, "Thoughts for the Times on War and Death," Freud said: "My death is unimaginable. Even the unconscious is convinced of its immortality."[40] In 1956 Lacan gave a reason for what Freud, like others before him, had observed. No person can truly consider his own death because "neither death or birth have a solution in the signifier. This gives existential value to the neuroses."[41] Like sexuality (which confuses the neurotic), death and birth lie at a juncture of impasse in the real. Because they are *enigmatic* at the level of cause and effect, death, birth, and sexuality are mentally unrepresentable. It is not surprising that children express the strangest notions of sex, birth, and death, often up to their teens: "Why was I not in your wedding?" my eleven year old asked as I asked my mother before her; "I'm worried I won't be able to breathe in my coffin after I die," my child says. As a child, I feared the worms that would crawl on me in my coffin. "Sex is having a baby," continues the eleven-year-old wisdom, "but how can I have one if the doctor sews me up like he sewed you up?" And so on. These questions from my eleven-year-old daughter and her friends flow along regularly, despite their reading appropriate explanatory books for their ages, discussing sex in school classes, and viewing anatomically correct dolls.

Lacan argued throughout his work that psychoanalysis is not a natural science, as Freud had thought, but a mathematical and a logical one. Still, Freud's texts spoke truths about human experience that Freud did not understand. *Civilization and Its Discontents* (1930), for example, reveals one such fundamental truth. The *malaise* at the heart of life is not caused in a simplistic one-to-one way by psychic conflict coming from the clash of superego dicta with id strivings. Nor does it come from identifications with bad parents, or from life frustrations—sexual or otherwise. The *malaise* is an indestructible inertia in *unconscious* desire that organizes all normative life around the fault or flaw of a sexual unrelation between men and women. Two cannot be one. Love does not stop the *malaise*. A certain unhappiness is the human norm.

This permanent flaw or *malaise* begins with the loss of the primary object. Such loss is requisite for acquiring an *internalized sense of social law*: learning difference as the law of boundaries. The law is the law of "no" to being One with the mother. It defines self in reference to the third term of difference, in terms of gender difference. Primordial separations first gave rise to desire as wanting a repetition of pleasure. Desire continues to be shaped by the so-called Oedipal experience of identifying with Mommy and Daddy. In consequence, language and *jouissance* command the transformation of desires and identifications into two systems of knowledge: the symbolic-order *savoir* of desire and the imaginary-order *connaissance* of *jouissance*. But no natural (biological) wish for incest obtains in the Oedipal structure, merely the desire for Oneness. A consequence of the function of desire in daily life is the drive toward mastery lest lack or loss undermine one's stability.

Lacan's recasting of the Oedipus myth to an Oedipal *structure* is crucial to his theory that there is a death drive at the center of life. Diacritically speaking, children learn to represent themselves in language by distinguishing one sound from another, by differentiating persons, tones, smells, and so on. But even before they learn grammar, the meaningful foundation of individual subjectivity is organized around the child's experiences of castration and the phallus. This "Oedipal" third term is itself constituted as the phallic signifier, or the unconscious realization that the mother is not All. Lacking this signifier for division, the psychotic depends on the drives to give meaning to his life. Thus, no signifier "means" except in reference to certain *a prioris*. The void in the Other resonates with this truth: lost primordial objects were never possessed in the first place. For most people, desire places loss in the "drive," in the demand ($ \diamond$ D). We *ask for*, aim for, the object *a* of fantasy ($ \diamond$ *a*)—any object that holds out the promise of attenuating loss and

perpetuating *jouissance*. But loss persists in the center of each signifying unit, placing all meaning on shaky grounds.

A subject's encounter with the mother as lacking (or not)—not
lacking an organ, but lacking the capacity to be all to her child—
marks that person's position in language as normative, neurotic,
perverse, or psychotic. The normative male or female acknowl-
edges the sexual difference while bemoaning it, extolling it or making of it a *cause célèbre*. But fundamentally he or she is satisfied
by symbolic order conventions. The neurotic denies castration—
that the sexual difference makes a difference—making a life theme
out of "It ain't necessarily so." The pervert disavows knowledge of
castration, claiming the place of both sexes: both/and. In psychosis—the position of greatest disenfranchisement from the social
masquerade—the subject bears the burden of being neither one sex
nor the other, the sexual difference having been foreclosed in the
unconscious. He or she is without a place in the Other.

The Oedipal principle means that each sex loses *being* the other
sex, loses the *jouissance* of being whole. The signifier for the Name-
of-a-Father serves as a principle for ordering the chaos of the drives
in an asymmetrical turning away from the mother *qua* same or
whole. Such a signifier deflects a child's demand for love away from
the naturalness of the mother toward the legal fiction of a father,
who symbolizes culture. Yet culture does not arise out of the symbolic turn, but as a response to the loss of the primary object.
Lacan's innovation in psychoanalysis was to propose the paternal
metaphor or symbolic father as a structure, but a structure necessary to social functioning. Psychosis is the true death state where
jouissance prevails over the law, which is simply the law of exchange. By exchange I do not, however, mean Lévi-Strauss's marriage exchange which is merely one symbol of a structural reality.
Lacan equates the capacity to exchange (to substitute) with the
dialectic of change. The alternative non-dialectical solution places
the limit of freedom in psychosis.[42]

But how can any freedom be found in psychosis where the primary object is never lost? I understand Lacan to imply that the *limit*
of freedom—a tenuous one—lies in the fact that many psychotics
can and do live in the social world, as opposed to the unmitigated
and relentless living death of no freedom experienced at the pre-
psychotic pole Lacanians call autism. Autism, an extreme case of
psychosis, is a death state where language serves little if any supplemental ego function. In psychosis, by contrast, the symbolic is
joined to the real; the imaginary order of representational differ-

ence (i.e., distance) being foreclosed. Insofar as autistic language is submerged in *jouissance*, it is not usable for giving the subject a position for the capacity to deploy language requires the distance from *jouissance* that enables one to represent a "self" in language for another. The autistic subject lives in language, if at all, rigidly and negatively.

In psychosis rigidity points to the continued reign of an Other's *jouissance* that bespeaks a successful symbiosis between child and mother: two real-ly functioning as one ($O \equiv J$). The third term—the signifier for difference—that ordinarily serves as a referent for linking one's proper name to an image of the sexual body (be it masculine or feminine in identification) is foreclosed. In consequence, the capacity for abstract thought—based as it is on projective imagination—is impaired. Instead, spontaneous, concrete memories arise to infuse secondary thought with primary-process displacements, thus transforming secondary-process thought, often creatively. The imagistic symbols underlying any coherent use of grammar infuse language with a dyadic shimmer that often makes of this subject a creator of art, poetry, music, or mathematics.

Lacan taught a sad lesson: Everyone loses. Even though the psychotic—who, in his failure to lose the primary object, implicitly refuses normative conventions—may create marvelous things, no one who works with psychotic patients would ever encourage a mother to rob her child of access to the social. The sheer unmitigated pain of psychotic suffering puts all other mental suffering in the shade. Yet, the lack most people live with has a death-giving side too. Desire moves in language as a temporal impulse, pushing us to seek objects worthy of attenuating the want-in-being. Working in the service of lack, desire is, nonetheless, a barrier against limitless *jouissance*. In this context, consciousness reflects the polar tension between an ego alienated in *jouissance* and a "beyond" in the drives that escapes understanding. Lacanian analysts work to separate the ideal ego ($I[O]$)—an unconscious formation—from the object *a* which is stuck to the ideal ego. The object *a* by which one tries to realize consistency, reifying ideals, is always excessive. Indeed, "it" blocks the realization of desire insofar as it denotes the surplus of *jouissance* Lacan called the remainder or leftover "semblances" of being from our past. Worse, these masks and myths remain present as dead matter, stopping the temporal movement of change in the present.

The subject, taken as *petit a*, is a semblant. At the level of semblance or appearance he or she masks the real where desire is battened down by *jouissance* which tells the story of what each person has sacrificed of ideals and hope. To what maternal lack does a daughter offer her identity in trying to compensate her mother's pain? To what paternal ideal does a son sacrifice his career? What physical organ is sacrificed in the family sexual/narcissistic/aggressive history of reward and punishment? Whose "family" name does one slave to clear? Whose unpaid "debts" become a child's burden? To what dead desires and muffled aspirations of others does an adult sacrifice him or herself within the generational history of familial/cultural debts? One sees myriad versions of these questions held in suspension in the analytic clinic. And any analyst can only wonder *why analysands continue to live half-dead in the wake of the epics of others*. And I refer only to those persons who cannot carry their burdens any longer and so fall out of sync with the rhythms of the symbolic order, addressing themselves to one of the many "institutions" they suppose can offer help.

The successfully repressed people one might describe as "normative" or normal obsessionals simply displace the question of their burdens onto group or community institutions (such as church, army, political parties, etc.). The material of their suffering is projected onto others (individuals or groups) in guilt/blame scenarios. But blaming others does not disperse the lethal substance of *jouissance* that clusters around the drives in meanings that concern "self"-worth. The real speaks the body anyway in the enigmatic language of the symptoms whose infinitely transformational capacity for displacement allows people to perpetuate illusions, to remain satisfied by a spurious Other. And another social establishment—the medical one—validates the semiotics of bodily *malaise* with a range of drugs, treatments, and "scientific" names describing any malady. Blaming others—the economy, doctors, history, and so on—such individuals ignore the death hold of *jouissance*, living by the closure Lacan equated with the master discourse; the religion of "being *me*" (*m'être*).[43]

Insofar as the earliest experiences of the world build up around Ur-objects that cause desire—the breast, the feces, the voice, the gaze, the (imaginary) phallus, the phoneme, the urinary flow and the nothing (Lacan, "Subversion of the Subject," 315)—unconscious formations coalesce from the beginning as matrices of meaning whose logic is corporal. Unconscious thought evolves in terms of love, desire, and satisfaction. So Lacan departs from Freud to argue that we do not desire objects *per se* to give us pleasure, but consistency. One begins to see how desire is hooked to the death drive. People must seek concrete satisfaction from others, and so risk the displeasure of disagreement or discontinuity. But the cost of submitting to the Other, giving up on one's own desire, is enormous. It means being satisfied by one's misery, rationalizing the repeated *jouissance* that is sustained by lies and illusions.

Not only is desire left aside, worse, it becomes lethally hooked to *jouissance* via the drives. For Lacan's "objects" of desire *cause* desire to function as partial drives that seek satisfaction via reminiscences of the forms that first gave rise to desire. Thus "drives" intervene in all our closures, splintering language and ego into infinite intimations of the real: of the gaze, the voice, the oral, and the anal, which all have one goal—to eradicate loss (*Sem.* II, 209). So we do not find object fulfillment. Nor is the ego curable by reparation. Lacan teaches that all drives are "death" drives. The partial drives always miss their aim: i.e., to ensure a permanent satisfaction by closing the void once and for all.

Obviously experiences and objects do satisfy. But the drives aim for something *more* than pleasure. They aim to repeat the sense of wholeness that constituted them in the first place as montages made up of concrete traits. As such, drives can only lead to missed encounters because closure never comes. So encounters ask for more, again, the next time, *Encore*. Lacan called this gap between desire and fulfillment the "fundamental disorder of instinctual life" at the base of all human dissatisfactions and problems (*Sem.* II, 209). In anorexia, for example, a psychic link is forged between the void constituted by primordial loss of the mother as the primary object of consistency, the *need* for food to maintain physical survival, and the demand for love. Ordinarily, the oral drive bears on the *desire* to incorporate the mother *qua* guarantee of love. In anorexia sheer *need* or primal hunger hooks up with the void in a lethal way. The stubborn demand for love turns into a drive to merge with nothingness itself, thus replicating the *void* feeling. The anorexic risks, and often loses, her life by refusing food. Anorexia may ensue any time a hysteric loses the love context that stabilizes her without any replacement to fill the loss she cannot repress. In refusing food, she *gains* the pleasure of being one with nothing, Lacan's *rien*.

Retaining, but defining anew, Freud's categories of pathology—neurosis, psychosis, perversion—Lacan insisted that the *cause* of the neuroses and psychoses is neither "natural" nor biological. Rather, the "pathologies" or clinically differential structures, mark precise patterns of desire (or not, as in psychosis). These ways of relating to lack do not point to semantics, however, but to the loss of the primary object which annuls a grounding signifier for gender. The effects of this primary loss show up in a person's efforts to compensate in language, via "objects," for the lack of a solution to the problem of existence. The *malaise* in existence comes from the fact that there is no harmonious *relation* of love with sex within a *natural union* of the masculine and the feminine, be it heterosexual or homosexual. Having redefined fantasy as a cover over a positivized void of loss, Lacan argued that the void is first constituted as that which gives rise to culture out of the fundamental lack of a "sexual rapport." There is no rapport of oneness between mother and child, or man and woman.

The idea that there is no fundamental harmony between the sexes (see *Encore*, 40), no ratio for sexual identity via gender, has been taken literally by poststructuralist feminists who think Lacan meant that people do not have sexual relations.[44] Lacan actually argued that people continually "relate" sexually in an effort to bridge the void. And he links the reality of an unbridgeable void between the sexes (usually denied or idealized), to a *malaise* or death drive in culture itself, attributing this *malaise* to an impossibility of Oneness between individuals or within individual being. Jacques-Alain Miller has interpreted Lacan's fixed formula—fixed in a mathematical sense because it concerns the relation of cause and effect—to mean that there is no way a boy or girl can acquire sexual identity (i.e., understand what it is to be a woman to a man, or a man to a woman) through observation of a mother/father type couple.[45] Rather, the effort of each child to correlate gender, body, language, and sexuality in a rational way via observation of a parental couple (or its equivalent in varying social configurations) leads to impasses and incomprehensions that are experienced as traumata. And where there is trauma, the real is constituted as palpable holes in comprehension. And an object *a* tries to fill in a void that is neither myth nor metaphor.

Thus, unconscious desire cannot be deciphered logically except in reference to the aim of the drive, which is to become one with the libido itself. And, Lacan attributed to Freud the intuition that meaning could have the power of death over life. Memory is plural, multiple, and inscribed in diverse forms, Freud said (*Sém.* III, 203). Even though Freud understood that memory is not simple and that people always look for meaning (*Bedeutung*), Lacan discovered *how* meaning is linked to memory. Intertwined in diverse forms of memory, meaning derives from *real* effects that inhabit the body as unsymbolized knowledge, from the *symbolic* body as incorporated in partial objects, and from the *imaginary* order of signifiers that cut up the body, mapping it for meaning. Through the combined effects of these three orders, we project a "world" of forms such that there is no mind/body split. In this scenario, "mind" is a metaphor—not a mirror as Richard Rorty says—for what is concretely held together in the Borromean unit or chain of real, symbolic, and imaginary material. In truth, knots, intersections, and blind spots appear in this material that constitutes what we generally call "mind," thinking of it as an organ or essence. Nor is mind rational thought *as such*, although it functions by the rationality of a logic of the unconscious, even in psychosis. Mind is an asymmetrical (in)coherence of imaginary traits, symbolic words and conventions, and the impasses created by a real order of radically lost meanings. These three orders all circle around a void. Early on in his rereading of Freud, Lacan said that "mind comes from memories that function as if they were objective: dead letters—signifiers that can be localized—that consider the speaking subject already dead" (*Sem.* II, 202). Later, Lacan would call these "dead letters" *jouissance* identifications wherein the subject is an object of the real, insofar as the *lettre* of language is joined to the body by the libidinal glue of agony, ecstasy, or anxiety registered differently in three separate orders.

Memory, thus portrayed, is immanent in humans. It drives them. Lacan translates Freud's *Wahrnehmungen* as primordial associations that occur simultaneously between the unconscious and consciousness, which are, nonetheless, lost to conscious scrutiny. Although they are lost to memory at the level of context, these "perception marks" still retain traces or traits of the cut that first stamped the preferences that determine individual choice by the real of lost *jouissance*. Thus language is materialized around libido. And this is not a mysterious idea. One need only think of poetry and music to understand the nostalgia that binds the present to the past by language, images, and sounds in a *jouissance* of the primary *lalangue*. By *Bewusstsein* Freud meant conscious, conceptual memories. But his *Vorbewusstsein* pointed to a dynamic of real presentations (Lacan's Ur-objects cause-of-desire) that mark synchronic memory by diachronic traces of something else, some *jouissance* yet to be said or found (*Sém.* III, 202–4).

Unlike the primordial realm of real traces or unary traits that are lost to memory, pre-conscious memories are structured in reference to the mirror-stage effects of alienation imposed on an infant from the outside world. As such, pre-conscious memories are structured by conjunctions of the cut (*qua* separation) joined to the disjunctions of alienation. Although these pre-conscious memories are *Verdrängt* (i.e., pressed under), they are not repression itself. Rather, one recognizes repression in the momentary *lapse of repression* when some*thing* falls from one order of signifying expression as it passes to another—be it imaginary, symbolic, or real (*Sém*. III, 202–4). The fall of the object *a* marks the *dropping* of a piece of condensed *jouissance* onto another vector. Whether one drops a pound of flesh, an imaginary bond, a cherished symbiosis of mutual suffering, a debt, or a gaze whose judgments are cruel, any shedding of superego skin—be it from the primordial lane of the drives or from Other pronouncements—will lighten the load of detritus each of us carries as a death within.

Lacan found death effects at the origin of life in the loss of *jouissance* that we seek to replace by repetitions which quickly become duties. He also discovered that language enables us to speak about those repetitions from a position of skepticism, even though loss *qua* structural reality [S($\emptyset$)] never disappears. This defect accounts for why "big" life questions are never answered once and for all. It also accounts for the plurality of interpretations and the effect of infinitization in meaning. Yet, it is almost impossible to believe there is either a void or a death drive at the center of life because the fleeting associative evocations of loss are not verifiable via corresponding realities. Moreover, the void continually propels *jouissance* into language and into the physical organism, causing the breakdown of consistencies. The void at the heart of being produces enigmata at the best, unbearable suffering at the worst, and anxiety, ecstasy (mania), depression, anger, or despair in between. But one cannot simply dismiss the void, for it is not undecidable or ambiguous. It opens onto the impossible real which never ceases to write itself in the object *a* (*das Ding*) that seeks to fill up the void (*vide*) of loss.

Lacan argued that the Other or symbolic order places itself in the human infant as a *symptom* meant to compensate for loss of the primary object (partial objects attributed to the mother). And these, in turn, create a limit place between what Freud called anxiety and inhibition. Speech gives interpretive value to this *lalangue* of images and sounds and seeks to cover over the void which imposes an *a priori* materiality of density, weight, and motion on language. It enters them, making of culture a circulating, rotating order of projections, introjections, incorporations, that give rise to the myths of an era and within specific families.

If, as Lacan said, the first losses are mother related, the incest taboo being the profound, but necessary loss of the primary object that prevents psychosis, it makes sense that personal and cultural myths will be assimilated within an Oedipal context. Woman is structurally lost as an absolute essence on the side of the real (*la Femme*). She is not lost philosophically, biologically, or affectively. Yet individuals interpret the link between loss, mother, and Woman at the level of a guarantee of "being" that denies this loss. Identification with language, rules, and lineage becomes a proof that nothing is lost, culture itself being the push away from the natural toward the cultural. But the real invades the symbolic anyway, the obscenity of *jouissance* appearing in the superego tones of cultural law—the language of morality—that tries to command others via one's *own* desire.

Individuals seek fulfillment via the alienation of language and the missed aims of the drives: this paradoxical quest places biological males and females under strange strictures. Human beings seek some ideal of being that would give life "meaning." The search, then, is for love, ideals, and satisfaction—not for "self." This is perhaps the unkindest cut of all in Lacan's teaching. Ego certainty merely mimics the void in the unconscious that beckons us forward in the first place. One can see that Lacan reversed the image of humans as always being in the process of creating themselves anew and placed them askew of what one calls a "self" or a "mind." Rather, human subjects are in the position of always *coming after* the unconscious, finding themselves at the interstices of their own lives, continually *interpreting* after the fact who and what they are in the world. Given the human propensity to "know" in advance, to plan, to strategize, life can only deal people unexpected blows.

Lacan's "determinism" is a pre-determinism, then, both more brutal and more hopeful than others from past histories. Insofar as subjects are blocked by the blind spots in their own language, identifications, and symptoms, they aspire to unity or Oneness via ideologies: the fixity of ego fictions and *jouissance* repetitions. Yet no one can hope to create a space of freedom or creativity without rearranging what one already is, reconstituting the *Sein* in the *Dasein* that contains the *esse* (essence) or *jouissance* Lacan called libidinal glue. Insofar as unconscious position—both in the Other and in *jouissance*—is a problematic first created by language that later resurfaces within language, language cannot answer its own questions about the "more in language than language" that is not finally reducible to grammar, syntax, or linguistics. But one can use the symbolic to treat the real impasses in language. In this way Lacan hoped to return psychoanalysis to its earliest meeting with Freud in the talking cure, where a suffering being is offered the chance to live beyond what first fixed him or her in the identical— in the death rut. The challenge Lacan confronts both academics and clinicians with is the offer to follow him in his complex and difficult recasting of psychoanalysis. He offers a new epistemology of the Freudian cut and a renewed clinic where the narcissistic ego and enigmatic symptom must be separated one from the other in order to allow *jouissance* to speak.

Only in this way can one use the symbolic to work on the re-pressed or fantasized "object" that remains one's secret goal, one's hoped for liberation. This repression is not of childhood or sexual fantasies, but of the "truth" we are used to, the real we refuse to know. In that place of impasse one is all or nothing—a human object (of the gaze, voice, void, and so on)—who desires the absence of pain and hopes for the absolution of love. Only when repression is lifted does an object *a* fall out of a fantasy, allowing one to confront unconscious desire in terms of the lethal *jouissance* that blocks it.

Notes

1. Ernest Jones, *The Life and Work of Sigmund Freud*, 3 vols. (London: Hogarth, 1962).

2. Sigmund Freud, "Beyond the Pleasure Principle" (1920), *SE*, 19: 3–66; 46.

3. Sigmund Freud, "Analysis Terminable and Interminable," *SE*, 23: 209–54;246.

4. Pierre Bruno, *Entre éthique et jouissance*, Les séries de la découverte freu-dienne (Toulouse: Presses Universitaires du Mirail, 1989).

5. Ellie Ragland-Sullivan, "Lacan, Jacques," *Feminism and Psychoanalysis: A Crit-ical Dictionary*, ed. Elizabeth Wright (Cambridge: Blackwell, 1992): 203.

6. Jacques Lacan, "The function and field of speech and language in psycho-analysis, *Ecrits: A Selection*, trans. Alan Sheridan (New York: W. W. Norton, 1977), 30–113.

7. Jacques Lacan, *The Seminar of Jacques Lacan*: Book II, *The Ego in Freud's Theory and in the Technique of Psychoanalysis* (1954–1955), ed. Jacques-Alain Miller, trans. Sylvana Tomaselli (New York: W. W. Norton, 1988).

8. Jacques Lacan, "A Love Letter," *Feminine Sexuality: Jacques Lacan and the école freudienne*, ed. Juliet Mitchell and Jacqueline Rose, trans. Jacqueline Rose (New York: W. W. Norton, 1982), 149.

9. Jacques Lacan, "The agency of the letter in the unconscious or reason since Freud," *Ecrits: A Selection*, 146–78.

10. Jacques Lacan, *The Four Fundamental Concepts of Psychoanalysis*, ed. Jacques-Alain Miller, trans. Alan Sheridan (New York: W. W. Norton, 1964).

11. Jacques-Alain Miller, "Language: Much Ado about What?" *Lacan and the Subject of Language*, ed. Ellie Ragland-Sullivan and Mark Bracher (New York: Routledge, 1991), 21–35.

12. Colette Soler, "Literature as Symptom," *Lacan and the Subject of Language*, ed. Ellie Ragland-Sullivan and Mark Bracher (New York: Routledge, 1991), 213–20.

13. Jacques Lacan, *The Seminar of Jacques Lacan*: Book VII, *The Ethics of Psychoanalysis* (1959–1960), ed. Jacques-Alain Miller, trans. Dennis Porter (New York: W. W. Norton, 1992).

14. Ibid.

15. Jean Guir, *Psychosomatique et cancer* (Paris: Points Hors Ligne, 1983).

16. Jacques Lacan, *Le séminaire XVI (1969–1970): D'un Autre à l'autre* (unpublished seminar).

17. Jacques Lacan, "The subversion of the subject and the dialectic of desire in the Freudian unconscious," *Ecrits: A Selection*, trans. Alan Sheridan (New York: W. W. Norton, 1977), 314.

18. Jacques Lacan, *Le séminaire XX (1972–1973): Encore*, text established by Jacques-Alain Miller (Paris: Editions du Seuil, 1975); Sigmund Freud, "Totem and Taboo" (1912–1913), *SE*, 13: 1–161.

19. Jacques Lacan, *Television: A Challenge to the Psychoanalytic Establishment*, trans. Denis Hollier, Rosalind Krauss, and Annette Michelson (New York: W. W. Norton, 1990), 34.

20. Ellie Ragland-Sullivan, "Masochism," *Feminism and Psychoanalysis: A Critical Dictionary*, 239–42.

21. Jacques Alain-Miller, "A and a in Clinical Structures," First Paris New York Workshop, (New York: Schneiderman Publications, 1987): 23.

22. Sigmund Freud, "The Ego and the Id" (1923), *SE*, 19: 3–66.

23. Elisabeth Roudinesco, *La bataille de cent ans: Histoire de la psychanalyse en France*, vol. 2 (1925–1985). (Paris: Editions due Seuil, 1986), 181.

24. Jacques Lacan, *Le séminaire IV (1956–1957): La relation d'object* (unpublished seminar), to appear March, 1994.

25. Russell Grigg, "Lacan on Object Relations," *Analysis*, no. 2 (1990): 39–50.

26. Jacques Lacan, "The function and field of speech and language in psychoanalysis," *Ecrits: A Selection* (New York: W. W. Norton, 1977), 53.

27. Jacques Lacan, "The subversion of the subject and the dialectic of desire in the Freudian unconscious," *Ecrits*, 301.

28. Sigmund Freud, "From the History of an Infantile Neurosis," (1918 [1914]), *SE*, 17: 38.

29. Jacques Lacan, *Le séminaire III (1955–1956): Les psychoses*, text established by Jacques-Alain Miller (Paris: Editions du Seuil, 1975), 215.

30. Jacques Lacan, *Le séminaire X (1962–1963): L'Angoisse*, November 14, 1962 (unpublished seminar).

31. Colette Soler, "The Real Aims of the Analytic Act," *lacanian ink*, no. 5 (Winter 1992): 53–60.

32. Christine le Boulenge, "Symptôme et psychose infantile," *Les Feuillets du courtil*, no. 4 (April 1992), 57–61.

33. Elisabeth Bronfen, "Death Drive (Freud)," *Feminism and Psychoanalysis: A Critical Dictionary*: 52–57.

34. Sigmund Freud, "Three Essays on the Theory of Sexuality" (1905), *SE*, 7: 125–245.

35. Jacques-Alain Miller, "Language: Much Ado about What?" *Lacan and the Subject of Language*, ed. Ellie Ragland-Sullivan and Mark Bracher (New York: Routledge, 1991), 21–35.

36. Jacques Lacan, *Seminar VII*, ibid., 209.

37. Jacques-Alain Miller, "Extimité," trans. Françoise Massardier-Kenney, *Prose Studies* 11, 3 (1988): 121–31.

38. Serge Cottet, *Freud et le désir du psychanalyste*, Bibliotheque des Analytica (Paris: Navarin, 1982): 114.

39. Voltaire, *Candide, ou l'optimisme*, ed. George Havens (New York: Holt, Rinehart and Winston, 1964).

40. Freud, "Thoughts for the Times on War and Death" (1915) *SE*, 14: 291–93.

41. Jacques Lacan, *Le séminaire III: Les psychoses*, 215.

42. Francois Sauvignat, "Histoire des phénomènes élémentaires: A propos de la 'signification personelle,' " *Ornicar?* 44 (1988): 19–27.

43. Jacques Lacan, *Le séminaire XVII (1969–1970): L'Envers de la psychanalyse*, text established by Jacques-Alain Miller (Paris: Seuil, 1991).

44. Alice Jardine, *Gynesis: Configurations of Woman and Modernity* (Ithica, N.Y.: Cornell University Press, 1985).

45. Jacques-Alain Miller, "To Interpret the Cause: From Freud to Lacan," *Newsletter of the Freudian Field* 3, 1–2 (1989): 30–50.

4
Causes of Illness and the Human Body

The Scriptures tell us that "you will know the truth, and the truth will make you free" (John 8:32). But when, in Lord Francis Bacon's words, "jesting Pilate asked 'what is Truth?', he would not even stay for an answer."[1] The teaching of Jacques Lacan (1901–1981) continues both Judeo-Christian and empirical scientific traditions of trying to ascertain what truth is. But Lacan's answers to the age-old riddle differ from any heretofore theorized. People suffer because they have no access to the "truth" which speaks them in a parasitical manner, as if they were robots or already dead objects.

Lacan's theories regarding the structure of the subject serve as a basis not only to discuss his discoveries regarding the causes of mental illness, but also as a point of departure for considering the psychosomatic causes of physical illness. I shall argue throughout this chapter that the question of truth (or the real as Lacan came to call it in his third period of teaching) is essential to the relation between mental and physical health. In developing Lacan's arguments, I hope it will become clear why I answer these three questions as follows. Do people choose their illness?—No, their illness chooses them insofar as they stay attached to their negative *jouissance*. Does the health-care system perpetuate illness?—Yes, to the degree that mental and physical health-care does not take account of this "truth": that the cause whose effect is disease in the human body goes beyond biological life. Do health-care providers hinder the patient's chance for a return to health?—Yes, depending on the degree to which they lack an adequate theory for their practice of treating illness.

The most radical thesis I wish to advance here is that the body may sicken in childhood or in later life as a result of the powerful role insignia play in pushing individuals to establish the identifications they then use to fill up a palpable void within being, knowledge, and body. Although certain diseases are inherited, Lacan suggests that the etiology of psychosomatic illness has little to do with genetic transmission. This suggestion may seem surprising unless one can imagine that gravely ill patients whom their doctors view as having come for treatment are already more than halfway through the fifth act of their life and death drama.

Lacan's Concept of Truth and the Structure of the Human Body

Focusing first on act one, or even setting up the stage prior to the first act, let us consider that nothing of Lacan's later teaching makes sense except in light of his first concepts of a mirror-stage logical moment—that is, the narcissistic instance of loving oneself in another—and the Oedipal structure, "structure" becoming clearer if we think of it as a Borromean unit enchaining associations in perpetual pre-determined movements. That is, the mirror phase moment and the Oedipal moment are concepts Lacan uses to explain the power transference operates in the assumption of sexual identifications. Although some of Lacan's terms sound like old-fashioned Freudianism, and others are new and unfamiliar, it is helpful in reading Lacan to remember he used Freud's psychoanalytic terms to pursue what Freud thought was "true" in those terms. But Lacan radically altered those meanings to verify Freud's intuitions and thereby produce a new teaching. By keeping those parts of a word or a concept that had already pinned something down, Lacan, at the same time, challenged his listeners to rethink the words and concepts they take for granted, use thoughtlessly. One effect was to demonstrate that prison houses of language can only be detonated with explosive force, be it of the musty and impalatable sense of a word like "phallus," or simply by the stunning effect of enigmatic uses of language. More specifically, Lacan led his audiences to rethink science itself from the 1950s on: "Every science arises out of the manipulation of language which is anterior to its constitution, and . . . it is in this manipulation of language that analytic action develops."[2] But long before language coalesces into a useable grammar system, the unconscious subject of desire begins to be structured by effects of the real of the biological organism, and by the images of the surrounding world Lacan called the imaginary, or virtual real.

Lacan considered perception (*connaissance*) to be imaginary. Indeed, the transference (or grafting) of images, words, and effects from outside the body onto the biological organism is never an automatic or natural developmental process. Autistic infants, for example, never achieve a mirror-stage illusion of bodily unity that ties together the corporal real of *jouissance* to a virtual *image*, an image which, in turn, is "supposed" to *re-present* the body and which is negotiated in language by metaphor and by sublimation of the drives. The exception is psychosis wherein the body is experienced at the level of the real, without the cushioning layer of imaginary distance we call "representation." But for most people the body *is* the imaginary realm of re-cognition that marks the already seen.[3] Put another way, an infant cannot identify with others—or with an image of itself in a mirror—if it is not able to do so against the backdrop (*tache*/spot) of a welcoming gaze cast from the minimal distance that allows motor coordination to develop *as if* it were a natural biological development that also gives rise to an image of the body.[4]

But to achieve a sense of *being* by identifying with an image of the body as a whole body is not a biologically natural process. Lacan called the mirror stage the first human experience of alienation, thereby arguing that identification occurs prior to any biological causality. Others, particularly the primary caretaker, form the infant's "interior" center of grounding from the visible world of image and effect. "Separation" from these alienating images and effects means, in Lacanian parlance, the impact of the loss of an image, the effect of a cut, not psychic or physical separation from an actual person as object-relations theorists imagine. Lacan designates such losses as the very referent of meaning itself: $[S(\emptyset)]$.[5] The logic of the cut means, very simply, that things are missing in subjectivity (except in psychosis whose definition might be the foreclosure of the cut). But since primary objects are, in fact, radically lost objects, a *Fort! Da!* dialectic of fulfillment by substitution—introducing the outside into *jouissance*—grounds most humans in the transference even prior to any coherent use of language.

By the time most children begin to use language (the symbolic) coherently, language *functions* to tie the biological organism (the real) to images of the body (the imaginary) and to objects in the natural world *by naming* or evoking the *form* of an image that replaces an absence. Later, a simple signifier—the name of a beloved place—can give rise to a welling up of nostalgia, a re-experiencing of loss itself. Thus, language enables most individuals to be "human" by talking about or writing about the world at one remove from it. That is, language defers the direct impact of a sensory merger with objects and experiences of the world. Even prior to a child's birth, language begins to describe the place that infant will occupy in the world, thus imposing a primordial split between culture and nature in the causality of being.[6] Thus, at the level of the biological organism culture always organizes "nature" around meaning, even if the meaning conveyed in certain relations to language is chaotic or incomprehensible (as in autism or psychotic episodes).

A second alienation experience begins in the second year of a child's life. The advent of coherent speech means that words link images to the body and to objects of the world. Lacan called this an experience of castration. By that he did not mean biological emasculation, however, but the imposition of a fictional being and body on the biological organism. Symbolic fictions are *inscribed* on various parts of the body, naming or designating (i.e., cutting up) the body. Such imaginarizing of the body occurs through the incorporation of signifiers that represent the person as a subject—"subject" marking the lack of a signifier for "self." Thus, the imaginary order of representations is anchored by symbolic ordering, which is the very definition of the differential. Indeed, the capacity for making dialectical meaning derives from one's "self fiction" (a *fixion*). And this fiction is always constituted in reference to the differential by which one *identifies* as masculine or feminine, identifications which do not cohere with anatomy or gender in any one-to-one way. Moreover, the lack of inscription for this difference (which Lacan called *castration*) in psychosis results in perplexity, confusion, and a propensity for continual *frustration*. Since the psychotic has not learned identification as sexual difference, he or she remains One with the mother in primary identification.

The sexual difference is an identificatory matter, then, founded on a turning away from the mother as primary object toward culture. This creates what Lacan called the Oedipal structure or the law of the Name-of-the-Father(s). But by *law* Lacan meant that which organizes one's perception, language (thought) and action at the level of structure. Not governmental law, or police "law and order". The psychotic "lack of lack" means that he or she refuses responsibility for his or her choices or judgments, always blaming the Other for any "mistake." As the object of the Other's *jouissance*, the psychotic always finds himself innocent of negative intention toward others. Having discovered that psychosis is the exception on which a rule of the norm is based, Lacan reinterpreted the Freudian superego thus: Freud discovered that identification with cultural values—the words of others—installs alienation in being, thus placing sacrifice to the principle of cultural law at the heart of the human.

The Law of the Name-of-the-Father does not necessarily invoke a literal father. Some principle of prohibition enters an infant's life to deflect identification of body and being away from a total merger with the mother. Whether one refers to a boyfriend, a stepfather, or a mother's brother (as among the Trobrianders), Lacan rereads Freud to argue that this first profound splitting determines a person on the path of neurosis, psychosis, or perversion. As we remember from earlier chapters, if no identificatory splitting away from the mother occurs, the fixity or petrification of psychosis is established. And the psychotic moves in language by a desperate clinging to non-dialecticized signifiers, his rigidity causing him to cling to the drives at the level of representation.[7] He or she tries, literally, to hold body and mind together via a continuity in *jouissance*.

The distress of acquiring an unconscious (i.e., being subject to being represented) opens up the gaps in language Lacan described as the insistence of the unconscious. The unconscious surfaces in language, in the associations catalyzed by images, sounds, words, and the effects of loss, revealing that unconscious fixations anchor the repetitions which constitute what each of us calls his or her "knowledge." Yet no one is consciously aware that "knowledge" is not natural, but arises from the particularity of one's own signifying chains. Lacan called this radically split-off place of knowledge, asymmetrical to conscious life, the Other. He taught that we repeat messages from the Other in order not to remember the pain of the real—the impasses in our lives. Thus, there is no final attainment of a whole "self" to be had, just a subjective split between identification and language, or between the Other as desiring or demanding. Human "being" is structured by effects, then, not essences.

All this talk of language and identification is anything but esoteric abstraction. Lacan's valorization of the processes of identification explains to brain researchers *how* and *why* a symbol system comes to reside in the "brain," by the implication of the voice, the gaze, the phoneme, and so on. That is, an infant in*corp*orates these partial objects via the path of identification become sublimation. If these "objects" give pleasure, they create desire as the desire for a repeated pleasure. If they cause radical displeasure, desire might not be constituted at all. For severe negativism can cause the refusal of "objects" we call autism. That is, in a person's experience of Ur-objects-cause-of-desire, an experience of object satisfaction itself is incorporated, or not. While lack comes from dissatisfaction, it, nonetheless, gives rise to desire. Satiation, on the contrary, gives birth to demand. In recasting Freud's work on object relations, Lacan taught that castration goes hand in hand with the lack that give rise to desire *because* a limit has been placed on demand. And that demand, meanwhile, is inseparable from frustration.

Lacan added the term "privation" to Freud's use of the concepts of castration and frustration. By "privation" Lacan sought to describe how "objects," or the things of the world, are inscribed within a place of lack.[8] Such object material—the residual traits left over in the wake of the cut (loss)—links the body to what we call the mind. But by object language, Lacan does not mean the "natural" language of psycholinguistics in which physiological organs—the brain and vocal apparatus—are said to dominate the language material imposed on them. Lacan's focus is, rather, on an infant's dependence on the powerful injection of images and sounds from the external world by its keen visual and auditory powers.

Of capital importance in Lacan's teaching concerning what causes a potential physical illness down the road, is the paradoxical presence of a continually widening split between one's "knowledge" (*savoir* as symbolic), one's being (*connaissance* as imaginary), and one's truth (the real of *jouissance*). People can repress the fact that loss dwells at the center of being by screening out the memories or messages that are unwelcome, by forgetting, by idealizing, or by not symbolizing what they cannot bear to know. By "whitewashing" unpalatable material, most people do, indeed, retain a "good enough" narcissism, based on the pretense (*semblance*) that whatever their life situation is, it probably could not be better. Whatever goes awry is blamed on other people, circumstances, economic realities, etc. And blame blocks change. Moreover, such rationalizations or misrecognitions do not abolish the knotted material in language (thought) that Lacan described as impasses of the real. But, unfortunately the ego and the network of language work as systems of defense or resistance. Indeed, language prevents people from confronting the real of the truths written in the primal scene of the "family novel" (Freud's *Familienroman*). Living their lives at the level of fiction and appearance, humans are semblances, then—not objective, rational creatures. As such, each person occupies an elliptical position to the truths that constitute his or her being.

Insofar as physiological and biological responses are secondary reactions to the meaning already imposed on the body, it is not surprising that Lacan reconceptualized Freudian defense mechanisms as essentially "normative" responses to a mirror-stage structuration of the ego from which the transferential effects of jealousy, grandiosity, fear, aggressiveness, rivalry, shame, anxiety, and so on, arise. These all refer back to the elemental human yearning for a Oneness to replace the centrality of loss against which being defends. At a second level of identification—sexual identification—the injunction to differentiate from the mother takes us beyond the Oedipus myth by which Freud tried to understand the mysteries of human sexuality. Lacan points to the unnatural assumption of a sexual identification. Indeed, at approximately the same age, a grammar system is acquired, the brain is lateralized, an immune-defense system is consolidated, and a sexual identification is chosen.

To equate anatomy with gender demands the impossible: that one align anatomy, libido, gender, and identification as either masculine or feminine in a harmonious way. Yet the split between being as masculine or feminine reveals the structure of the "mind," emanating as it does from a child's experience of castration and the phallus—in desiring categories Lacan (following Freud) called neurotic, perverse, or psychotic. We know that psychosis is the condition of having no split between the masculine and the feminine, while hysteria is the condition of being permanently split in identification both with the masculine and the feminine. In perversion, one may identify as masculine or feminine, as long as the feminine is fetishized. In these variations one sees clearly that the phenomenon of division between the masculine (symbolic) and feminine (real) refers to the phallus, or the third term of a differential that is itself a signifier: away from the mother in the name of the difference that signifies limits or lack. In Lacan's description of the unconscious, we remember that all identifications are structured around four key signifiers: birth, love, procreation, and death. Thus, universal experiences underlie the substantive material of narratives, telling each person's story in an anticipatory/retroactive kind of dynamism. In *Seminar* II where Lacan first described a topology of the human subject that can be taught and studied in a formal manner, the human subject was said to exist "on several planes, caught in networks that intersect.[9] Later, he depicted such intersections via the Borromean signifying chain of imaginary collusions, symbolic differentials, and real cuts that intersect, giving rise to the fourth order Lacan named the symptom or *sinthome* in 1975.[10] In this final period of his teaching, he placed truth on the side of the real, describing it as something that limps into view and fades out of sight just as quickly. And he argued ever more demonstrably that one can formalize a study of structure (the Borromean topological unit), of the signifier (what represents a subject for another signifier), and of the letter (the body joined to language), although their meanings are particular in every person's language and desire.

The Causes of "Psychic" Suffering: The Neuroses and Perversion

Before discussing physical illness in Lacanian terms, let us suppose what health might be within the framework of a traditional psychology. A person's sense of "having" or "being" an identity would be solidly grounded in reference to who he or she is. Such a person would be able to take into account, even to create, his or her desire. Psychic health would go hand in hand with having the freedom to recast one's own subjectivity, the capacity to make ethical judgments, and the ability to live life as an interconnected subject rather than as an oppressed and alienated object only playing at being free. Most psychologies are based on the positivistic model of container and contained: pouring the right answers into the "mind" container. They assume that "good" behavior can be learned voluntarily. But Lacan considered this nineteenth-century concept of learning to be wrong.

Indeed, Lacan took up a problem of which he never let go. Why are people unable to change? Why can individuals not create their own new legends or give birth to their own desire? He answered thus: What holds one together is the same libidinal glue (*jouissance*) that causes his or her pain, *jouissance* indicating a "psychic" symptom in the real.

The Greek meaning of "symptom" (*symptomat*)—a happening, attribute; a subjective evidence of disease or physical disturbance; something that indicates the existence of something else—applies quite literally to the concept of the subject as a response of the real, an object of condensed *jouissance*. When Lacan added the symptom to the imaginary, symbolic, and real as the fourth order that links fundamental fantasy to conscious life, he stressed that a symptom is not a double meaning in the traditional sense of symbol or met-aphor, as he had theorized earlier. Rather, the symptom is living evidence of any person's repressed—thus unconscious—truth whose material presence marks an *absence* of comprehension about the enigmatic aspects of one's life. Paradoxically, Lacan taught, symp-toms do not conceal the truth of the real, but speak its meaning "loud and clear" at the surface of a life. But since individuals cannot decipher the language of symptoms that point to the *envers*, the reverse side of discourse, they remain blind to the cause of their own suffering. Yet the very existence of symptoms, Lacan argued, proves that there is a place of knowledge in being that knows noth-ing of itself. And indeed when a person's ego fictions are unraveled, and certainties pushed askew, an analysand can speak differently about his or her symptoms, revealing something of their mystery in stories of buried pain and suffering. Some truth always emerges about the familial identifications and myths anchored in signifying chains as "necessary" *fixions*. But the beliefs formed by these child-hood fixations must be detonated if distance from the psychic al-ienation that causes suffering is to be attained. Most people, how-ever,—analysands included—refuse to question either the fictions of childhood or the real of parental desires.

Yet the structures that yield *psychic* suffering are formalizable and speakable, at least in part: they do not have to remain mysteries to both patient and doctor. So universal is the *malaise* of the human condition that one can say, in the broadest sense, that neurotic suffering arises from a confusion about gender identifications. A "fuzzy" notion about "who one is" gives rise to confusion about what to say and how to say it. Indeed words are the material we affix to being and desire in our efforts to describe what *is* or what *will be*. As such, the neuroses bespeak an inability to say what one wants—a kind of mental paralysis that goes hand in hand with not knowing for sure who one is. One of Lacan's more radical theories is that even though the kinds of problems brought to a psychoan-alytic clinic will always reflect the historical *malaise* of the consti-tutive moments of a person's story (*histoire*), these stories *can* be rewritten if the death drive is taken seriously. Indeed, the ethics of psychoanalysis requires that identifications be rewoven in this life.

Lacan redefined hysteria (usually a female suffering) as a neurosis and a discourse structure characterized by a question about one's gender: Am I a woman or a man? The obsessional (usually a male) clings to the feminine that he, in turn, denies. Neither the hysteric nor the obsessional has squared the circle between biological sex and psychic identity. The hysteric is plagued by the chaos of identifying as neither/nor. In analytic treatment she will choose this or that: masculine or feminine. Lacan described hysterics as being *hors-sexe*. By this he did not mean transsexual, but that the hysteric has no firm set of sexual identifications that can serve as an identity basis for being. Obsessionals, on the other hand, suffer from trying to eradicate desire, desire being the sign of the feminine in sexuation. The obsessional's question is: Am I dead or alive? This eternal "son" enjoyed an excess in his mother's desire. The price he pays for this childhood joy is the adult burden of inertia and passivity, emanating from the guilt that goes with the unconscious knowledge that he replaced his father in his mother's affections.

The hysteric and the obsessional literally carry the family burden of parental "rejection" on the one hand and election on the other, as perturbations that surface in language, showing too little distance from a primary object (particularly the *rien* in hysteria). Put in other terms, Lacan viewed the neuroses as arising from an exaggeratedly incomplete "psychic" separation from the mother's desire and from a conflictive set of experiences and expectations surrounding the Father's "Name." The rejection in hysteria is of *being* as a woman, while the obsessional identifies with an unworthy Father signifier.

Lacan placed perversion between neurosis and psychosis. While the neurotic does not know what he or she wants, the perverse subject knows very well. Like Freud, Lacan located the structure of the fetish in perversion. It can appear substitutively—i.e. metaphorically—as an addiction to drugs, money, or any other "object" that *displaces* basic anxiety surrounding the issue of lack or loss as it refers back to the mother and bears on her child's early efforts to link gender and anatomy to sexuality. Where neurotics have a question mark—Am I a woman or a man?, Am I dead or alive?— the pervert places a *jouissance* object. And while the neuroses are in and of themselves an indirect question about who one is (was) in the parents' discourse, perversion substitutes one particular object for what is repressed, unknown, or unconscious. Of course perverse traits mark all the structures, while perversion proper reveals a *repudiation* of castration.

Perhaps one begins to see the unique difficulties for unique patients. Each person carries the real of his or her suffering as a psychic weight, a literal ball-and-chain that defines who one is in the real. Moreover, *jouissance* is maintained in the shock of recognition of one's pain which one loves even more than one's freedom, for suffering defines each one with a consistency that prevents change. The analytic impasse is obvious. Asking individuals to give up the consistencies within which they live—even if by sheer negativity—is not a simple matter of showing people how to drop death weights, for the analyst is demanding another kind of death: a relinquishing of the illusions that serve as masks.

Lacan figured out that the repetition "beyond the pleasure principle" which Freud could never really explain, is equatable with the reality principle taken as the death drive. Repetition is synonymous with ego fixity, then, and provides the means by which the death drive functions. People do not suffer from neurosis because they are immature, fantasizing, emotional, pleasure-seeking children, as Freud thought. Rather, people repeat certain patternings of ego consistency which is all they know for sure. And people suffer because the verbally constituted ego resists change in favor of familiarity. One sees, then, how the unicity of the systematization of language helps people to lie about who they are, what they want, and how they feel. Given that most things work against the possibility of a person's changing his or her life, Lacan shifted the emphasis of analytic praxis to argue that the actual resistance to a patient's request for cure is the analyst's resistance.

But only the patient knows what his or her fantasies mean or what desire is really in play, even though this "knowledge" alone will not provide a cure. The change in a "psychic" symptom is marked by the traversal of a fundamental fantasy which, in brief, is totally unlike everyday day dreams or fantasies. The fundamental fantasy as Lacan described it, and Jacques-Alain Miller clarified it, is unconscious and, by definition, organizes all one's thought and language. Miller says, "It is the structure from which everything makes sense for a particular subject. This universality of his fantasy is, as a rule, unknown to him precisely because the subject is inside it."[11] But how can a fundamental fantasy ever surface, given that it is unconscious?

The answer lies in the transference where the analysand *re-forms* himself in language and love, thus disassociating from the absolute fantasy that governs him unaware. But Lacan reconceptualized Freud's theory of transference wherein the unconscious is catalyzed into evidence—or awakened—within the field of verbal and affective interplay. Lacan placed this interplay between the analysand's own ideal ego and the ego ideal the analyst represents for him or her. Viewing transference as the only means for getting back to the truths inscribed in the Other, Lacan differed from Freud by teaching that transference *must be used as a tool* to break up the *jouissance* of ego fixities that stops people from realizing their desires. Always emotive and erotic, the imaginary order of transference relations serves the analyst as a pathway to use the symbolic to help the patient speak lost pieces of meanings, to untie the "knots" of the real in her language that have not been symbolized as knowledge because they were too disturbing to know. The analyst's goal is to trip up the orderly gait of a patient's recited memories, conscious fantasies, normative discourse, ego fictions, or believed self-descriptions, in order to push him askew of his assumed ways of seeing himself. As imaginary wholes, individuals seek the paradoxical fate of remaining consistent at the price of identifying with the unbearable real. F. Scott Fitzgerald once wrote: "We feel so damned secure as long as there's enough in the bank to buy the next meal, and enough moral stuff in reserve to take us through the next ordeal. Our danger is in imagining that we have resources—material and moral—which we haven't got."

It is well known that Lacan criticized American psychologists and psychiatrists for equating the "true" with adaptation to some preconceived notion of reality, with someone else's idea of "the good" taken as realistic behavior. Lacan thought such a view of behavior had its roots in pragmatism. Indeed, he could have said as Edward Tolman did early in this century that the very idea of "behavior" reeks with utilitarian purpose, and meaning as well. The Lacanian analyst's goal is to help the suffering person attain absolute and total difference from the analyst's own desire or being. Sitting in as a *semblant* for what the patient cannot see or say in his life, the analyst knows only this: that the patient can choose to stay attached to what weighs him down, or he can drop it. Insofar as truth is on the side of the real, cure lies in the space opened up when a person speaks about his horrors and his shame.

Lacan defined truth as going in the opposite direction from the certainty underlying moralistic principles. Post-Freudian theories have made precisely the error of equating unconscious truth (Freud's *Realität*) with adaptation to some experiential notion of reality that Freud tried to describe by *Wirklichkeit*, or the "reality" of sense data. Aiming at primordially repressed truth, Lacan argued that one's truth is not one's Good. Rather, truth is the real residue of traumatic experiences—and the kernel of an object *a*—that are virtually unsayable by the sufferer. In this sense truth or the real overdetermines and subjectivizes all knowledge and discourse, making it impossible to test either language or the unconscious empirically. Thus, one cannot make a pragmatic or utilitarian argument for retaining a consistency of being, for to do so means clinging to the death drive. And this is unethical. Thus, Lacanian analysts listen for the "truth value" by which a person gives his or her life meaning, finding problems where that "value" constitutes a negative identification with an Other's desire as law, or with the Other's *jouissance* as law.

The Causes of Psychosomatic Illnesses

Lacanian analysts who work with physically ill patients refer to Lacan's teaching in *Seminar* XI to characterize the following diseases as psychosomatic: asthma, eczema and other skin ailments, rectocolitis, hemorrhaging ulcers, anorexia, and, most surprisingly, cancer.[12] At stake in psychosomatic illness is the concrete etiology of diseases whose causes today's medical science would attribute to the biological organism itself. The most unfamiliar, and some would say the most "unscientific," idea I will develop here is that the sick body carries a message from the patient's family novel. Not only does the body speak the story of symptoms blind to their cause, certain organs are actually marked as potential targets of disease within a family history of identifications and language effects.

But before characterizing psychosomatic illness further—which is not synonymous or contiguous with any one of the differential categories of psychoanalysis—I shall return to Lacan's definition of structure as that which organizes our knowledge, after being organized itself, even that which falls outside the parameters of transparently accessible conscious knowledge. Structure means the *functioning* of the imaginary, the symbolic, and the real, the I-S-R. In the analytic experience language tries to symbolize the imaginary, unfolding itself up to the point of verifying that certain things are impossible to say.[13] Jacques-Alain Miller points out that the psychosomatic phenomenon actually inverts the I-S-R circuit to an S-I-R movement. In the psychosomatic instance the symbolic is imaginarized such that it imposes an impotence of the real on an organ. A petrified *jouissance* renders a particular signifier non-dialecticizable, absolute (p. 126).

In "Quelques réflexions sur le phénomene psychosomatique" Miller bases his thoughts on Lacan's comments on the psychosomatic phenomenon in *Seminar* XI and in the "Geneva Lecture."[14] Taking the field of language as his point of reference, Miller places the psychosomatic phenomenon at the limits of the structure of language, at the point where the dialectical meaning of signifiers is lost because certain signifiers have welded together in a holophrase, or lack of aphansis (Miller, "Quelques réflexions," 114). He describes the psychosomatic phenomenon as that which skirts the signifier or the field of the Other, by contrast with hysteria that puts the Other in question. The psychosomatic phenomenon is marked by a seal, a scar, a hieroglyph, where a certain *jouissance*, displaced from the erogenous zones, imprints itself, rather, on one signifier (i.e., giving a particular organ an imaginary meaning). In this instance one can use Lacan's definition: "The Other is the body" ("Quelques réflexions . . . ," 122). Moreover, the Other taken as body—rather than as the place of the signifiers—is transcended by the biological organism insofar as it includes the libido as an organ (the *lamelle*) and the objects represented by *a* that Lacan described as dwelling "outside the body." (124) Relying on Lacan's distinction between the body and the organism in "Position de l'inconscient,"[15] Miller suggests that in psychosomatic phenomena the libido becomes corporified—an inorganic lesion (Miller, "Quelques réflexions," 125). He concludes his article by asking if the psychosomatic response is susceptible of becoming a question about (unconscious) desire (126).

If one works with the idea that psychosomatic illness is caused by a confusion between desire and libido (a *jouissance* "mode of being"), one might consider that the message spoken by psychosomatic symptoms concerns a lack of clarity regarding desire, gender, and one's "narcissistic" position in the symbolic. Although Lacan agreed with Freud that there is "pleasure" to be found in suffering—that masochism is fundamental—he stressed, however, that pleasure and pain are constructed. They are not innate. Moreover, certain unconscious repetitions, fixations, or non-dialecticized meanings block change. And these have the Borromean structure of thought: language (the symbolic), the body (the imaginary), and the real (the organism). At the level where each of us suffers, psychically or physically, one finds a person cohering in the only manner he or she knows. Yet, the suggestion that psychosomatic illness tells the story of traumatizing childhood memories or events, that disease is related to repressed memories or emotional traumas—that it has precise and concrete meaning—is generally unacceptable to patients and doctors alike.

Yet, the cause of certain illnesses is potentially *psycho*somatic precisely *because* it is disconnected from the story of a person's life. What was primordially repressed as the Ur-object that causes desire presses back on the body. But such painful material does not appear as "knowledge" in fantasies or dreams. For such material bespeaks the impasse of the real where knowledge is unsymbolized, even though inscribed on the body. Thus, its roots lie beyond the imaginary body (cut up in signifiers that say one has Aunt Jo's chin, Uncle John's "bad blood," etc), anchored in the real of the partial drives that function in the voice, the gaze, the breast, and the feces. One might describe psychosomatic phenomena as "holophrases" in the real that return in the body as displaced *jouissance*. More explicitly, Lacan described a psychosomatic structure as formed around the sacrifice of some part of one's own body. Such a sacrifice, made in childhood or early youth, may have been a bid to win maternal love or meet with parental approval. In the most extreme case, one could even view autism as the attempt to win approval by self-annihilation, whose symptom often appears as a refusal of the gaze, as well as of the proper name.

Recently American psychologists Seymore Fischer, April Fallon, and Paul Rozin have written that a negative body image can distort a person's psychic well-being.[16] In the 1930s Lacan linked body image to primary narcissism—that is, to an ideal ego, the first countable trait in the symbolic order, and traced the history of its evolution through the defiles of the signifiers of familial desire and Oedipal law. In 1975 Lacan gave a lecture on the symptom in Geneva, Switzerland. Of the psychosomatic effect, he said, "the body gives way to writing something in the order of the number."[17] Linking Lacan's statement here with another statement he made in the same lecture—that in the case of psychosomatic phenomena, the body is like a cartouche, delivering its proper name—Eric Laurent hypothesizes that we are confronted, not with a *proper* name, nor with the Name-of-the-Father, but with the *jouissance* that would be the *true* proper name ("Les noms du sujet," 33, 36). We know that the number is in the order of the real for Lacan. That is, in the psychosomatic instance a signifier One unifies two bodies (such as a mother and child) in a unary trait that erases the ideal ego as a dialectic. Instead *jouissance* is linked only to activities such as corporal care (Josselin, "L'identification," 47).

Dr. Lucien Israel of Strasbourg, France, teaches Lacan's topology of the human subject to medical doctors whom he tries to urge away from positivistic thinking about the body, enjoining them to recognize that it is dangerous for them to treat only the patient's *complaint*, or to believe a patient's description of his or her illness. Doctors do not know *why* a person suffers, Dr. Israel insists. And any claim that they do implicitly enjoins the patient to admire the doctor's expertise and professional training, rather than go on a quest for the *reason* he or she is sick.[18] Indeed, Lacan's interest was in the fact that suffering itself is a passion. And, insofar as the truth of the ego is a fiction, a lie, this basic fact alone means that any person can die because he or she has no means of getting at the fictive roots of his or her disease in identifications.[19] Lacan criticized medical doctors for their failure to realize that patients can endure suffering with indifference and the stoic heroism of silence. The hope Lacan held out to medical patients is this: Lost and repressed stories are not buried in the substrata of childhood memories as Freud thought. Nor are they made up only of language traces.

But even if a doctor or analyst agreed with Lacan's teaching here, he or she would still face the problem of how to fish out the real truths that make psychosomatic illness at the limit an unconscious choice for death. Put another way, why is cancer the number two American illness today? "Stress" certainly means nothing here. Nor does diet. In a Lacanian purview, one would do better to think first about which organ is affected. What powerful gaze from the Other could be said to penetrate an immune defense system, making the body speak a suffering so unbearable it cannot be verbalized or even symbolized in knowledge? At the point where disease appears, Lacan taught, the body is a desert, a "desert of *jouissance.*" Insofar as the body is an imaginary signifier where each vital organ is inscribed for meaning, trouble with a body part may well tell a story of desolation, despair, hopelessness and self-sacrifice. Indeed, the silence of the drives speaks the language of an absolute *jouissance* where a knot or impasse in meaning may have engaged some vital organ.

The psychosomatic inscription on a body retraces the story of a parental body, even as that story goes back to another parental body beyond where some part of a child's body was sacrificed in a family history of libidinal "organ" exchanges. At these points of matrix one may hear stories about a child's performance where the measure of a mother's "self"-worth is her child's success which she failed to give her own mother. The child's body later speaks its tale of sacrifice and woe, giving voice to the mother's silent "cry" for recognition. The symptom is no longer a metaphor, as Lacan first defined it, but is as redefined in 1975: "that which comes from the real."[20] That is, the unconscious is a knowledge first articulated in *lalangue* which is tied to the physical organism by the real. The symptom may later appear in a son's colo-rectal cancer where a latent plea for recognition and affirmation is spoken to the Other via the malady.

If we think of disease as a scar left over from the Other, we might consider it a knot of the real in a person's life that has become a petrified lump or tumor in the fibre of the biological body, mater-ialized by meaning. Although genetic material may *seem* respon-sible for lesional manifestations, a doctor might, rather, look for a libidinal lesion: a battery of signifiers, not a battery of genes. But psychosomatic phenotypes are not to be confused with neurotic structures. Instead, psychosomatic symptoms point to an auto-erotic drama, to a story of *jouissance* surrounding the Ur-objects-cause-of-desire that gave rise to the (partial) drives in the first place. The *jouissance* in play would be the "third" one, then, the *jouiss-ance* of meaning.

But this theory does not blame cruel parents. Indeed Lacan found no saints or sinners, only endless chains of victims. Lacanian an-alysts go very slowly in helping psychosomatically ill patients learn how to listen to the haunting words that stand behind their suffer-ing. Dream narration, for instance, is the umbilical cord between words, the imaginary body, and the real of the biological organism. Unconscious touching of body parts can also signal hidden mes-sages. Proper names referred to frequently can be crucial signifiers insofar as they are linked to repressed identificatory resonances. Working with medical doctors, such analysts also pay close atten-tion to the names of medications chosen or rejected by the patient, for these may hold the key to an unconscious meaning to which a patient clings, even at the cost of his or her life.[21]

Let us consider a male cancer patient who died within an eight-month period at the age of fifty-one. Prior to his illness, brilliant Professor X had just won a prestigious fellowship to study "empty first person discourses." No one asked him why he thought persons did not inhabit their own speech. No one asked him why *he* always spoke in the passive voice, what it meant that a division or split dwelt at the surface of his speech. But he told stories loud and clear of having long ago ceased having sexual intercourse with his wife, of eating meals apart from his family, of taking showers in the dark so he would not see his body, of the bathing beauties he secretly watched from the window, and desired. But while he refused his wife's carefully prepared food, he remained sexually faithful to her lest he forsake a debt to his religious roots and further disappoint a minister father whose approval he had never won. In Lacanian terms, he was a man who had given up on his desire. Indeed, his dying words were a rejection of contemporary theorists (like Lacan) to whom he had been drawn. These words were enunciated in conjunction with a new-found peace of certainty and religious One-ness which his father's sermons had long ago promised. I could not afford to doubt, he said at the moment of death.[22]

Lacan taught that the affair of life and death is waged between the ideal ego and the superego.[23] So ferocious and obscene did Lacan find the superego that he said the only guilt lies in giving up on one's desire (*Sém.* VII, 321). This is a complex axiom, we re-member, not a simple injunction for getting one's own way.[24] For desire and judgment go hand in hand in dealing with the resistance to change that *jouissance* marks. Besides guilt, another index used in scanning a patient's speech for the real, concerns his or her fantasies about the origins or causes of a sickness. However sub-jective the explanations may be, such material is valuable because it points to the Oedipal structure the patient internalized in child-hood. What fantasy lies behind a mother's unconscious desire, for example?

Many mothers will readily tell you that their children are clearly genetically determined in their gender behavior, thereby evoking proof for the preferences of their infants, even from birth on. A "real boy," for example, is said to have chosen a football over a doll at six months of age. A "real girl" is a child who simply adores carebears and pink rainbows. And as mothers and other family members talk on, one could speculate that infant calm or agitation may well be connected to intense maternal anxiety experienced around the issue of gender. As one discovers the depths of a wife's desire to please her husband, her mother, her father, and so on, one begins to suspect that there is nothing *purely* biological at issue in the constitution of gender. Indeed, the familial unconscious drama regarding gender aspirations begins to shape an infant's life by denials and repressed desire, even prior to birth. Some Lacanians pay great heed to the name given an infant. Who chose which name? What name was not chosen? For whom *is* a child named? What identifications and expectations lie at the base of a seemingly in-nocent proper name?

And one may well ask how such ordinary and seemingly mean-ingless things could possibly cause a breakdown in someone's im-mune-defense system. To believe that identifications and gender issues can govern a person's capacity to fight for or give up on life requires one to consider that an ideal ego must find some viable accommodation between the demands of desire and the possibilities for *jouissance*. Insofar as the gaze is the primordial agent of both recognition and judgment, it also serves as the law governing ideal ego narcissism. Within this theoretical context, one might consider a diseased organ as a knot in a family history, telling the story of a person's desire in relation to the first form of law, the gaze. But only words enable an analysand to flush out the unspoken suffering that underlies ontology, making of it a *hontology* (a being of shame). Indeed, the genetic family tree that doctors already construct could be used by those same doctors in a different interpretative mode: to constitute the desire that lies at the point where impasses block the patient's hopes.[25] For "cure" lies in separating out who one wants to be (desire as the timing of the unconscious) from whom one believes one is or must be (the *jouissance* that subtends superego ideals). In this context, the oral, anal, scopic and vocative drives would be taken seriously.

The male cancer patient I mentioned above died with the sorrow that he had never earned the prestige his mother felt would elevate her, canceling her own humiliations from growing up in rural poverty. He was obsessed with his *own* failure at never having obtained his minister father's approval, for disappointing his parental family by having chosen what they consider an inferior profession, i.e., one that did not directly serve God. Professor X died filled with hatred for everyone, especially those who had not praised his father—the same father who had disdained him. His inner ghosts literally crowded love out of his life, and any hope of fulfilling his desires. Ten days before his death he said he felt love and compassion for the first time in his life. He began to thank God for the cancer which had let him feel love. But, the balance between love and hate is too fragile and precious to risk on life, he said. Death was, paradoxically, his only hope.

Based on the theory that psychosomatic illness often hides an uncertain, murky body image, Lacanians treat psychosomatic patients by sitting face to face with them. By identifying with a "solid" body image in the transference, such patients may become free to speak from the real of impasses in desire that may force an unconscious choice of life over death, if not spoken. In this context, let us consider a young Protestant minister who recounts the story of trying during his whole life to deflect his mother's adoring gaze away from his brother, and toward himself. She refused to comment on his success in scholarship and in sports. So he chose the career of Protestant minister because his mother loved "church" as much as she loved his brother. Yet she refused to attend his ordination, his marriage, and his daughter's christening. She never even came to hear his sermons—not once. In his early thirties, this young man developed a tumor in his chest, in the place of his masculine pride (i.e., at the site of the muscles developed in sport). His mother never visited him when he went into the hospital with cancer. And yet he kept living long beyond medical expectations, particularly after he began to speak of his rage toward his mother and his sorrow for his father, who also rejected him. But just before he "decided" to die, he spoke in bitterness and hatred, forswearing life (his wife, his daughter, his friends, his success) in favor of hating his mother. He had one last hope: that she would attend his funeral and feel guilty.

Jean Guir argues in *Psychosomatique et cancer* that it often emerges in analysis that the patient's affected organ was subject to a hysterical or phobic symptom in adolescence (13). At that time a traumatic meaning was soldered onto a particular physiological organ ensemble and then repressed. In adult life, the return of the real to the same place in the symptom seems disconnected from the person's life; it seems autonomous. Yet Lacan taught that the imaginary body is made seemingly consistent by the signifier. And the specific *jouissance* of the unary trait (Freud's *Fixierung*) that ties a child's body to its mother's in alienated desire may well give this meaning to the psychosomatic illness: The illness is itself an effort to turn away from an imprisonment in the *jouissance* of sameness, toward the Otherness of the father. Lacan said in 1975 that the paternal metaphor does not work correctly in psychosomatic illness and that, indeed, the father is in the final analysis a function or structure that refers itself to the real.[26]

Thus, the ethics of psychoanalysis would bear on medical problems too, demanding a separation from the *cause* that is the mother's unconscious desire. Let us take another example. Susan X's mother had been a disappointment to her own parents. She was not the replacement child they wanted for the boy who had died at six months of age. When Susan's mother gave birth to her own first child—a girl—her repressed sorrow of being became her daughter's legacy. This daughter was given, affectively, to the grandmother by the mother. Here the unconscious desire for forgiveness and the hope of finally winning her own mother's love were intertwined. As Susan's identifications developed, she lived from two master signifiers: as a piano virtuoso she pleased her grandmother; as an "A" student she pleased her father. But she was not given any signifier for *being* as a girl (either in role behavior or body image).

When Susan developed breast cancer in her 30s, no one would have thought to link her own childlessness, her by then militant rejection of her *feminine* sexuality, to an ongoing battle with the hysteric's question of whether she is a boy or a girl. The reappearance in adult life of an episode regarding her breasts seemed unrelated to the earlier moment in her adolescence when she had cut up and buried her first bra (given her by a friend) deep in a field lest her mother suspect her of wearing a brassiere and, thus, revealing her deepest secret: she wanted to be a woman.

Variations on these stories are endless, but all revolve around the universal key signifiers of birth, procreation, love (desirability, sexuality, gender), and death. Many disturbing factors must coalesce, however, to allow a psychosomatic illness to develop. A number of unconscious messages must suddenly signal to each other that the person is no longer capable of meeting the challenges presented by life. Certain Lacanian analysts have suggested that prior to the onset of psychosomatic illness, a precise dynamic reveals itself in three temporal, logical moments. First, psychosomatic illness covers up a primordial separation from a beloved person. Even the trauma of early "loss" of the mother during the period of nursing or feeding at the birth of a second sibling can cause trauma. In Lacanian theory, it is axiomatic that during the mirror-stage logical moment, food (physical need) and the desire for recognition become intertwined with the demand for love, such that the real of the biological body becomes the bedrock to which identifications and desire will later refer. In the second logical moment, something that resembles the early trauma is repeated, (as in divorce, death, job loss, etc.). Such an event may *break up* the imaginary defenses—illusions and fictions displaced onto bodily organs—that generally keep the immune defense system consistent (i.e., well "formed"). A third logical moment in psychosomatic occurrences happens about a year after the second (repeated) trauma.

Many of the children that Lacanians work with have become sick after the birth of another sibling.[27] Some Lacanian analysts have suggested that psychosomatic illness tends to occur in families where there is considerable confusion about generational guideposts, where some children are "lost"—not given a clear position—within a large family constellation. Indeed, if psychosomatic patients seem flaky or poorly centered, it is because they lack the representational anchoring—the signifying text—that grounds them in clearly defined identities in the imaginary and symbolic—that is, in a linkage between body and language and in a linkage of language to paternal law.

In the *genesis* of a psychosomatic illness special "signifiers" or insignia occur in at least four different orders: in dates that denote special events in the patient's life; in proper names; in confusion between gender and sexuality; and in the unconscious persistence of holophrases, i.e., a complex of ideas soldered together in a single fixation of petrified, nondialectical meaning. At the point where a "psychic" critical mass is unconsciously reached, a signifying date— such as a father's birthday—may catalyze repressed material, triggering the genesis of an illness in the breakdown of the denials and ideals that characterize conscious thought. Insofar as dates are rigid designators, fixed points in the real, not just any signifier, they do not belong to the order of the signifier, but to the repetitious return of the real to the same place.

Psychosomatic subjects sometimes change their names, hoping to gain a new identity thereby, or even a new (and worthier) Father's Name. For proper names are also a major anchoring point of identificatory fictions. Lacan gave the example of James Joyce's textual play around the poverty and degradation of worthy fathers within his family lineage. Indeed, Joyce was physically well when he was writing, anchoring his ideal ego (I) in the words and rhythms that carried him along as a subject represented by writing and the voice. When he was not writing, he suffered from a severe glaucoma that disappeared spontaneously once he took up the pen again (Guir, 17). But one must remember to distinguish between psychosomatic symptom and psychoanalytic structure. In Joyce's case, the glaucoma is not synonymous with the structure of psychosis that marks his language.

A third marker in the genesis of psychosomatic illness is the confusion between sex and gender. Insofar as the assumption of sexual identification is not natural for either males or females, the confusion that typifies neurosis or psychosis will put some organ into suspension at the level of unconscious meaning. The neurotic or psychotic child may begin to transsexualize him or herself in adolescence by unconsciously fantasizing that some part of his or her body can be sacrificed to the "change of sex" asked for in the family novel, although not in any direct correspondence with physical anatomy. A boy may give up the idea that having the penis means *being* the phallus, for instance.[28]

Finally, in the genesis of psychosomatic trouble, a holophrastic statement often unveils the meaning of a disease insofar as it points backward to the family Oedipal structure. For example, just prior to his final showdown with desire, the male cancer patient I referred to first summed up his life drama in the holophrase, "empty first person discourses." In a privileged dream, the female cancer patient I spoke of above dreamed the word "Tchaikovsky"—a word that summed up the gender identificatory confusions of mother/ daughter/grandmother/father/husband around the interwoven themes of music and love. That the first and last letters were those of her father's name is meaningful in that psychosomatic illness is itself a call to the father. It is a "cry" to the social order to offer a path for distance from the primary *jouissance* that emanates from a subject's links with the mother as the primary object *supposed* to annul the effects of loss.

In a Lacanian purview, a sick body speaks as an icon of pain. A patient's affected organ may well tell the story of the interlinked suffering among family intimates where the demand for love is always in play as a demand for signifying position in a very *real* drama. And the afflicted organ speaks the pain that cannot be spoken to a parent or grandparent, or to a marital partner who substitutes for a family member in an identificatory drama. For this is the stake: vital organs themselves tell stories of disappointed love, thwarted desire, unbearable loss, and faulty nurture. And all family "novels" leave inscriptions on the flesh of their children, inscriptions whose opaque meanings can be deciphered as patients narrate their imaginary histories wherein seeing, breathing, and digesting all refer to the primordial drives that were themselves constructed for meaning as the outside world imposed a story on the body's parts, cutting it up into a network of signifieds that speak on the side of the real (the unknown, the impasse).

Lacan taught that the scopic drive plays a large role in psychosomatic illness. Skin disease cries out at the surface of the body, commanding others to look at a pain that cannot be spoken or spoken about. Skin disease also enables the subject to avoid looking at his or her own suffering, and thus to keep at bay the truth of the unbearable real. Some analysts see the common passage from eczema to asthma, for example, even in very small babies, as an absence of the screening-out defense that skin disease reveals. Asthma is a quite literal plea for recognition spoken by the loss of breath in its proximity to love and death (Guir 19).

Some analysts believe that psychosomatic illness can be attenuated if the impasse behind the disease can be symbolized by the patient. Such an unconscious enunciation is not a grammatical statement, however, but proof that *jouissance* forms a meaning system. Lacanian analysts who work with psychosomatic patients take care to listen to the *patient's* version of the family story, unlike the object-relations psychoanalyst who, for example, insisted that Mrs. X recount her incest with her father and take a good look at what *she* had done to her mother. The analyst was heartbroken when this patient shot herself, but perplexed as to why her suicide, planned with great care, was executed on her father's birthday: the ultimate ironic gift. Life or death is the stake in constituting the real as a "knowledge," rather than retaining it as a passion of ignorance. When the meanings of the real penetrate the imaginary-symbolic covering of the void, a breakdown of the immune system of the biological organism may occur, penetrating the "self"-believed fictions that generally cover the void place and protect us from the real.

Any analyst who points out to an analysand *the true elementary kinship structures* in the heart of a family may even put a patient's life at risk. Rather, the freeing up of repressed knowledge must come *from* the patient, *within* the timing of his or her own desire to see its consequences and then act on them. When a cure does occur, it brings about a radical change in the patient's relationship to the dynamic of family kinship bonds.

In conclusion I will try to answer some of the questions implicit in this chapter. First, medical doctors cannot be blamed for stating the obvious, for describing disease in terms of the biological maps they read so expertly. Indeed, at the level of biology the body is complete. Vitamins, grain, and fibre do improve our health. But reductionist formulae such as "you are what you eat" or "broccoli is known to prevent cancer" leave out this fact: the *essence* of life lies in the "you *are* . . . "; in identifications, not material goods or products. As long as doctors view the body as a biological organism that causes its own effects, their chemical view of illness will not include the idea that language materializes the organs of the body for the *quantitative* meanings we call representational and for the *qualitative* meaning value of *jouissance*. "Nothing is made from nothing," Lacan taught, "thus we must rethink the issue of 'matter' around which all Ancient philosophy turns" (*Sem.* VII, January 27, p. 121). Indeed, the primordial building blocks of the matter that constitutes what we call perception are representations (*Vorstellungen*), "forever and from the beginning at the origin [and they] have the character of a signifying structure" (*Sem.* VII, February 3, p. 138). As long as doctors think biological effects are the equiv-

alent of their own cause, they will dismiss any theory of psychosomatic disease that would urge them to look beyond the physical
organism for cause. Specifying cause "inside" the organism (hormones, genes, etc.) or outside in the environment (food, toxins,
virus) bypasses the particularities of trauma that appear as impasses
in the language that governs the body.

Such headlines as "Alternative Medicine Going Mainstream"—
alternatives such as chiropractic and herbal medicine—are not surprising given the inability of medicine to cure or explain cause.[29]
Christine Pasquet, writing in *L'Ane* in 1990, suggested that the tendency toward medical specialization is an implicit admission of a
failure to understand disease that opts for the technical (positivistic)
solution of studying ever smaller isolated parts.[30] Lacan dispensed
with the impersonal medico-organic metalanguage and looked at
the dimension of effect that establishes cause. "What the unconscious teaches us," Lacan said, "is that everything is already within.
We do not have to invent anything."[31] That is, words, images, and
the effects of lived experiences have built up a representational
memory bank out of which we repeat words, rituals, and so on,
without recognizing that they come from us, that the question about
origins is within our own signifying chains, not outside them; that
we are our own support systems.

That the unconscious is "structured *like* a language"—i.e., *functions* by transforming its material through substitutions and displacements—means this: A glitch shows the error in arguments that
mistake difference for sameness, "same cause/same effect," "dif-
ferent/but equal" kinds of arguments. Yet, because memory disappears as its own source, we cannot *see* the "things" that cause
us to move in language by substitutions built on ungraspable libidinal objects that cause desire. Such functions prevent us from
recognizing what drives us. But when we see the truth behind the
fact that substitutions only seem to move us on to the new, that
actually these laws of primary (metonymy) and secondary (metaphor) processes fixate us in a stasis of repeating familiar *jouissance*
material, we see how our lives are lived in the shadows of our own
childhoods.

Since we do not have ready access to the unconscious Other *qua*
knowledge, we are, by definition, not whole beings. In relation to
"self-knowledge" we are One-minus, in Lacanian parlance. We depend on new others to give us value, and yet draw our opinions
from suppositions of knowledge given by familiar others. But in
that space of lack between being and knowing, signifiers can be

reformulated. One can de-cathect the *jouissance* that holds together one's life lies. In those gaps between signifiers we can start quite literally to reweave our fictions, to learn a new way to speak, a "well-saying" (saying the truth of our lives) that constitutes good "form." But language never directly reveals the repressed lies that compose meanings in the Other. Thus, "well-saying" does not mean correct speech (à la Quintillian) or recognizing descriptive tropes. It means saying the truth that Lacan came to call the real. In this context, Lacanian analysts are necessary to the medical clinic because they listen differently than doctors, away from believing that words mean what they say toward a "listening askew" to the *jouissance* fixations where death reigns over life. What the patient *says* (and does not say) counts for everything—especially mumblings, asides, and denials. Although Lacan disagreed in 1975 with Noam Chomsky's idea that language is an organ, Lacan taught that the libido is an organ that materializes language.

Language cohabits with the biological body, constituting the particular truths underlying the Oedipal traumas of castration, frustration, and privation. But such truth is only ever speakable when treatment aims to the left or right of a symptom, surprising individuals out of their belief that they are unified, or unities of some whole. In psychosomatic difficulties, a person speaks endlessly about the affected organ. But doctors resist listening to a patient's language, fantasies, and desire, perhaps sentencing a person to death. Since the listener who proffers health must perforate the teller's smooth narrative in order to tune into the story behind the organ dysfunction, suffering can be said to "call" to an analyst who can help the patient separate the ego (i.e., [a]) from the symptoms that tell a story of the real. But since the real is blocked by ego fictions (*fixions*) that believe in imaginary harmonies, the analyst's task is hard.

Speaking the "language" of enigmatic messages, symptoms, starting with Freud's inhibition and anxiety, are an implicit call for cure spoken from a level of "thoughts that lie too deep for tears" (Wordsworth). In undertaking the impossible—to help a person stop *being* who he or she is—Lacanian analysts place an ethics of truth over the human propensity to cling to the alienations of the death drive. This is no easy task since individuals want the positive recognition they identify as love or approval, over truth. With few exceptions, individuals seek out and acquiesce to those who represent the socially acceptable position of the time (historical moment) rather than speak from the alienated desire of the unconscious Other. Furthermore, when a symptomatic plea is treated behaviorally by advising the patient to adapt to social norms—Get married; Have a baby; Be a better person; Be successful—that person *may indeed* get better. Later, when the same person dies an untimely death, no one connects the disease of cause to a failure to treat the specificity of cloistered desire in that person's life drama.

Finally, one must realize that even though Lacan's teachings here might seem to resemble holistic medicine, a major difference lies in the basis of his teaching: the recognition of an intrinsic lack-in-being (both in body and knowledge) psychoanalytic cure does not lie in a union of disparate parts into a whole, a structural impossibility. Cure occurs when a person changes his or her unconscious relationship to the effects left over by the mother's unconscious desire functioning in reference to the Father's Name as they organize *jouissance* around dead letters and petrified scenarios.

People do not consciously choose their psychosomatic illnesses. Their illnesses may well choose them—from the unconscious. One might even suggest that the health-care system perpetuates illness insofar as it refuses to see the *cause* of a given disease as an effect of the specificity of a subject's life. Lacan mapped the intricacies of how language and visual images are structured by the interlinking of three categories—the real, the symbolic, and the imaginary—that constitute what we call "mind." These structure the biological body in a logic of language, identifications, and traumas which play out a life and death scenario in relation to the symptom, the fourth category marked by a dialectic between desire and *jouissance*.

Finally, health-care providers actually hinder the understanding of health (or *well*-being) when they look away from meaning, assigning first cause rather to biology or environment. Unless it is accepted that the route to change *is* the talking cure—the only path on which the truth (*aletheia*) behind symptoms can be uttered—the real part of a symptom (psychoanalytic or psychosomatic) cannot be unraveled. When the meaning of an enigmatic symptom is constituted or reconstructed, a subject's life is seen and heard in a *different* way. A suffering person will speak of the passion that exists just beyond seemingly transparent meaning where a symptom "bespeaks" troubled desire, alienated desire that renders its subject guilty, masochistic, and unable to change. At the point where desire attaches a subject to someone else's *jouissance*, one finds a body in pain.[32]

Notes

1. Lord Francis Bacon, *Essays: Of Truth* (1625). Cf. Richard Whatley, *Bacon's Essays: With Annotations* (Freeport, N.Y.: Books for Libraries Press, 1861; rpt. 1973), 1.

2. Jacques Lacan, *The Seminar of Jacques Lacan*, Book VII: *The Ethics of Psychoanalysis* (1959-1960), ed. Jacques-Alain Miller, trans. Dennis Porter (New York: W. W. Norton, 1992)

3. Alexandre Stevens, "Version de la fin de l'analyse," *Les Feuillets psychanalytiques du Courtil*, no. 4 (avril 1992): 93-104.

4. Jacques Lacan, *The Four Fundamental Concepts of Psychoanalysis*, ed. Jacques-Alain Miller, trans. Alan Sheridan (New York: W. W. Norton, 1977).

5. Bruce Fink, "The Lacanian Subject," *Analysis*, no. 3 (1991):7-28; 25. See also Jacques-Alain Miller, "Language: Much Ado about What?" *Lacan and the Subject of Language*, ed. Ellie Ragland-Sullivan and Mark Bracher (New York: Routledge, 1991).

6. Bruce Fink, "Alienation and Separation: Logical Moments of Lacan's Dialectic of Desire," *Newsletter of the Freudian Field*, 4, 1-2 (1990): 78-119.

7. Alexandre Stevens, "Two Destinies for the Subject: Neurotic Identifications and Psychotic Petrification," *Newsletter of the Freudian Field*, 5, 1-2 (1991): 96-112.

8. Jean-Jacques Gorog, "Actes Imposés," *La Lettre mensuelle de l'École de la cause freudienne: Au-delà de l'Oedipe, Actes* 103 (November 1991): 18-21.

9. Jacques Lacan, *The Seminar of Jacques Lacan: Book II, The Ego in Freud's Theory and in the Technique of Psychoanalysis* (1954-1955), ed. Jacques-Alain Miller, trans. Sylvana Tomaselli (New York: W. W. Norton, 1988), 227.

10. Jacques Lacan, *Le séminaire XXIII* (1975-1976): *Le sinthome* (unpublished seminar).

11. Jacques-Alain Miller, "Duty and the Drives," *Newsletter of the Freudian Field*, 6, 1-2 (Spring/Fall, 1992).

12. Eric Laurent, "Les noms du sujet," *Analytica*, no. 48 (Paris: Navarin, 1986): 29-36; 36.

13. Jacques-Alain Miller, "Quelques réflexions sur le phénomene psychosomatique," *Analytica*, no. 48 (Paris: Navarin, 1986): 113-36; 126.

14. Jacques Lacan, "Geneva Lecture on the Symptom," *Analysis*, no. 1 (1989): 7-26.

15. Jacques Lacan, "Position de l'inconscient au congrès de Bonneval reprise de 1960 en 1964," *Ecrits* (Paris: Editions du Seuil, 1966), 829-50.

16. Article by Daniel Goleman and Marla Camp, "Psychological Distortions Prevent Us from Seeing Ourselves as We Really Are," in *The Ann Arbor News*, Monday, July 8, 1975. Reports research done by Thomas Cash, Old Dominion College, Norfolk, Va.; Seymour Fisher, Upstate Medical Center, Albany, N.Y.; April Fallon and Paul Rozin, University of Pennsylvania.

17. Françoise Josselin, "L'identification dans la maladie psychosomatique," *An-*

alytica; Le phénomene psychosomatique et la psychanalyse," no. 48 (Paris: Navarin, 1986): 47–56; 47.

18. Lucien Israel, *Initiation à la psychiatrie* (Paris: Masson, 1984). Interview in *L'Ane, Le magazine freudien,* "VRP en psychanalyse," by Jean-Pierre Klotz, no. 20 (January–February 1985): 35.

19. Michel Silvestre, "Le rêve du psychanalyste," *L'Ane, Le magazine freudien,* no. 15 (mars–avril 1984): 24.

20. Jacques Lacan, "La Troisième," (1975), given at the VIIth Congress of the *Ecole Freudienne de Paris,* no. 16 (1975), 178–203 in Rome (1974).

21. Jean Guir, *Psychosomatique et cancer* (Paris: Points Hors Ligne, 1983), 11.

22. Taken from a personal case study.

23. "La depression: le mal du siècle?" in *L'Ane, Le magazine freudien,* no. 11 (Juillet–Aout 1983): 3–5. See also Lacan's discussion of the superego and ideal ego in *Le Séminaire VIII* (1960–1961): *Le transfert,* text established by Jacques-Alain Miller (Paris: Editions du Seuil, 1991); and Catherine Millot, "Le surmoi féminin," *Ornicar?,* no. 29 (April–June 1984): 114–15.

24. See Jacques Lacan, "Kant avec Sade," *Ecrits* (Paris: Editions du Seuil, 1966): 765–90.

25. Ellie Ragland-Sullivan, "The Phenomenon of Aging in Oscar Wilde's *Picture of Dorian Gray*: A Lacanian View," in *Memory and Desire: Aging-Literature-Psychoanalysis,* ed. K. Woodward and M. Schwartz (Bloomington: University of Indiana Press, 1985).

26. Jean Guir, "Phénomenes psychosomatiques et fonction paternelle," *Analytica,* no. 48 (1986): 57–69; 57.

27. See the numerous studies of various kinds of psychosomatic illness among children recounted in the book *Psychosomatic et cancer;* see also *Analytica,* no. 48 (Paris: Navarin, 1986); and *Analytica,* no. 59 (Paris: Navarin, 1989).

28. Jacques Lacan, "Signification of the phallus," *Ecrits: A Selection,* 281–91.

29. Leslie Miller, "Alternative Medicine Going Mainstream," *USA Today,* Thursday, January 28, 1993, 1a to 4d.

30. *L'Ane,* no. 41 (November 1990).

31. Jacques Lacan, *Le séminaire XX* (1972–1973): *Encore,* text established by Jacques-Alain Miller (Paris: Editions du Seuil, 1975), 122.

32. "Actualités: 6 'Seminario lacaniano,' "; *Ornicar?* no. 33 (Summer 1985); 171.

5

Lacan and the Ethics of Desire

Freud's last paragraph in "The Question of Lay Analysis" was written as a postscript from Vienna in June of 1927:

> The resolution passed by our American colleagues against lay analysts, based as it essentially is upon practical reasons, appears to me nevertheless to be unpractical; for it cannot affect any of the factors which govern the situation. It is more or less equivalent to an attempt at repression. If it is impossible to prevent lay analysts from pursuing their activities and if the public does not support the campaign against them, would it not be more expedient to recognize the fact of their existence by offering them opportunities for training? Might it not be possible in this way to gain some influence over them? And, if they were offered as an inducement the possibility of receiving the approval of the medical profession and of being invited to cooperate, might they not have some interest in raising their own *ethical* and intellectual level?[1]

Freud speaks here of the inherent value of psychoanalysis independent from its application to medicine, thus laying the foundation for Lacan's later concern both for the development of what Freud termed "lay analysis" and for an *ethics* of psychoanalysis. Freud wrote: "The real point at issue, it will be said, is a different one, namely the application of analysis to the treatment of patients; in so far as it claims to do this it must be content, the argument will run, to be accepted as a specialized branch of medicine, like radiology, for instance, and to submit to the rules laid down for all therapeutic methods. I recognize that it is so; I admit it. I only want to feel assured that the therapy will not destroy the science" ("Question of Lay Analysis," 254).

Jacques Lacan devoted his *Séminaire* VII (1959–1960) to the question of what an ethics of psychoanalysis would be, taking up Freud's questions: How does one change the suffering of a patient? and how does one teach analysis? Thus, the ethics of Lacanian analysis is concerned both with changing oneself and with teaching analysis as a potentially new "science"—of the real. Lacan's idea of working with the real teaches that one can effect ethical change for individuals in the clinic (and in society) insofar as a person's actions lead to change. Lacan did not view the unhappiness or suffering of mankind as caused by medical symptoms or economic ones *per se*, but rather as symptoms derived from the basic human propensity for narcissistic self-deception, despite the best of intentions. Against the reformist programs of the ages, Lacan argued that most change is only superficial. It is on this premise that he calls for a new ethics. But change can only come from a reworking of the unconscious history of the letter where being (*l'être*) and body join the word of the symbolic to the real of *jouissance* that one might define as the absolute sense of one's value. The presence of *jouissance* can be "measured" as a meaning system of energetics based on *quality*, then, that resides alongside the empirical or *quantifiable* meaning system of language or representations.

In his introduction to "The Question of Lay Analysis" Freud says:

> There are some complications, which the law does not trouble about, but which nevertheless call for consideration. It may perhaps turn out that in this instance [the instance of analytic practice] the patients are not like other patients, that the laymen are not really laymen, and that the doctors have not exactly the qualities which one has a right to expect of doctors and on which their claims should be based. If this can be proved, there will be justifiable grounds for demanding that the law shall not be applied without modification to the instance before us (184).

Over thirty years later Lacan taught that radical, ethical change can only come from reworking the unconscious trajectory of the letter that Jacques-Alain Miller defined in 1987 as "a sign, but which defines its nature as object, not its effect as signified."[2] In other words, there are two sides to the letter: repressed meaning and a "beyond" in meaning that Lacan called *jouissance*. Indeed, in 1957 Lacan said one ought to change the title of his inaugural teaching, "The function and field of speech and language in psychoanalysis" (1953), to "Function, instance and field of the word, the letter, and language in psychoanalysis." His addition of "instance" and the "letter" refers to fields of meaning beyond semantic consistency, to fields where *jouissance* marks the limit of interpretation (Miller, *Joyce*, 11). In these fields, the imaginary "being" of the body joins the word of the symbolic to the real of *jouissance* effects, both in the body and in language.

These may seem to be drastic, even ridiculous, propositions. Ethics is generally thought of as a set of criteria for human action, both narrower and broader than the dictates of law. Etiquette, for example, is its diminutive. In ethical matters, most people take the acting subject for granted and concentrate their inquiry on the field of actions *per se*, or on the belief systems that give rise to action. I am concerned, rather, with the theory that the acting subject is not, in fact, the *agent* of its action. Surely it is axiomatic that the status of the agent must be a consideration preliminary to any question concerning action itself.

In the second period of his teaching (1964–1974), Lacan questioned precisely what occupies the position of agent in a given discourse.[3] "Agent" as I use the term here does not, however, mean the mind or will.[4] Vicente Palomera says "the agent is what we [Lacanians] call a place of power" (p. 43). That place can be occupied by a master signifier (S_1), by knowledge itself (S_2), by lack ($), or by a pleasure of suffering where a person is identified with the real impossibilities of an impasse. Moreover, in Lacan's third period of teaching (1974–1981), he emphasized that people do not think from a preordained place called the mind, taken as a container holding knowledge. Rather, as we have said previously, thought is composed of interlinked signifying chains, made up of Borromean units of the three *overlapping* orderings of real, symbolic, and imaginary material, whose intersections spawn a fourth order of the particular.[5] Lacan used orthography to distinguish between the symptom (Σ) as a category or order, and its enigmatic veiling of the precise relationship of desire to lack in a given life by reinstating the medieval French spelling, *sinthome*. *Sinthome* replaced the late-learned Renaissance borrowing of the Greek word "symptom."[6] A *sinthome* appears in the analytic clinic, Lacan taught, if one pays heed to the moment when a word is suddenly pierced by *jouissance*. The "sense" of a transgrammatical meaning appears in language, giving the analyst a way to work on the unsymbolized real in a patient's discourse, whose meaning has, nonetheless, left its mark on key signifiers.

But no paradigmatic theory of what is wrong, or of what will cure, can actually lift the *jouissance* thrall whose archaic death effects come from the lies that hide in impasses already constituted by familial and cultural desires; lies that were imposed on a child as fact or "truth" by language and identifications. But since the experience of identity (as a consistent "I") supposes some totalizing thread that unites anatomy, selfhood, gender, biological anatomy, and sexuality as a coherent whole, it is difficult to grasp the multiform nature of "being." Yet such totalizing harmony is a patent lie, covered over by idealizing cultural and familial myths and by carefully orchestrated historical "self"-narratives. Paradoxically, these large units of signifying associations are held together by the real in a life: what cannot be thought or said because it is too painful to know. When a person is eventually able to face a trauma, it can be spoken or dreamt and gradually "dropped" as an unbearable burden one carried. One can let go of pieces of the real that defined him or her in the order of the symptom.

No one is actually *in* the symbolic, then, but is represented there by the imposed language and identifications that signify a person as a subject. In this sense, a subject is nothing more than a placeholder in a chain of representations composed of words, images, and a proper name. These constitute a "self" myth that seems sufficient to itself. Yet, the "self" is not "self"-reliant. Rather, being and desire are not only co-dependent, but are also both co-joined *and* opposed. One wants what one lacks (what one does not know about who one is) but cannot attain this knowledge because of what one does not know, but *is*—absolutely—in the real. Quite literally, we lack *in being*; the real takes a bite out of what we call being.

In Lacan's rereading of Freud, the *cause* of individual suffering comes from the dissymmetry constituted between the feminine and the masculine in their relationship to the phallus: not the phallus as a penis, a signifier, or a mark of power, but the phallus as the primordially repressed signifier for difference that structures how desire is (or is not) constituted: neurotic, psychotic, or perverse.[7] In one sense, the phallus can be taken as a question mark about what one lacks (or does not lack), that is, what one is worth in the field of desire as a *jouissance* object. Yet, this surplus value that appears in whatever bears on desire's cause as a limit or blockage *in* the field of language ties sexuality to the drives via unconscious fantasy, which seeks to fulfill desire by circumventing the effects of alienation and separation.

Still, the real is difficult to conceptualize because it functions by contradiction, i.e., by a logic of double negation. On the one hand, it is absent as symbolic order meaning, but is present as *jouissance* that stops desire from achieving its goals. Because *jouissance* is already a fixed libidinality that fills in the void [S(Ø)] with semblances of being, (*a*), it provides a sense of consistency which is actually correlated with the death drive. Yet *jouissance* is continually evacuated from the void, even as all life's ups and downs rip at the veils of its continuities and consistencies to reveal loss as the human *cause* par excellence.

Now, as Freud suggested in "The Question of Lay Analysis," having credentials in the positive sciences of medicine or psychology does not prepare a specialist for treating someone whose dilemma concerns desire: be it the hysteric who identifies with lack, the obsessional who distances himself from desire, the pervert who tries to make his desire the law of the other's *jouissance*, or the psychotic who lacks the distance from *jouissance* that would enable him or her to desire at all. Moreover, *jouissance* points to a leftover residue (*a*) constituted by the *effects* of lack and loss that place a hole in the Other, whose fundamental referent is the foreclosure of a signifier for sexual rapport.[8] At the void place in being and language, the object *a*—a *logically* deduced consistency—stops up the hole. But its function misses the mark, making of it an excess, a kernel of nonsense, or a piece of trash which only marks the human failure to achieve or maintain *jouissance* as a consistent state, be it of pleasure or pain. As a stopper to the effects of loss (anxiety, confusion, etc.), the object *a* is not, however, a partitioned-off set of feelings, separable from thought. Rather, the object *a* introduces heterogeneity into the signifier, creating a "grammar" of the drives that concerns loss.

Here, the subject identifies, not with language taken as an imagined infinitude of noises or meanings, but with the pulsation of libido in his or her language that bespeaks the presence of *jouissance* as a knowledge that comes from the drives, as well as from the signifiers. Introducing a libidinal logic into meaning whose syntax is that of the sexual divide, *jouissance* is both fragile and rigid,—what Lacan calls the essence of the human, and of which Colette Soler will say: "There are certainly . . . biological bodies of different genders, and signifiers related to sex: man and woman, father and mother, as well as all those which erect sexual ideals, such as 'virgin,' 'whore,' 'wife,' and so on. None of these inscribes the object which would annul the sexual lack, and they all fail to compensate for the hole, for 'the partner of *jouissance* is unapproachable in language.' "[9]

The quest for *jouissance*—for absolute consistency, Oneness, or satisfaction—sets language on the paradoxical path of seeking to fulfill desire by quelling the "I want" that speaks a lack in being that Lacan denoted by the negative small phi ($-\phi$). But the want-to-be (lack in being) is not innate. Lacan indicated two structures of knowledge constituted by the logical operations of alienation and separation, designating them by a *vel* which means "the place of" ($\Diamond$). Alienation is the function created because knowledge is imposed on the body by an Other's myths and desires. And language is parasitically infested with this material. Two things ensue from this structuring that keep humans from being able to appease lack once and for all. Because we are fixated as "selves" or egos in words and identifications that re-present us as subjects of desire (lack) or objects of the real (loss), we wear our masks comfortably, happily repressing the knowledge of who and what we are. Yet our desire is isolated in an absent Other knowledge we assume to be pregiven, natural, or innate. But, we are bothered by the Other's *jouissance*, by proximity to the object-cause-of-desire which perturbs the symbolic *order*. One can write the alternating dialectical effect at play by these formulae:

$$\frac{\text{Jouissance}}{\text{Other}} \quad \frac{\text{(Quantity of affect)}}{\text{(Representations)}} \quad \text{or} \quad \frac{\text{Other}}{\text{Jouissance.}}[10]$$

The second operation, separation, is the primary operation that causes humans to identify with the traits of the objects they lose insofar as the cut—the impact of loss on the body—elicits the primordial response of anxiety.

Now let us look more specifically at the Seminar on the ethics of psychoanalysis.[11] At that period (1959–1960), Lacan was particularly concerned with the alienating effects of words *when taken as acts committed*. Miller stresses Lacan's reliance here on Freud's concern with ethics, as early as *Civilization and its Discontents*.[12] But Lacan did not mean speech acts performed in a public arena. Rather, he pointed to the alienating effects of words on and in the body. In the phrasing of philosophers Baas and Zaloszyc, "the subject does not inhabit the body, but commits itself into the body."[13] At the level of loss or trauma, the effects of this conjuncture between body (separation) and world (alienation) constitute the order beyond the symbolic and the imaginary that Lacan called the real. This order is not, we know, an undecidable, nor an empty negative space of *noumena*, like the Heideggerean vase. Nor is it simply the sensory real of objects in the world or of biological organs. The real is constructed as a logical order of palpable densities and enigmata. Lacan calls its effects knots or positivized negatives that disrupt language's smooth flow and cause disorder in life. But since the real is unsymbolized within representation, it appears in luminous or dark points of opacity and density, not unlike the "navel" in the dream. Such instances "say" that there is *more* to know than we grasp, but we cannot quite get it by studying, by squinting, or by furrowing our brows.

Baas and Zaloszyc speak of a primordial commission in the *conjunction* of the symbolic and the real. By "commission" they mean making something operative that precedes any other act of commission that might grant authority. That is, before the signifying chain can function,—whose entry into a certain finitude marks a play between a sense of the finite and infinite—space itself must be created. An infant's lips must be made to open in desire for something in order that a word can later be enunciated by them. Indeed, this is the condition of breathing itself. "By comparison to this *commissure*, sense, the desire for sense, the test of finitude, the distance separating word from idea, the abyss between the sign and meaning, the opposition of the signifier and signified . . . are secondary. Indeed, not accessory, but secondary" (Baas and Zaloszyc, *Descartes*, 81). For desire is this *cause* that makes the infant *want* to eat, walk, speak, learn, change.

Lacan always viewed philosophy as secondary to psychoanalysis. He argued that in the wake of Aristotle, philosophy has decomposed itself. By going ever further away from its concern to explain *cause*, philosophy has evolved as "complexification" for its own sake. This is not, in Lacan's estimation, a Good (*Sém.* VII, 88). Moreover, Lacan distinguishes his psychoanalytic ethics from Aristotle's, portraying Aristotle's universalist categories as always ending up in an ethics concerned with power; that is, with morality as it tries to find better paradigms for behavior by way of rules and law. Because Lacan's ethics focuses on the function of which each of us is a "case" in the singular, a *sinthome* of the particular effects constituted by experience of the paternal metaphor, he made distinctions between his ethics and Aristotle's, as well as between his ideas and those of Kant, Hegel, Schopenhauer, Nietzsche, and others.

Lacan based his ethics on a rereading of Freud. He did not claim to go beyond Freud, however, but described himself as displacing himself into the interior of Freud's text (*Sém.* VII, 245). To do what? On the one hand, to show how psychoanalysis subverts philosophy.

Indeed, Lacan argued that Freud had skewed centuries of philosophies in which ethics were treated in terms of law and morality. How? By introducing the pleasure principle and the reality principle into the field of ethics in terms of the Good which he called psychic health (*Sém.* VII, 256).

In recasting Freud's pleasure and reality principles, Lacan linked them to the death drive, even in the first period of his teaching in his seminar on ethics. In *L'acte psychanalytique*, a seminar given during the second period of his teaching, Lacan referred to Aristotle's claim that the first measure of an ethics is *the fruit of an act*.[14] For this very reason, Lacan says, there is a necessary relation of ethics to analysis, primarily because the desire for pleasure links our actions to death. Because we desire repeated satisfactions, desire drives our actions, the very nature of repetition meaning a return to the same (or similar). The insistence in desire is that pleasure repeat a lost sense of Oneness experienced as a consistency, a consistency "paradoxically" known as such only because "it" has already been lost. Insofar as the death drive arises from the real—impasses that never stop writing the impossible—to bear on individual and cultural history, Lacan viewed the ethical dimension as situated in the broader historical one. From the 1970s on, Lacan gave such increasing scope to the death drive that he said his ethics seminar should even be rewritten with this in mind. Indeed, the pervasiveness of the death drive calls for an ethics of psychoanalysis that Lacan will later develop as a science of the real.

Most important, the *new* idea on which Lacan bases an analytic ethics—and which gives rise to his reinterpretation of Freud's pleasure and reality principles—comes from his rereading Freud on the question of what *causes* repetition, what makes repetition so telling, what makes radical change so difficult, and why "historical" change reflects myriad surface illusions of difference while the *different* always comes back in new variations of old dilemmas, at least as far as ethics is concerned. In "The Project for a Scientific Psychology" (1895), Freud broke away from the neurological model from which he had taken the idea that an unbroken chain of physical events is causative of memory.[15] Having failed to explain the unconscious in terms of memory or thought, Freud evolved his new concepts of a pleasure principle and a reality principle. But he did not know where to place them within his overall theory. Gradually, he decided that the pleasure principle belonged to primary-process (or unconscious) thinking and the reality principle to secondary-process (or conscious) thought.[16] Lacan's realignment and reconceptualization of these two principles clarifies what he called Freud's "enlightening" confusions of pleasure with reality. The Freudian pleasure principle seeks to cancel displeasure's sensations: i.e., a certain amount of tension. Yet a quantity of tension remains. Lacan called this irreducible amount the object *a* (Miller, "Ethics in Psychoanalysis," 19). This irreducible tension turns pleasure into reality, not an opposing force. Thus, Lacan broke with Freud's development of his own thought.

Arguing that *there is no pleasure principle*, Lacan finds his basis for veering away from the classically read Freud in "Beyond the Pleasure Principle."[17] That Lacan would find the basis for rethinking the reality and pleasure principles in "Beyond the Pleasure Principle" is not surprising. While working on this same text, Freud referred to the "death instincts" for the first time in a letter he wrote to Max Eitingon on February 20, 1920.[18] In Freud's book that appeared in December of that year, he gave great scope to the idea of a compulsion to repeat, which he had previously considered a clinical phenomenon manifested only in moral masochism (or unconscious guilt) and negative therapeutic reaction. In "Beyond the Pleasure Principle" he imputed the characteristics of a basic instinct to these phenomena and also added the new idea of a dichotomy between Eros and Thanatos. Moreover, he emphasized the *problem* of human destructiveness ("Beyond the Pleasure Principle," 4–5). Decades later Lacan would argue that there is a "beyond" *in* the pleasure principle only because our quests for pleasure always include dissatisfaction and loss. And this occurs, not simply because the pleasure "principle" or quest for satisfaction pushes us to repeat, but because we become affixed to repetitions rather than to satisfactions. Freud saw that "beyond" the pleasure principle, we stumble onto death in the guise of repetition.

In Lacan's terms, the pleasure principle turns sour because repetitions constitute satisfactions that hold us in a death thrall. Since our love of our symptoms is synonymous with the love of consistency, the reality of the pleasure principle is not a biological principle of homeostatic constancy aiming at zero tension, then. Nor is it the quest for a non-conflictual entropy resembling death. Rather a *sense* of pleasure can only be experienced retroactively, i.e., in relation to a before which is "known" as pleasurable, simply because the "after" is not pleasurable. Put another way, repetition is itself marked by the unary trait that first joined the infant's body to the world by a trace of identificatory *jouissance* which remains embedded in the flesh long after the loss (or cut) of primordial objects.[19] Since these primal traits constitute a fixity of libido inscribed on the body, *jouissance* appears in language in seemingly disassociated signifiers or in dreamlike images that break up a pat narrative content.

But one can be more precise about *jouissance*. Lacan described it as any meaning that refers to sex or death. Indeed, if desire is taken as the desire to repeat prior satisfactions, and is seen as constituted in three logical moments that coincide with the dividing of the subject, one may begin to grasp the logic in play. These three moments are: *jouissance* experienced at the time of pleasure; anxiety experienced at the moment of loss; and desire/lack created as a permanent structure in subjective fantasy.[20] Between the absoluteness of *jouissance* and the impossibility of sustaining it as a state of pleasure, one encounters a range of phenomena from renunciation (superego) to castration. But Lacan's innovation here is surprising. Castration does not mean that law is constituted in some pregiven or innate form that forbids *jouissance*, but that the Name-of-the-Father, or language itself, functions to produce a "no" (Miller, "Ethics of Psychoanalysis," 23). When the paternal metaphor malfunctions, *jouissance* reigns supreme—it is not renounced. This happens in psychosis where *jouissance* serves as an internal limit to its own impossibilities.

Bringing back the Latin word *causa*, Lacan used the French word *la chose* to translate Kant's and Freud's *das Ding*, calling this Freudian "thing" truth. The truth of the real that we hide is fleeting and partial because we do not want to see that we are narcissistic creatures who seek *jouissance*, not truth or wisdom.[21] For at the level of *jouissance* we value ourselves supremely in our worth as "things" of supreme being or devastating nothingness. *La chose*, our cause, is the desire which calls for repetition as repetition of the known which shows itself as whatever fills the hole of loss to reaffirm in us a sense of constancy and (well) being. This reality, in turn, serves as a barrier to change. But what does this paradox mean? It means that we depend on archaic fixations that repeat certainties which we value, lest loss, questions, or doubts leave us open to an encounter with the unbearable real of anxiety. Thus, desire is constituted as a dialectic that gives rise to fantasies of fulfillment via the drive which aims at the impossible: the maintenance of a consistency of primary *jouissance*, or a primordial masochism.

Since both drive and fantasy aim at keeping things as they are, they *function* as barriers to changing action in the ethical field of desire. That drive and fantasy occupy the realm of the death drive, turns upon an impasse that makes sense only if one keeps in mind Lacan's claim to have made a break with philosophy in the field of ethics. Relocating the ethical question by means of the topological theory he called the Freudian cut, Lacan elaborated a logic in which etymology was not his guide. Nor were twists and turns of poetic sound his concern. Although Lacan says the usage of the signifier constitutes the "lettre" or *l'être* in its *synchrony*, it is not an alphabetical letter in question, but a unary trait that links the body to the world via precise identifications. Lacan makes the point that the "letter" introduces not only censure or repression, but also the unconscious as a timing of desire. Denoting repression by S_2, the matheme for knowledge, Lacan gives a new meaning to "knowledge": We use conscious knowledge in the service of repressed word, sound and image associations, and primordially repressed "objects" that *cause* desire. Such knowledge (S_2) subtends the enigmatic signified of symptoms. But *diachrony* concerns structure, not knowledge, the structuring of desire that comes from a relation to the phallus which appears clinically in the differential categories of neurosis, perversion, or psychosis.

At the level of such structures, there is, however, the knowledge of *jouissance* effects, there where the subject is an object *qua* response of the real: The object *a* is defined here as condensed or materialized *jouissance* with which the subject identifies itself as an object that causes its own desire. If one thinks of the *petit a* as a positivization of the negativity of loss—a retrieval of a wisp—one may speak of the enjoyment of meaning or *jouis-sens* wherein ego becomes an object reducible to the death drive. The *jouissance* of meaning is another name for the attempt to valorize the inconsistencies that are already in the symbolic: [$S(\emptyset)$]. Put another way, when libidinal energy is dislocated—neither assimilated in conscious knowledge nor lost—its effects return anyway. But they return discordantly in the symbolic to disrupt the *jouissance* of oneness and attest to the traumatic presence of something strange in being. We are not in the realm of philosophical ontology, clearly, although lack has an almost ontological status in Lacan. Rather, we are in the real of *ontotautologie*.[22] While the object *a* is not *das Ding an sich*, it is not a logically decipherable *presence* either. Rather, it is an excess or surplus in *jouissance* that bears witness to a tie between the world and the body at the level of the already constituted meaning one might call the symptom (*Sém.* VII, 56).

In *Séminaire* XV, *L'acte psychanalytique* (1967–1968), Lacan says that since even reason is not rational, it *is* rational to seek to know what makes reason fail. *His* answer is *das Ding*, the cause, *la chose freudienne*. But "it" is not what "it" was for Kant, nor even for Freud. "The thing," says Lacan, "is the passage of a conflict between men *to* the symbolic order." But by conflict, Lacan does not refer to some battle between the id and the superego to be resolved by the ego. Nor does he refer to some intersubjective disharmony between self and other (or "ego") to be mediated by a third person. Rather, conflict is whatever, in each of us, is already there as irresolvable. In *Extimité* Jacques-Alain Miller depicts the object *a* as logically deducible at the point where an excess appears in what seems to be a libidinal consistency. At that place one finds that the real of some signifier, some drive, some trauma, some experience of sexuality, cannot be symbolized. Normally, people identify with constellations of consistency (objects, activities, effects), seeking a semblance of unity, attempting to cover over the raw anxiety and discontinuities produced by the real.[23] In unconscious fantasy we reach for familiar satisfactions that give us the sense of doing things, acting on our desires, passing from place to place. But in truth we simply have the *illusion* of movement which enables us to deny that conflict always enters the symbolic from the unsymbolized real, disrupting our fond hopes of unity and our beliefs in a guarantee.

In *Seminar* XI Lacan gives the name *lamelle*, a thin plate or scale, to the libido and describes it as an organ, moving from person to person. Redefined by Lacan, the biological lamella becomes an invisible, mythical organ whose palpable effects come from the real. Indeed, all the forms of the primordial object *a* that one can enumerate as organs separable from the body as a whole (i.e., the breast, the placenta, and so on) are its equivalents. And they appear in the Other, not only as signifiers, but also as elements of what one must lose by having to pass, for reproduction or copulation, through the sexual cycle.[24] In the place where *jouissance* marks a loss, the desire for an object seeks to compensate for the loss. But the loss remains irreparable, structural. In the late 1950s, however, Lacan had not yet located *das Ding* in the symbolic order, spawning objects that try—inadequately—to fill up the holes and inconsistencies in being. In the 1950s he described *das Ding* as passing into the symbolic order in the form of a conflict between individuals. One might well ask how this differs from the conflict model in Freud's theory of the drive. Why would Lacan's concept of *das Ding* call for a *new kind* of ethics? Let us hold that question in suspension for a moment.

Lacan makes it clear in *The Ethics of Psychoanalysis* that *das*

Ding—"it"—does not pertain to an ethics which would present itself as a science. Nor does "it" constitute a superego knowledge of what *must* be done in order to establish an adaptation that will enable individuals to participate in a certain ethical order, or even submit to it. Rather, veering away from the Freudian moralistic/adaptive ethics, Lacan agrees with the writers of old that ethics always bears on the issue of the "good," even on the Sovereign Good. To emphasize his point, Lacan notes that most of Aristotle's *Nicomachean Ethics* treats this question: Why, when *everything* has been done to ensure good action, does intemperance subsist? Lacan does not hope, as did Aristotle, that ethics will succeed up to the point that a particular order will become a universal knowledge whose ethics can then constitute a politics, in imitation of the cosmic order (*Sém.* VII, 31).

Ethics can never become a universal politics, Lacan argues, because culture is an agreed upon set of exchanges concerning two sexes who have no *natural* relation one to the other. Culture, indeed, cannot exist except in the conflictive terms of this imagined rapport *which is not One*, whether the non-rapport results in overt conflict or whether it remains denied or repressed. Aristotle's question about why intemperance subsists after everything has been done to ensure good action, is not so different from the one posed by the Marquis de Sade (and others before and after him). To wit, in what does the *jouissance* of transgressing the law consist? (*Sém.* VII, 229–30). To say that the pleasure in transgression comes from the desire for total fulfillment is not such a shocking reply. But such desire is not attainable—desire by definition marking a structural lack, a place of *unconscious* desire. The problem lies, rather, in that each of us must always contend with our dependence on others for satisfaction, while the primordial Other who set the terms of each person's satisfaction in the first place is the Other sex *qua* gaze or voice, as well as the Other place of repressed signifiers, or cultural knowledge.

Yet Lacan points to a major flaw in the theory that the desire for a totalized (thus impossible) satisfaction gives rise to conflict or intemperance. And in so doing, he puts his finger on a problem Aristotle never solved: the relation of the universal to the particular. Passing through the defiles of Lacan's signifiers, we find that desire is not universal, but entirely particular. One need only consider the specificity of each person's dreams, life story, sense of humor, sexuality, not to mention many other examples. To state the obvious: each of us is unique, whatever our similarities may be. And when the particularity of one's desire appears visibly in the *sinthome*, it also marks the libidinal metonymy Lacan designated as a signified, not a signifier.

Lacan's concept of desire is not equatable with Freud's concept of pleasure. Since desire gives evidence of something "more" always sought because something is always lacking, the "more" bears on the dialectical conflict between a *jouissance* of being (ego fictions and ego ideals) and a *jouissance* of sexuality (drives). But by sexuality, Lacan does not mean sex acts or gender. He refers, rather, to sexuation or the subjective position that anchors each person's desire in networks of unconscious fantasy (*Sém.* XX, 73). Lacan's logic of the real—new to the theory and practice of psychoanalysis—resides in the interplay between representations he denoted as quantities (empirical meaning) and the *jouissance* by which he described affects as qualities. If desire were universal or universalizable, as both Aristotle and Freud thought, and if its wants could be fulfilled by understanding, then the field of positivistic psychology (with its descriptions of the childish pleasure that remains in the man) would have already answered our questions concerning why human conflict is ineradicable. And we would be further along the path to curing human suffering than we are (*Sém.* VII, 33). Moreover, if the child remains in the adult, how can this be so? And how does this give rise to ethical dilemmas caused by indestructible desire that leads humans to repeat destructive "behaviors" in their own stories, as well as in history?

Lacan argues that in such psychological theories, "the child" stands in for what he calls the subject. But unlike the "subject" of desire, the signifier "child" does not lack, while the Lacanian subject is the *function of lack* itself. Castration $(-\phi)$ is the name Lacan gives to the child's incorporation of the Oedipal "no." The castrated "subject," therefore, is not *in* language as an essence of self, but is re-presented there by the images and words that serve as its clothing. The identificatory traits that mark the subject of desire ($) indicate what is lacking in a fantasized *jouissance* ($ $\lozenge$ a). Lacanian unconscious desire is not, then, another name for an ego or self that reifies lack as some totalized entity, i.e., an essential subject. Rather, Lacan used a mathematical x to denote *the function of desire*. After the 1950s, Lacan's response to genetic psychoanalytic theories (wherein ego is equated with "the child in the man" and behavior with an index of truth and cure, or wherein ego means the child as an object determined by the mother wherein narrated fantasy leads the way to truth and cure) was to argue against the biological bias of these ego-based theories. The signifier, the Other, the object a, structure—i.e., the Borromean structure of signifying orders—offer another psychoanalytic logic than the linear phenomenological one preferred by developmental theories.

There are no "laws" of the unconscious such as the pleasure principle or the reality principle; there are only the laws of language (metaphor and metonymy) and the laws of *jouissance*. In 1974 Lacan presented a paper in Rome entitled "La Troisième," which refers to the third kind of *jouissance*: the *jouis-sens* of meaning or of the unconscious. He described the three as the *jouissance* of being or meaning, the *jouissance* of the body, and the *jouissance* of the physical organism.[25] Lacan had started to define *jouissance* in 1960 in "The subversion." In *Encore* (1972–1973) he gave clear articulation to the first two *jouissances*: the phallic (sexual) one of the unconscious and the bodily or imaginary one linked to the Other sex. Turning on the oscillation between pleasure and displeasure, the term *jouissance* is clearly not the equivalent of Freud's pleasure principle.

Freud's theory of a pleasure principle may have been derived from Franz Brentano's philosophy course. In Vienna, Brentano taught the Aristotelian theory of the universal good as something realizable via physical *imbibing* of the sweet (as the good) (*Sém.* VII, 39). Whatever the influences on Freud's thinking, there is no question that the twin principles of pleasure and reality postulated in "Beyond the Pleasure Principle" caused as many new problems for him as they solved old ones. If cultural dicta (the superego *qua* reality) thwart sexual pleasure, causing conflict in the id, then removal of prohibitions to sexual freedom *should* have already brought about universal pleasure. This has not happened either in Freud's day or our own. Unconscious guilt, (castration) anxiety, and (penis) envy remain even after all is done, Freud said in "Analysis Terminable and Interminable" (1936).

Lacan says Freud failed to see *what* the tension was between the pleasure and reality principles because he had not solved the problem of *how* an "unconscious" could think. Opting, rather, for biological answers in his second topology (1923) Freud depicted the pleasure principle as instinctual. In the 1890s Freud had conceptualized the unconscious as a progressive stream of sensations that cling to a pleasure principle through memories of infantile pleasures and literal bodily sensations, thus reverting to an eighteenth-century mechanistic sense-data model of intelligence or thinking.[26] In his second topology, Freud tried to link fantasy and pleasure to instinct through the id. Thus, he became increasingly preoccupied with the issues of energy and drive. This second Freud leaned ever more heavily toward the idea that the same cause produces the same effect. Replacing the conscious/unconscious/preconscious models of his first topology with the id/ego/superego agencies, he stopped worrying about symbols, Oedipal conflicts, and sexuality in his new-found certainty that biological first causes lay at the heart of human conflict.

In giving his *own* answer to what the pleasure principle is and to what lies "beyond" it, Lacan argued that Freud had skewed centuries of ethical systems proposed by philosophical tradition in showing that *reality* is not, as they had thought, something already there. "Reality" is not a comfort that is *itself*, be it named God, the *cogito*, the *Dasein*, *das Ding an sich*, the undecidable, unconscious fantasy, the trace, the genome, or any other internal pre-given on which an opposition between pleasure and reality is "supposed" to be based. Moreover, Lacan read Freud as intimating that *reality* is not even opposed to pleasure. Reality is threatened by pleasure. If reality *is not itself*, Lacan said as early as 1959, but is precarious and deceptive, going in the direction of the displeasure of repetition, one must grasp what reality actually is in ascertaining why something like reality would be threatened by pleasure (*Sém*. VII, 40). Lacan relocates Freud's *ça* or id in a moment in grammar that tells only one thing: that the trace of the cut has been foreclosed from grammar onto the body itself where it delivers itself up to the game of repression, to what is not "I". In "Pour une logique du fantasme" Lacan calls the Cartesian "I do not think" a kind of "not I," or that which in discourse is "not I."[27]

But how does one bridge the gap between a "not I" and its source in language? The answer is the fantasy, supported by desire, that creates a bridge between body and language, filling in for the subject lacking in language. As such, the fantasy is fundamental and ineliminable. Insofar as it is closed in on itself, and is without referent, the "reality" to which the fantasy refers itself in grammar is not a real thing, but an empty and derisory term.[28] To what does "The King of France is bald" refer, except to centuries of Anglo/French competition? That is, there is no reality *qua* reality to which the fantasy refers; there is only the fantasy constituting a person's reality.

But what has this to do with the Freudian reality principle? In "The Project" (1887–1902) Freud identified thought with neurons. In the "Interpretation of Dreams" (1900) he identified symbols with perception. The early Freud, elaborating such correspondence theories, clearly did not think of conscious thought as flawed, even though he thought similar things could be the "same" as each other. In the early 1950s Lacan dubbed the errors of logic wherein one argues that like produces like, imaginary thought. One could learn more from the later Freud who thought repetition lies "beyond the pleasure principle," and found no easy explanation for this. If repeated acts turn into the death drive, thereby defining laws of what one might equate with resistance to change (even when change is willed), this implies that the subject is caught in the fantasy. But fantasy supports the Freudian reality principle in the sense that "reality" means accepting things as they are.[29] And, indeed, by 1937 Freud had concluded in "Analysis Terminable and Interminable" that psychoanalysis is an impossible profession precisely because of the impossibilities for change in fundamental masculine and feminine fantasies, despite the best analysis.[30]

Lacan's logic of sexuation shows a way out of the bind of Freud's theoretical impasses here. Focusing on the *cause* of the impasses, Lacan argued that one can learn to "do something with" one's symptoms in a creative way. Listening to the reality of fantasy spoken in repetitions, Lacan discovered an ordering of the particular in each person's suffering that he named the *sinthome* in the 1970s. With this fourth order which tells the story of how a given life coheres by the knotting of the orders as constituted by a mother's desire in reference to a signifier for a father's name, Lacan rewrote the Freudian Oedipus complex as a failure or success of the paternal metaphor. The differential structures of the analytic clinic are constituted as precise functions of desire, then, not as pre-existent diagnostic categories as Barnaby Barratt maintains.[31] .

In repetitions, the subject *appears* as a libidinal object, a response of the unarticulated real of effects primordially repressed in a pre-symbolic real (R_1). Libido eddies up heterogeneously from the *Urverdrängt* in a post-symbolic real (R_2) where symptoms are repetitions (or signifieds) that tell the story of a person's life strangely—by aiming askew of the real or the "thing" that is not yet sayable, speakable, or thinkable. Nonetheless, symptoms were formed in the past. They were first laid down in pre-symbolic matrices of the real and they return as a post-symbolic real. And although one may see that some*thing* blocks the smooth flow of symbolization and memory, one does not know what causes a symptom. But "it" is not completely opaque for its traces are written on the body as the death drive that Lacan describes as the "more than you in you" that does not wish your good.

Lacan argues the unthinkable. *Das Ding* or the real is the *agent* on which thinking and acting depend. Yet this not-recognized *thing* (Freud's *Unerkannte*) is not an impersonal project driving one toward death or old age. Nor is it a myth or a metaphor. Rather, the death drive is supported by two kinds of meaning. On the one hand, each person is alienated into the "knowledge" produced by the interlocking orders of his or her Borromean signifying chains. On the other hand, the subject as object *a*, response of the real, is an irreducible piece of an insoluble kernel at the heart of every chain. The object is "simply the presence of a hollow, a void, which can be occupied, Freud tells us, by any object, and whose agency we know [Lacan adds] only in the form of the lost object, the *petit a*" (Lacan, 180). And Miller describes it as "this irreducible amount that the functioning of the pleasure principle cannot cancel out" ("Ethics in Psychoanalysis," 19). Even though the object *a* is not an actual object, it is, nonetheless, logically inferable at the level of identification where the imaginary and the real intersect. And one can "see" its effects when *jouissance* breaks down in the castration, frustration or privation that follow the loss of a consistency.

Paradoxically, the object *a* is also Lacan's name for the primordially repressed effects that *cause* desire in the first place. Thus, desire will forever after retain its link with its origins in loss, its hankering after radically lost Ur-objects that constitute a pre-symbolic real. Insofar as the drive is a request for recognition, it emanates from desire and culminates in the "I ask this of you." But desire, taken as the object that causes "demand," disappears into primal repression, as Lacan says in "Subversion of the subject and the dialectic of desire"

> with the single exception that the cut remains, for this cut remains present in that which distinguishes the drive from the organic function it inhabits: namely, its grammatical artifices, so manifest in the reversions of its articulation to both source and object. . . . The very delimitation of the "erogenous zone" that the drive isolates from the metabolism of the function . . . is the result of a cut (*coupure*) expressed in the anatomical mark (*trait*) of a margin or border—lips, the enclosure of the teeth, the rim of the anus, the tip of the penis, the vagina, the slit formed by the eyelids, even the horn-shaped aperture of the ear. . . . Observe that this mark of the cut is no less obviously present in the object described by analytic theory: the mamilla, faeces, the phallus (imaginary object)

> the urinary flow. (An unthinkable list if one adds, as I do, the phoneme, the gaze, the voice—the nothing.) (314–15)

Reminiscent of the desire for "more" created by first cuts or separations—be they of weaning, a lulling away from the world of images, voices and gazes into the silent one of sleep, and so on—the cut gives literal birth to desire as a function of the real of loss. The well-known *Purloined Letter* story on which Lacan based a seminar bears the mark of the cut if one thinks of the theft as itself a cut that displaces *jouissance* onto the stolen letter that moves from one place to another. Whoever holds the letter is then marked by its power, which imbues various persons with the effect of being "it" for the time the law of the symbolic is subverted. But the letter is only a lure "object," supporting this unconscious fantasy: that in "having" the letter one is the phallus, i.e., the object of desire. The metonymic chain of thefts, driven by each person's desire to be "it" by having "it," moves along the drive circuit of the gaze. In the field of the visible, "having" objects confers power because objects *appear* to compensate for lost *jouissance*.

If I suggest that the primordial loss in the realm of the visible is the feces, readers may be confused. But the anal drive is no simple acquisitive drive in Freud's sense that retaining the feces lies at the heart of greed and sadistic grabs for power.[32] In his *Seminar* X on anxiety, Lacan argues that the first *social* demand placed on an infant—the demand for exchange and reciprocity—concerns the production of feces. These are taken as a "gift" given to the mother. In this *social* act the child is *seen* as disposing of waste, as leaving behind the animal comfort of being cared for, as achieving social approval. Yet the real effects of anxiety remain, Lacan argues. The infant is judged as both good and bad. He is praised for disposing of a piece of his body he is told is disgusting. He or she is told simultaneously that the feces are dirty *and* a "gift" that pleases others. Not surprisingly, the anal partial drive intersects with the gaze in its relation to loss where desire for recognition and success catalyze the experience of anxiety.[33]

If palpable loss is the beginning that forms its own center, it makes sense that a battle is waged between Eros and Thanatos, simply because Thanatos continually sabotages Eros. In Lacan's theory, there is no simple binary opposition between the two, but rather a relation to loss that is itself a third thing: the real of the void that exceeds grammatical meaning at moments when the cut enters language, showing the subject of grammar as an object set adrift. This "subject" refers itself to something enigmatic, finally, to the void as a positivizable negative where each person's most intimate *cause* is—not a conflict between death and life or sex and repression, but—the Freudian "thing": the truth underlying the desire that holds one in a death thrall. For Lacan, we remember, the void is not a metaphor, nor a myth of negativity, nor emptiness as in the Heideggerean vase, which Lacan describes as itself a signifier for a piece of pottery that we remember represents only the *potential* for fullness or emptiness.

Lacan characterizes loss as an effect that positivizes the void, giving it a palpable sense beyond the significations of grammar. If each person finds the Good in the way he or she replaces loss, thus avoiding anxiety, then the void can be filled by nonmaterial things such as love, belief, community, work. Filling its own void, the subject can be conceptualized as an object of a gaze, a voice, and so on. Lacan's subject is not a subject of thought, then, but an "object" subjected to another kind of knowledge: *jouissance*. The split between the *jouissance* of being (body and organism) *and* the language of thought means that no person is ever One, ever whole, for lost objects are not replaceable. Thus, the illusion that there are consistencies of body, being, or knowledge requires forced harmonies and harmful lies.

Indeed, one's "good" is appreciated, if at all, only retrospectively, in the *re*telling of stories, in viewing photos, in *supposing* a pleasure of wholeness in memory or anticipation, but not in present time. In *Séminaire* XXII (*R.S.I.*) Lacan reordered his exigencies, the real becoming the first order, the one that infers discontinuities into the seeming unities or continuities of the symbolic and imaginary. The real makes the void spaces between the orders appear, showing the Other as inherently inconsistent. Oneness or unity is nonetheless repetitiously sought by all individuals. And most ethical systems argue for a unity based on prescribed actions. Whether one seeks Oneness in the White Mass or the Black Mass, in Immanuel Kant or in the Marquis de Sade, Lacan's point is this: *structurally* speaking, the quest for union and (re)union is itself the effort to repeat *jouissance* as a Good. And such an energetics of repetitions paradoxically constitutes the obstacles of its own death weight.

That Lacan situated ethical problems in the dimension of the unsymbolized, thus unsayable, real which *functions*, nonetheless, to block speech and memory explains his insistence that the real exists as the impossible to bear. Any freedom won by extracting oneself from incorporated traumas allows one to drop the weight of certain repetitions, the enjoyment of which is archaic and tau-tological. Yet the satisfaction implicit in identifying with dissatis-faction bespeaks a closed circuit of *jouissance*. Lacan found such death pleasure to be typical of the master discourse which, by def-inition, denies pain and represses the fact that the traumatic roots of *being* are fixed in unconscious desire. Moreover, such denial occurs at the expense of the freedom to change place within one's own discontent.

In *Seminar* VII Lacan says: "The death drive is to be situated in the historical domain, insofar as it articulates itself at a level which is only definable by function of the signifying chain, that is to say, insofar as it is a guide, which is a guide of order" (250). That is, the real in any historical chain is isolatable *because* it was first inscribed in an associative network of meanings that go back to questions concerning a fundamental lack in the Other: (Ø). They go back to the words and images that oscillate around lost mem-ories. If an analysand speaks of the pain of anxiety felt from age four on as a physical opening from stomach to throat, an analyst might ask what happened when this sensation first appeared. The answer would not reside in a global narrative, nor in the memory of good or bad parenting. Rather, the answer will be told, if at all, in disconnected images and signifiers which unveil the discordance between illusion and reality as an experience of the cut.

Insofar as the cut produces the unary traits Lacan called "letters," language is linked to anatomy by the *jouissance* Lacan called li-bidinal meaning. Producing inertia, *jouissance* brings together af-fective pain, organ function or dysfunction, and meaning. But La-can's teaching takes a surprising turn here. We tend to ignore the libidinal meaning in the signifying chain where secondary-process thought simulates the chain itself. Nor can we *adapt* this knowledge to the so-called external reality of *a priori* meaning (*Sém.* VII, 211). If the signifiers "four year old" and "a pain from here to here" (just mentioned) are to serve as analytic guides for re-ordering the un-bearable meanings in a life, such re-ordering can only be done by the analysand's talking until he knows what lies behind. *Jouissance* knowledge, then, belongs to structure as it concerns desire (neu-rotic, perverse, psychotic), not to narrative or conscious memory.

Moreover, structure itself cannot be eradicated or repaired, al-though a person can change position within his own structure. Lacan argued forcibly that the reality principle is equatable to the *jouissance* of superego dicta. Adaptation to such dicta, be it via the acceptance of an analyst's morality or of an institution's, is to accept the Other that has already (de)-formed and (trans)-formed one by alienation and *méconnaissance*. Such paradigmatic (superego) moralities are unethical for there is no "natural" or true identity between being, signifier, gender, and body. There is only the pair of unfulfilled desire and the familiarity of *jouissance* that give rise to the quest to identify with ideals. Nonetheless, one *can* come to know some of his or her signifying chains in their *historical* dimension by the pathways of primary process where pleasure was *first* written as a corporally recorded experience of *das Ding*. Such "meaning" imposes itself as primordially repressed traits that link together loss, the rims or edges of the body, and erotic preferences or sensations. Yet, *das Ding* designates that which *has* no name precisely because *jouissance* precedes language (Miller, "To Interpret the Cause," 47). Not only can *a priori* memories not be recalled in well-made narratives, or as memories of experienced pleasure, they can only return at all as *a timing of the real*.

But—and this is crucial—these instants return in a *second* memory Lacan called the timing of the superego or the "reality principle" of Thanatos, which appears when judgments confer the blow of a negative gaze on ideals: shunning, exclusion, and disgust. The timing of the real *re-turns* in the voice of reprimand and blame, or in praise and love: Eros's oscillating tones. But, how does one recognize the *return* of something radically lost to memory? One recognizes the real, says Lacan, in what does not return as pleasure, but in the form of a symptom that *no longer* wishes one's Good. Paradoxically, this thing-in-itself was once a good, a pleasure. Otherwise, it would not have persisted as an "instance" of memory, recorded in enigmatic or erotogenic "letters" that tie the body to the world.

Here, Lacan's reshaping of Freud's thought is awesome. In that the effects he calls the object *a* are not visible objects with properties one can describe phenomenologically, one heeds palpable— that is, "visible"—properties such as the litter of the letter, i.e., a message not "meant" to be heard in the *double entendre* of tone or word play. The *jouissance* effects that are all-powerful and omnipresent in organizing what we disregard, dismiss, or overlook, play havoc with the notion of intention. Yet everyone recognizes this shadow language of the real, although we pretend it does not count. And, indeed, it does not count when we reduce meaning "that counts" to grammar or to linguistics or to philosophical or scientific propositions. Effects of the real do not correspond to words, images or objects of desire in any one-to-one way in terms of secondary process. Rather, they produce confusion, disruptions, lingering questions, vague hopes, and inexplicable sufferings around which an object *a* is "essentialized" by the *jouissance* emitted from a pure void—an empty place *that does not exist, but which functions* anyway.

The void resides in language as a positivity, actually piercing holes into words in the guises of panic, anxiety, nostalgia or longing. Lacan teaches that some*thing* is always already laid down in the void, prior to memory, the *a priori* libidinal stuff of *jouissance* that glues the world of objects, sounds, images, and the body together in an absolute knowledge about how one values things. We are far away from the Lockean concept of sense knowledge here, or from Condillac's man machine. The particularity of *jouissance* as constituted meaning enables analysands to find a logic to their symptoms as they unravel the stories of their attachment to suffering, which returns in the future perfect of repetition. In this *future perfect tense of repetitions* meaning oscillates in a temporal movement between anticipation and retroaction. The referent of such oscillations is the *jouissance* evacuated from a void around which one invents meaning *in language* because the real can only ever be approximated (Miller, "Much Ado about What?" 31–32). The return of the real points to something lost as a *cause*. One knows only that upon repetition some effect which once caused pleasure has turned into displeasure. But why would there be a gap between the *pleasure* of an *a priori* moment and its return as a *reality* of displeasure, marking a second logical moment in the real that bears on the death drive?

What is this real order of traumata that dwells in all human beings—at the heart of culture—producing Eros in a first moment that turns into Thanatos in a second one? It is not *das Ding* as the imaginary lure object (*a*), nor does it infer a consistency of subjectification in *objective* statements. The real takes on meaning only after the fact when surprise or disruption of grammar (the enunciated) or of a narrative unveil the unconscious fantasy that supports any part of speech (*Sem.* VII, 72). A primordially repressed object *a* causes the desire that supports the fundamental fantasies ($ \cancel{S} \lozenge a $) that form unconscious (or repressed) thought in coupled pairs of signifiers (S_1, S_2). These paired signifiers also serve as the inaugural point of the ego ideal images by which one tries to stop up the void. Jacques-Alain Miller has developed Lacan's formula for the ego ideal to show that the social order itself forms ideals which, in turn, plug up the inconsistencies or gaps in the truth surrounding the ideals:

$$i\frac{(a)}{O} \to \frac{\emptyset}{a}$$

(Miller, Extimité).

If *das Ding* is pure or primary *jouissance* entering the symbolic, why should it produce an effect of shock? Precisely because it produces cuts, setting parts of us adrift in the temporality of the drives where the Other is itself split between the id ($\emptyset$) and the ego (a). Separation, Lacan says, is akin to Freud's *Ichspaltung*, but the "I" never comes to *be* itself.[34] Rather, "I" hovers at the edges of meaning and body, ever dependent on language, identification, and desire which continually alienate the "I" from itself. The reality of the "I" is that of repetitions, symptoms, failures, questions one has never formulated, as well as hesitation, doubt, prayer, and so on. At the level of primary process, desire starts out in the repetition of an infant's cry, meant to bring back a prior satisfaction. Repetitions quickly become their own *raison d'être*, anchoring us in a sense of being whole or consistent.

But because the "object" being sought to satisfy desire does not displace something that was actually possessed in the first place, no substitute can ever be the "real thing." Thus, repetitions bear the structure of obsession, pointing to the death in desire, i.e., the impossible task of finding Oneness. Yet, in a paradoxical effort to skirt anxiety and uncertainty by identifying with closure, people cling to the notion that repetitions give us comfort, even though it is the comfort of fixity Lacan called "death." In psychoanalysis, the meaning of repetition concerns pain re-pressed in the body that catches us in the very *cause* we seek to avoid. But we encounter our displeasures over and over anyway, because they define our limits in the real of splits, cuts, and enigmas that constitute the formal envelope of the symptom.

In the ethics seminar Lacan discusses Sophocles's *Antigone*, depicting her as a heroine of desire. Why does Antigone not just accept to forgo the burial custom for her brother, one might ask. Is his mortal soul really the stake in her wager? Or does she refuse, rather, to allow Creon to defile the weight of her suffering? Does she hope one social act will redeem "a pound of the flesh" of her accursed lineage, and an echo of a once proud family name? (Lacan, Sem. VII). Lacan calls her desire pure desire, indeed, desire which cannot brook compromise. One could take a simple line and argue that her desire is to retain the hysteric's "pleasure" of showing others that the social law is empty, made up of Wizard-of-Oz stuff. I shall take another tack and suggest that capitulation to Créon would have taken away her last shred of dignity. So Antigone is not guilty, for she does not give up on her desire. But which desire? Let us say the desire for a *new*, untainted name, forged out of claiming a dignity for her old name. There is no cowardice in Antigone.

Jacques-Alain Miller explains Lacan's Sophoclean ethics thus: *das Ding* is the agent that chooses, decides, and responds from the real, at the limit point or impasse in a given reality. Insofar as *jouissance* is locatable in an extimate object *a*—a point where inside and outside coalesce—guaranteeing consistency to the doubting, fading, and oscillating subject of desire, one might say "reality" is based on an objective fact: the point at which one breaks (Miller, *Extimité*). For Lacan, the mental function one usually calls "reality" is actually unconscious fantasy. By repeating its quest for *jouissance*, fantasy retroactively endows an act with an anticipatory meaning, producing a grimace in the real. Lacan gives no Cartesian guarantee. Indeed, Descartes's *cogito* mis-takes the act of thinking something for the truth of the thought. Astonishing as it may seem, the consequences of believing one's own suppositions, even as one argues against doubts, are these: one ends up in the hands of the supreme superego Lacan called ferocious and obscene. The only *ethical* way out of this dilemma, in which one feels anchored in thought by identifying with moralizing alienations, requires one to address the death weight of individual suffering. Serge Cottet has written: "The more one gives up on *jouissance*, the more demanding the superego is."[35]

In "The Construction of Imaginary Time," feminist theorist Teresa Brennan concludes that although Freud saw primary-process unconscious thought as timeless, Lacan's "linguistic" turn has obviated the need for a primary process by showing us that secondary process produces language. Thus, "there is no warrant for the assumptions made about the nature of the primary process. For the primary process can only be known through the perspective of the secondary process."[36] Indeed, Lacan does reject Freud's notion of the primary process. But he replaces it with another logic. Primary process places loss *in* language, functioning in a metonymic movement whose cause is the desire for *jouissance*. A quantity of affect (*jouissance*) is (dis)placed into the battery of signifiers as inertia or fixed consistencies. Miller writes the function of primary-process metonymy this way:

$$\frac{\text{Other (battery of signifiers)}}{\text{Jouissance (quantity of libido)}} \; (a) \; \text{[the leftover residue]}$$

(Miller, "To Interpret the Cause").

In Lacan's return to Freud, he argues that the pursuit of pleasure is stimulated by the real of primary process whose *cause* is that of replacing radically lost *jouissance*. The *primordially* repressed Ur-objects that elicit desire start the chase that ties the body to the world by the desire for *jouissance* (be it positive or negative). The infant first desires the Oneness of *jouissance*, not objects per se. Unity or wholeness is the goal. Yet if the infant stays fixed in the mirror illusion of being one with another, he is "rewarded" with a sense of always being right: BEING FULFILLED. For such a person no lack in being begets the desire by which most people *function* as flawed (i.e., human) creatures of potential redemptions and endless hopes.

In this sense, unconscious thought (*jouis-sens*) *is* time and timing, the time of the real marking fantasy by desire. The timing of the unconscious occurs in the trace of a moment, in a lightening fast movement along a Möbius strip, in a moment which defines the space of human inter-actions by the time it takes to make a turn around the gap between word and image. Lacan shows logical time to be an effect produced in the Other that elicits an unconsciously "calculated" response.[37] The timing of one's destiny dwells, then, in the repetition of desires that respond to a temporality whose logic is neither chronological nor linear. It is a response to a mother's unknown desire—unknown because inseparable from primordial ties to her body, her smell, her *lalangue*, her touch, her voice, her gaze—correlated with her way of presenting the signifier for a Father's Name. That is, the identificatory difference away from the primordial mother is itself a signifier. The specificities of any person's life story revolve around the issue of losing the primordial mother as a guarantee of being (or not). Lacan viewed such progressive losses of partial objects as the cuts that produce a *jouissance* of the body and the organism. As a surplus value, *jouissance* is non-utilitanian in any practical sense, then, although it defines a person's value(s).

Primary process, thus conceived, continually inserts itself into secondary process, showing that language is rooted in the body and in the time of desire. But desire is the desire to repeat, not the "desire to know." In this sense, desire is caught up in the death drive that Lacan situates in the historical domain. Laid down even prior to language, the death drive aims first for pleasure but misses. In this miss the dimension of an *ex nihilo* is introduced into language and knowledge (*Sém.* VII, 252). Lacan called the *ex nihilo* a void. That is, the infant "knows" to aim for satisfaction because he or she has experienced the dissatisfaction (anxiety) of loss. Thus, the drive intersects with desire in a *Fort! Da!* game of seeking, finding, and repeating that turns into the structure of wanting-not-to-lose. One can see how actual objects become so highly valued in matters of loss or gain. Yet ethical theories have generally disregarded these repetitions whose meaning is the pain of loss itself, even if it is manifest only in the bittersweetness of nostalgia.

Freud knew that repetition lies beyond the pleasure principle, that it gives the unconscious a law of signs. These signs guarantee that the subject is Good for nothing, not ideal, a "bad object" (*Sém.* VII, 89). In Lacan's paraphrase of Freud and Melanie Klein, no primordial sign system sends any message to any other. The real of unconscious identifications tells the story of imperfections, failures, mistakes—"original" sin, so to speak. Given the omnipresence of loss and lack in life, one can see why moral law has always aimed at silencing the real as such by holding on to the illusory hopes that keep anxiety at bay. To avoid encountering the void place in ourselves, we prefer any guarantee of wholeness or righteousness that promises to make things better. To make this point, Lacan goes to the extreme of arguing that Kant's universal maxim for human relations—the good of one is the good of all—pronounced in *The Critique of Practical Reason* (1788), and the Marquis de Sade's law of universal debauchery—you can do anything *to me, I* say to you— enunciated in *La philosophie dans le boudoir* (1795) show us the same thing at one level: the desire for a "law" to mediate the unhappiness and *malaise* of the human subject.[38]

The impossibility of such a law, as Lacan sees it, is that each person decides or chooses from the unsymbolized real, not from free will. Yet how can one choose from an ordering of traumata inscribed on the body and in language, but *un*assimilated in memory? Lacan gives this answer: *Because* the repetitions that predetermine choices as forced choices—either/or, this/that—find their roots in an unbearable limit in trauma. Thus, the meanings that govern habit point to something laid down before, both in the symbolic *automaton* of alienated language and in the contingent traumata of the real. Again and again choices bring us up against the object *a* at points of impasse in thinking. There, loss is positivized as a palpable density of *jouissance* whose cause appears in the enigma of any person's *douleur* (suffering) taken to its limit. And any means of closure—belief systems, transference relations, knowledge systems, and so on—can serve as an object *a*, as fillers for endless, bottomless holes of loss that, nonetheless, cough out narcissistic pieces of *jouissance*.

The primordial object *a*—partial objects-cause-of-desire—become partial drives linked to four primordial partial objects: the breast, the feces, the gaze, or the voice. Not only are such "objects" libidinally dispersed and splattered in the partial drives, language rites and ritual acts are built around them as well. Yet no "object," no matter how fixed or consistent, can eradicate the obduracy of the void as a palpable "thing" whose effects continually splinter and split language and body in repetitious impasses. Posing questions and inferring paradoxes, impasses send us on continuing searches for intellectual—and ethical—answers we elaborate as "content." Yet, the humble questions behind our great endeavors are: Can you see me? Do you hear me? Is my gift enough? Do you love me?

But why would a search for a subject's Good in *psychoanalysis* bring something new to ethics? Lacan says it is because we find *an unnameable subject of experience* there that seems to correspond to (imaginary) *oppositions* such as reality and pleasure, thought and perception, the known and unknown, and so on. Insofar as perception is imaginary—mixing the part with the whole—people take binary oppositions for true antitheses, whether they choose this or that or opt for the ambiguity of both/and. Lacan names the excluded middle in the relation between oppositions the vel ($\Diamond$) or the operation of union. Bruce Fink writes: " 'Vel' in Latin means 'or' where it is understood that *only one* of the two propositions can be true, not both."[39] But the imaginary (or perception) totalizes, not seeing that choices are first constituted, then forced. Thus, imaginary thinking deadends in identifying—and spuriously equating—antinomical terms: pleasure and the Good, for example (*Sém.* VII, 44).

In *Civilization and Its Discontents*, Freud's human being experiences a *malaise* because civilization or the social law demands too much. The product of such law, the superego, does battle with the id's demand for total pleasure. For centuries, the "human" answer to civilization's excessive demands has been ethical councils of goodness. Law has served as a balancing measure. In Lacan's picture, such councils reveal the ongoing truth of lack, loss, and the lies that subtend the best efforts at goodness: "All have sinned and come short of the glory of God."

Let us now try to understand what Lacan meant when he said that ethics emanates from one fundamental law: the incest taboo. His is not a moral injunction concerning literal sex acts, nor does he point to a literal primal scene, conceived as the observation of parental intercourse. Nor is his point a Kleinian one: that the mother, or parts of the mother's object-relations body, are in and of themselves experienced in fantasy impressions of Good or Bad objects that psychoanalysis can repair later on. In Lacan's rethinking, the incest taboo is the taboo necessary to the existence of culture itself—a taboo against an identificatory Oneness with the mother *qua* primary object taken as a guarantee that nothing will ever be lacking to her child. By *not* fulfilling her infant's desire to overcome the anxiety and sense of fragmentation accompanying loss through a totalizing identification with her, a mother prepares her child for the world. In a Lacanian ethics, the mother lets herself be lost, part by part. But this does not refer to the mother as a person or being, only as the structural source of ongoing *jouissance*, for *das Ding* is outside the signified (the symptom). It is recognizable, however, for it reeks of too much, of an excess. But because people enjoy whatever appeases their loss, one finds the paradoxic of a discontent in *jouissance*. In that place of "pleasure" one is bitter, confused, wounded, disappointed, perplexed, waiting.

Lacan taught that an ethics of psychoanalysis can truly help analysands change, while theological prescriptive moralisms or the pluralisms of contemporary atheism cannot. Moreover, contemporary atheism denies its own new god: Science. But whether one points to religion or conventional wisdom, people take on a sense of Being by identifying with their *semblables* as good and "naturally" well-intentioned. This illusion tells a lie, for individuals may wish their own good or that of their intimates. But not that of mankind. The idea of incest as *taboo* is also a lie, for incest occurs both in sexual acts carried out and in unconscious fantasy. Lacan enlarges the concept of the primal scene beyond the sex act to the family novel: one is *in-cest*/in-this. Yet the only *universal* taboo is the incest taboo, which is not even included in the ten commandments. We break the ten commandments, Lacan noted. And we misunderstand the incest taboo—*not* included in Moses' law—thinking it means only sex acts. In incest the problem is not that the mother *wants* her child to fill up her lack, or to *be* her mirror.

Problems occur when she wants to possess her child to the exclusion of others, of the social. And the greater a child's proximity to this symbiotic bond, the greater the affective disturbances caused by proximity to the primordial real.

Lacan's discovery is a structural one: what is *impossible* in the incest taboo is the Oneness it forbids. The illusion of two persons functioning mentally as one person constitutes the structure of psychosis where the subject's limit in *jouissance* finds the master and the slave occupying the same position. The social usually prevails over incest, however, insofar as sexual difference is the founding law on which the possibility of exchange in the social link is built up as an identity position based on lack. The foreclosure of a primary signifier ($ or the signifier for lack) creates an anti-social impasse which shows that whatever form a relation to the mother as primary object might take—whether a symbiosis of nostalgic romanticism or a Sadean destructive fantasy of social revolution substituted for destroying the mother herself—something else is at stake. Every human decision, action, or choice repeats the dilemma of a continually forced choice in sexual identification: either/or, both/and, boy/girl. In that symptoms announce nothing other than the presence of real knots in stories, memories and bodies—knots that persist in ego fictions—it is not surprising that they function as resistances to change one can only link to the death drive. Although people tell their life stories as signs of hope eternal, showing the power of the wish to change, such stories partake of imaginary and narcissistic illusions, revealing the human inability to give up on myths one has come to identify with one's Good. Indeed, ego illusions revel in the fantasy that the other—or Other—has one's own Good in mind. But while rationalizations abound, the Good stays out of reach.

Freud opined that psychoanalysis had not promoted the importance of moral issues. Lacan countered with an ethical issue: the primordial mother as primary object is lost (unless one is psychotic), yet we negotiate "it" as if an actual object were there. In "La réalité depuis Freud" Jacques-Alain Miller comments: "It is not the same thing to describe and articulate the reality of love and then to transform it. To make a subject grasp, for example, that his love life gravitates around the object mother, does that put him in a position to detach himself from the orbit which has been proscribed for him?"[40]

In the ordinary trajectory of our daily lives, we reify this primary object to equate static *jouissance* with the Good and to defend our miseries by narcissistic ideologies that bespeak unconscious stakes. Such master/*m'être* discourses $\dfrac{(S_2}{a)}$ of narcissistic certainty depend on the illusion of unity provided by language suppositions that screen out the primary-process effects of fantasy. Put another way, master discourses—discourses that tailor the unconscious to the visible—put the mother in a place of repressed fantasy. And both women and men speak master discourses that repress knowledge of the primary mother as a center of gravity (the *norme-mâle* and the *nor-mâle*). Most people, then, push for sameness, Oneness, wholeness, and agreement, revealing that imaginary logic prevails in conscious thought. Lacan says the temptation to tame the Other, and the loss at its center, is irresistible for anyone who speaks. So most individuals push loss away by their relations to things and others, basing most "ethical" systems on a high evaluation of the other, one's *semblable*. Fantasies of altruism, equality, group "good-will," solidarity, philanthropy, and expansions of the Goodness of Youness abound.

Such fantasies run counter to the limit that ethical systems always encounter: too much suffering. De Sade pushed this limit to its extreme to proclaim what Lacan calls the "truth" of *metipsimus*, myself, the same, the same-ty of others. "Love your neighbor as yourself," says the *Bible*. Lacan says that instead, we "love the image by which [our] ego was formed" (*Sém.* VII, 230). Love finds its identification in those who share one's own *jouissance*. Mankind *needs* an ethics of psychoanalysis precisely because human beings constitute each other first in the name of love, and then love only that in others that reflects themselves. At the interior of the ego, each person's narcissistic "self"-replications move in a continually rapid oscillation from nothingness to being, and back. Our most intimate part is "that": I am "it"; I'm not "it."

By showing conflict between people as the unstoppable inter-vention of the real in the symbolic, Lacan demonstrates that I/thou theories of subject duality (or inter-subjectivity) lead to false hopes of open interchange, of authentic debate, of longed-for empathy between "you' and "me." Rather, each person's intrasubjectivity includes a master/slave relation within oneself where *jouissance* bears on power, not love. Here we are at the bottom line for human "behavior" where a sense of being is a sense of "being" best or worst. Guilt lies somewhere in-between. One is guilty for falling short of being loved by ego ideals, and of not realizing one is already constituted in fantasy as a real "object" made of *jouissance* stuff.

But why would the ego incur guilt? Because *it* is already constructed as a death principle of resistance that keeps one from being able to re-constitute desire. Yet desire is the only path to change in the real, where the subject is reduced to a condensed object of *jouissance*—a voice, a gaze, a piece of shit, a scent, a breast, a penis, a vagina, and so on. And since *jouissance* holds the ego together, repetition has always already returned to mock (desire) with the impossibility of achieving a position of Sovereign Good.

How do we bear the impasse between wanting and being that imprisons each of us? Love is not enough. We have the images of pornography and the "dirty" words for sexual organs by which we try to bridge the unbridgeable sexual divide. Indeed, these very images and words prove the pain of frustration that arises from the unrepresentability of sexual difference. So we personalize. A breast becomes a tit; a penis, a prick; a vagina, a cunt; an anus, an asshole. And each part stands in for the whole of a gender, placing metonymy squarely on the side of libido where the *jouissance* of being speaks a language of the real. When words fail, when the ego is shoved askew, desire appears in the place of lost *jouissance*, referring itself to the "substance" of old: the Good of the subject.

Freud sidestepped the issue of defining the Good in terms of a morality or a set of laws. By finding the Sovereign Good at the level of the pleasure principle, he equated pleasure with a place where the mother is the forbidden good. He reversed the foundation of moral law with this idea (*Sém.* VII, 85). But, unlike Freud, Lacan did not see the issue of an ethics of psychoanalysis as arising only from the fact that each child's world revolves around the mother. Ethics bears, rather, on the particularity of how desire is structured by language, identifications, and loss. How are we constituted by others such that we evolve into fixed "selves" to which we quickly become blind? Since *jouissance* is itself absolute and non-dialectical within its own terms, *a pure non-utilitarian real which wishes nothing*, it makes sense that dumb, nonsensical, blind repetitions function *only* to satisfy the drive: the drive *to be* . . . seen, heard, fed, loved, and so on.

If the "drive" to be *cognized* is based on the necessity of being *re-cognized* then drive is doomed to express itself by repetitions which have quickly become mechanical responses, guarantees of no Good other than the familiar. Yet this seems better than anything else because it is certain. *Jouissance* constitutes reality's ego on the slope of narcissism, then, ensuring the fixity of symptoms. It retains consistency and familiarity over the Good of freedom, laughter, the creativity of everyday life, or the sublimation of art or making love.

Lacan taught that the analytic ethical act consists in recognizing the *jouissance* which has already set a subject afloat as an object of the real, identified with his or her symptoms. Only a reconstitution of the desire that has become the desire for suffering allows one to drop the *jouissance* that maintains itself as the cause of being, even though useless and archaic. The analytic task is enormous, then, requiring a separation of the "pleasure" of familiarity in ego fixity from the harm one does to self and others through symptoms. But such separation is possible. Although the real is split off from memory, its *jouissance* effects appear everywhere (in symptoms, images, language, and the body). *Jouissance* speaks the enigmatic language of limits and borders: nonsense, illogic, pain. Lacan's idea that cure requires one to open up a split between the ego and the symptom shifts the emphasis in Freud's celebrated formula: *"Wo es war, soll Ich werden."* Lacan shows the split as residing between grammar and desire, in the Other. Divided between the id (inconsistencies produced by the real) and the ego as *semblant* (as object *a*, filler of the holes in the Other), neither Freud's *Es* nor his *Ich* can be a whole agency (equatable somehow with id, ego, or superego).

In Lacanian treatment, either sublimation or a use of judgment *may* replace the death weight borne at the place where *jouissance* encumbers the analysand's being. When the analyst's action focuses on the limits of an analysand's suffering, making use of the cut to mark a point *between* images or words by a sound, a movement, or an end to the session, this analytic act is equivalent to the double buckle of the signifier that cannot signify itself (Granon-Lafont, *La topologie ordinaire*, 35–42).

The paradoxical solution to a particular life dilemma requires that the analyst cut into the density of language or desire at the place where the patient is enjoying suffering. Such action is ethical insofar as the subject is an object there, an excluded interior of the (hypothetical) real of its own structural organization. As such, the subject is *that* in life which is already dead, but "insists" on appearing anyway in searing moments when the object *a* shines through flesh, image, and language, projecting an anamorphic light. One could well agree with Lacan that the *weight* of duty in Kant's *Critique* parallels his own idea of the real weight that is the subject as object of *jouissance* (*Sém.* VII, 130).

But how can this psychoanalytic ethics help us to live in the world? Is this not just another version of Camus's "Il faut faire comme si." (One must act as if . . .)? I would say not. Lacan argues something different. Any degree of cure, of learning new ways to negotiate one's impasses, derives from a different kind of knowledge: the truth which admits we were formed by intimates and then deceived by them and will be again. The truths that form our lives emanate from unspeakable knowledge. Moreover, such truth accepts that there is always a failure of correlation between what we hope for from the symbolic and the responses we get back from the real. This "knowledge" is based on acceptance of the fact that there will never be a (sexual) *relation* of Oneness (*Sém.* VII, 123). In a Lacanian ethics we know we will not be loved (enough), that neither our goods or our Good will bring total happiness, and, paradoxically, that we can live more freely and kindly by dropping our romantic illusions.

One way to live with the impasses that never entirely disappear is to practice an ethics of "speaking well" (i.e., truthfully). Herein efforts are made to attenuate the brutal effects of the real by suspending judgments, by recognizing our narcissistic identifications, by calling things what they are. Yet such a *bien dire* is not easily learned. At the barrier between the desire to change and the *jouissance* that blocks change, the idea of the Good itself is a barrier separating us from it. Put another way, the quest for the immediate pleasure of narcissistic gratification only intensifies our fallacious notions of the Good. The esthetic phenomenon of sublimation is another barrier stopping us from the radical destruction of "absolute" desire. In sublimation pleasure is equated with the beautiful, which, in turn, seems true. Whatever one finds to be true, one finds beautiful. And vice-versa. Given this Keatian paradox, Lacan stresses that the sublimated beautiful often dwells closer to evil than to what one might call his or her good (*Sém.* VII, 256). The master discourse—the norm—closes out the truth of this paradox, clinging instead to the death drive, to repetition, to lies, to narcissism.

Of what should one be cured, then? Of the illusions produced by ideals and unconscious fantasies, Lacan says. Because they *fix* us on the path of death, cementing repetitions that place us in double binds. We love our symptoms more than doing what it takes to realize our desires. The real skews our vision such that we find beauty in whatever we do or think, readily defending things that hurt us and others. And we must because the paradox is this: we only survive at all *because* we make ideals of the first forms we live from, be it Ming vase or tomato soup can, high art or low art. Lacan's insight concerning ethics is this: To change the real—the impossible or contradictory—is so difficult, making freedom(s) so elusive, that our only hope for less suffering lies in smashing the impossibilities in our dreams, in breaking with the lies we tell ourselves. Only then can we begin to empty out the illusions that compose Being. This requires relinquishing that in us that is *more* than us, the excess *jouissance* in desire whose price is the stranglehold of the familiar that constitutes a false consistency.

Lacan's ethics of psychoanalysis is brutal. It asks us to work against the grain of the normative in our own desire, our own pleasures, our own timing. In analysis another person sits in as a symbol of a silent cause: the desire the analysand cannot speak. Lacan's texts go a long way toward exercising a similar effect on his readers. However, a text is not an analyst, although an "authentic" teaching can enable persons to maintain a question over an answer. When Lacan first spoke in a public seminar, only a few students attended. As individuals heard his words, the numbers grew into the hundreds and thousands. The "Lacan effect" is now being reproduced in more than forty countries since his death in 1981, in and of itself proof of an ethical action in his teaching, which is itself an injunction to act.

But what is the cause of the Lacan effect? Is it, as some say, a cult effect that produces "true believers"? No. Lacan shreds traditional notions of "truth" and "belief" in as thorough and brutal a way as has been done by anyone, ever. But, and this is perhaps a paradox, he speaks from the place of the truth of the real which is the place of human suffering. He teaches that freedom and change come from breaking with the concrete pieces of death we cling to. Insofar as the agent of our speech, behavior, choices, and actions is the *jouissance* of the death drive, Lacan's ethics of psychoanalysis is not a new set of prescriptive laws or standards for behavior. There are no new gods, least of all the god of narcissism. Rather, Lacan's is a *new* ethics which breaks with epistemology and ontology as they seek *answers* over truth, certainty over questions, closure over doubt or anxiety. In Lacan's science of the real, whose logic is that of the Freudian cut, truth has always concerned the truth of man's godlike power in his inhumanity to others, even including himself. And this truth speaks the language of rationalization, denial, and idealization in the myths we live by to justify what cannot be justified. Lacan gives us a new subject of lack, a new object of limit, and an injunction to live *with less attachment to our symptoms* because—and this is crucial—our masked suffering makes us harm ourselves as we harm others.

Notes

1. Sigmund Freud, "The Question of Lay Analysis" (1926) *Standard Edition*, trans. James Strachey et al., vol. XX (London: The Hogarth Press, 1959), 179–258; 258 [emphasis in citation my own].

2. Jacques-Alain Miller, *Joyce avec Lacan*, "Préface," directed by Jacques Aubert (Paris: Navarin, 1987), 10.

3. Jacques Lacan, *Le séminaire XX (1972–1973): Encore*, text established by Jacques-Alain Miller (Paris: Editions du Seuil, 1975), 19–27.

4. Vicente Palomera, "The Ethics of Hysteria & of Psychoanalysis," *lacanian ink*, no. 3 (Spring 1991); 41–53.

5. Jacques Lacan, *Le Séminaire XXIII (1975–1976): Le sinthome* (unpublished seminar).

6. Jacques-Alain Miller, "To Interpret the Cause: From Freud to Lacan," *Newsletter of the Freudian Field* 3, 1–2 (1989): 30–50.

7. Jacques Lacan, "Réponse donnée à Marcel Ritter," *Bulletin de l'EFP*, 1976.

8. Colette Soler, "The Real Aims of the Analytic Act," *lacanian ink* 5 (Winter 1992): 53–60; 53.

9. Colette Soler, "Literature as Symptom," in *Lacan and the Subject of Language*, ed. Ellie Ragland-Sullivan and Mark Bracher (New York: Routledge, 1991), 213–219; 215–16.

10. Miller, "To Interpret the Cause."

11. Jacques Lacan, *Le Séminaire VII (1959–1960): L'éthique de la psychanalyse*, text established by Jacques-Alain Miller (Paris: Editions du Seuil, 1986), in English, W.W. Norton, 1992.

12. Jacques-Alain Miller, "Ethics in Psychoanalysis," *lacanian ink*, no. 5 (Winter 1992): 13–27; 13.

13. Bernard Baas and Armand Zaloszyc, *Descartes et les fondements de la psychanalyse* (Paris: Navarin Osiris, 1988), 80.

14. Jacques Lacan, *Le séminaire XV (1967–1968): L'acte psychanalytique* (unpublished seminar).

15. Sigmund Freud, "The Project for a Scientific Psychology" (1895), *SE*, 1: 283–397; 300.

16. Sigmund Freud, "The Ego and the Id" (1923), *SE*, 19: 3–66; 14.

17. Jacques Lacan, "Pour une logique du fantasme," *Scilicet* 2/3 (1970): 223–73. See also Sigmund Freud, "Beyond the Pleasure Principle" (1920), *SE*, 18: 3–64.

18. Max Schur, *Freud, Living and Dying* (New York: International Universities Press, 1972).

19. Charles Méla, "Monade, Tétrade, Pentangle," *Ornicar?* 34 (Fall 1985): 139–42; 139.

20. Catherine Millot, "Désir et jouissance chez l'hystérique," *Hystérie et Obsession* (Paris: Navarin, 1985), 219–27; 221.

21. Jacques Lacan, "The Freudian thing, or the meaning of the return to Freud in psychoanalysis" (1955), *Ecrits: A Selection*, trans. Alan Sheridan (New York: W. W. Norton, 1977), 114–45; 123–24.

22. Jacques Lacan, "Postface," in *Le séminaire XI (1964–1965): Les quatre concepts fondamentaux de la psychanalyse*, text established by Jacques-Alain Miller (Paris: Editions du Seuil, 1973), 251–54.

23. Jacques-Alain Miller, *Extimité* (unpublished course at the Department of Psychoanalysis of Paris VIII, 1985–1986). See "Extimité," *Prose Studies* 11, 3 (December 1988): 121–31.

24. Jacques Lacan, *The Four Fundamental Concepts of Psychoanalysis*, ed. Jacques-Alain Miller, trans. Alan Sheridan (Paris: Editions du Seuil, 1973), 197–99.

25. Jacques Lacan, "La Troisième," *Lettres de l'Ecole Freudienne, Bulletin of the EFP* 16 (1975): 178–203.

26. Jacques Lacan, "The subversion of the subject and the dialectic of desire in the Freudian unconscious" (1960), *Ecrits: A Selection*, trans. Alan Sheridan (New York: W. W. Norton, 1977), 292–325.

27. Jacques Lacan, "Pour une logique du fantasme," *Scilicet* 2/3 (1970): 223–73; 243.

28. Jacques-Alain Miller, "Language: Much Ado about What?" in *Lacan and the Subject of Language*, ed. Ellie Ragland-Sullivan and Mark Bracher (New York: Routledge, 1991), 21–35; 34.

29. Lacan, *Le séminaire XX: Encore*, ibid, 75.

30. Sigmund Freud, "Analysis Terminable and Interminable" (1937), *SE*, 23: 211–53; 254.

31. Barnaby B. Barratt, *Psychoanalysis and the Postmodern Impulse* (Baltimore: The Johns Hopkins University Press, 1993).

32. Sigmund Freud, "Three Essays on Sexuality" (1905), *SE*, 7: 125–245.

33. Jacques Lacan, *Le séminaire X (1962–1963): L'angoisse* (unpublished seminar).

34. Bruce Fink, "Alienation and Separation: Logical Moments of Lacan's Dialectic of Desire," *Newsletter of the Freudian Field* 4, 1–2 (1990): 78–119; 107; cf. Jacques Lacan, "Position de l'inconscient" (1960), in *Ecrits* (Paris: Editions du Seuil, 1966), 829–50; 842.

35. Serge Cottet, *Freud et le désir du psychanalyste* (Paris: Navarin, 1982).

36. Theresa Brennan, "The Construction of Imaginary Time" (unpublished manuscript), 8.

37. Jeanne Granon-Lafont, *La topologie ordinaire de Jacques Lacan* (Paris: Points Hors Ligne, 1985), 4.

38. Jacques Lacan, "Kant with Sade" (1963), *October* 51 (Winter 1989), trans. James Swenson, 55–75; Marquis de Sade, *La philosophie dans le boudoir, Ouv-*

rage posthume de l'auteur de "Justine," 1795, 2 vols; Immanuel Kant, *Critique of Practical Reason*, trans. by N. K. Smith (New York: St. Martin's Press, 1929).

39. Fink, "Alienation and Separation," 81.

40. Jacques-Alain Miller, "La réalité depuis Freud," First European *Rencontre* of the Freudian Field, Lyon, France, May 5, 1991.

6

The Paternal Metaphor

From the First to the Second Paternal Metaphor

The Lacanian idea that language enters an infant in a divisive, splitting fashion has become rather commonplace by now. The "I think" of being is split by the *jouissance* of Freud's *Es*. Yet one still hears the idea stated in reverse: that the infant enters into the symbolic by acquiring language, as if some prior condition made it possible for an infant to passively receive language.

Lacan taught that language is acquired in the uniting of three correlated—but not corresponding—orders: sounds that become attached to words and to a proper name (the symbolic); identifications that constitute the body (the imaginary); and the effects of loss insofar as they leave a trace on the biological organism (the real). The libidinal qualities produced by the gaze, the voice, and so on, are repressed as "objects" that give rise to unary signifiers marked by a primary *jouissance*—an attachment to reminiscences of oneness. These signifiers bind the outer world to a seemingly "inner" void in one single stroke. This minimal Borromean structuring of a signifying chain constitutes what we call "mind" in a series of triadic units. And since one of these units—the real—infers constant loss, which, in turn, produces anxiety, people use language to seek the emotional comfort of closing out the real.

Lacan teaches that language is acquired in a series of conjunctions and disjunctions that run counter to historical or chronological time and that it is loss, desire, and anxiety that introduce a temporal dimension into language. And since loss produces anxiety—an opening onto the impasses of the real—desire constitutes itself in language as the desire to annul loss, language itself becom-

182

ing the filler of the gap between wanting and being. The necessary condition that renders human animals capable of becoming speaking beings—subjects of unconscious desire—is that a proper name be tied to an image of the body and joined to the libidinal experience of loss. The symbolic (word) binds the imaginary (image) to the real (the traumata of a missed encounter). At the point of overlap, one encounters three kinds of *jouissance*: phallic *jouissance*, (the symbolic), the Other *jouissance* (the real), and the *jouis-sens* of meaning or the Other (the imaginary). For Lacan, the signifying chain is not a chain of language sounds and concepts, then, but a necklace made up of associations whose logic is both synchronic and diachronic. These three orderings, three different kinds of "material"—the symbolic, the real and the imaginary—are the *Stoff* of memory and meaning that governs thought by *jouissance*. Thus, any semblance or appearance of a "naturalness" of language is paradoxical insofar as the prohibition to full satisfaction first creates lack. Lack, in turn, mediates between the false fullness of visible images and the traumatic effects of the real that remain as positivized loss, speaking a language of excess and pain.

In 1966 Jean Laplanche disagreed with a major Lacanian precept. The unconscious makes language possible, Laplanche argued, perception being its basis or guarantee. The unconscious is the condition of language, Lacan taught.[1] His revolutionary discovery—that language provides a distance from the real of *jouissance* which enables individuals to represent themselves by words—shows that the unconscious is constituted as a product of language.[2] Laplanche's argument does not differ from any other theory that takes an innate pre-given as the cause of being or knowing. Starting with the cut into *jouissance* that produces an awareness of loss, Lacan portrays language as that which clothes the void, covering it over with images and words that serve, in turn, as the material into which the real returns, cutting into language, being, and flesh. The impasses that constitute the real make holes in grammar and in the apparent fullness of the perceived (or visible) world. And since most infants displace the mother as the primary object (the function of metonymy), this primary sublimation guarantees that a certain stability be maintained by the function of substitution (metaphor). And things, persons, games, words, are all "objects" that substitute for this primordial loss. Thus, metaphor "operates" the mental apparatus long before it is called a linguistic or literary trope, enabling infants to play repetitious games around the edges of a real void of anxiety they try not to fall into. And this is not a metaphor.

Between the imaginary (i.e., perceptual) illusion of a fullness of the visible world and the real of anxiety, language imposes itself as a parasitical "body." As such, language plays a paradoxical role. It provides a guarantee of consistency that is lacking in persons, things, beliefs, or in the body itself. Although substitutions of one thing for another *seem* to create new meanings and to foment change, in reality, the static movement of substitution only produces superficial change. This function, nonetheless, describes the energetics of language which Lacan called the law of the signifier, itself constituted as a dialectical movement between *Verdichtung* (condensation or metaphor) and its referent, *Verschiebung* (displacement or metonymy).[3] The symbolic imposes differential *order* on imaginary identificatory fusions and also tries to name the real losses that are not symbolized as grammatical meaning. And while the symbolic and imaginary collude to give the illusion of totality, the gap caused by the necessity of representation itself prevents such closure. And this structuring of being-for-lack—the gap between the thing and the saying of it, written $(-\phi)$[4]—is the negative phallus which has concrete loss as its principal referent. Lacan finds the *jouissance* of being here, locating it in the overlaps between the real and the symbolic.[5]

We know that Lacan replaced the Freudian Oedipal myth with his concept of the phallus whose terms are those of identification— being "it" or having "it." One is either desiring (the position of lover) or desired (the beloved). In contrast, Freud's patient efforts to describe a phallic phase of reality always bore on his effort to distinguish *Wirklichkeit* (sense-data reality) from *Realität* (psychic reality).[6] Lacan argued in "Desire and the Interpretation of Desire in *Hamlet*" that "it" refers to the organ *per se* only in the imaginary register. Rather, the concept "phallus" names a process of signification wherein *jouissance* inscribes the biological organism for "psychic" sex.[7] A dialectic between desire and *jouissance* does not bear on heterosexual or homosexual difference, then—the choice of the same or different sex for a partner existing in "normal," neurotic, psychotic, and perverse structures—but on identification with the position of the masculine or the feminine in reference to castration and the phallus. In the masculine position one has "it" in the sense that identification with the *jouissance* phallus (Φ) means identification with a master signifier (S_1) or the reality principle.[8] The effect produced by identification with a symbolic order position is a belief *in*, or considerable certainty about, the knowledge one takes as reality.

In the feminine position, one identifies with being "it" (*a*), thus establishing a knowledge on the side of the demand for love. From the masculine position, language is spoken in the imperative and in the declarative modes. Feminine identification bears on the question; that is, it unveils impasses in the knowledge that bases its claims on certainty. Lacan gave the name sexuation to the unconscious choice of masculine or feminine sexual identification. One loses one part of the Other sex (S[Ø]) by identifying with the same (the mother) *qua* feminine, or with the masculine that turns away from the mother in the name of difference, itself a signifier. Because the losses are not symmetrical, an *obstacle*—or divide—is erected between the masculine and feminine, creating a "beyond" *in* language at the points where sex, anatomy and gender are not aligned in a one-to-one way precisely because one does not "get" one's psychic sex from one's biological sex.

In the 1970s when Lacan reconceptualized the structure of the paternal metaphor in relation to the order of the symptom (Σ), which he rewrote in the medieval French spelling, *sinthome*, to capture its particularity in each person's life story, he attributed to the *sinthome* a logic of consistency that he called *jouissance*.[9] In his early work on the symptom, Lacan had described it as having the substitutive structure of metaphor insofar as it is enigmatic, undeciphered meaning. As such, the symptom was said to cover over its own *sinthomes* or particularities, the metonymic causes of desire from which each person draws the libidinal energy that gives meaning to his or her unconscious fantasies in the circuit of the drives. Indeed, this fourth category is an ordering of the knot itself. That is, the "structure" Lacan calls Borromean is created out of an *extrinsic* knotting that *sections* a cord *in places,* a cord woven of the concrete threads of life itself. "When the cord is worn down to the thread, the thread shows through, showing that the weave is not distinguished in fabric [which] . . . could be an image of substance itself. But there is not fabric without weave."[10] The name Lacan gave this knot or cord was the *paternal metaphor,* or the fourth element that holds the three orders together, or not.

Lacan used knots to elaborate his second theory of the symptom in which the real inhabits metaphor as *jouissance.* In this definition, metaphor is not a secondary constellation of substitute meanings. Rather it carries the *jouissance* of the drives as a libidinal meaning system equal in importance to the representational system of words.

Yet knots are, by definition, opaque. Appearing at the interfaces of all the orders, they mark impasses of the real as it returns, cutting into consistencies to create discontinuities that appear as anxiety or conflict. "I am trying to constitute another geometry," Lacan said, "which would deal with the being of a chain. It has never, never been done. This geometry is not imaginary; contrary to the one of triangles, it is real; it is knots of string" ("Conférences," 56). While remaining quite clearly defined as to "kind" within their discrete orderings—language differentials (symbolic), identificatory collusions (imaginary), the effects of loss that create trauma (real)— these serial Borromean chains of association are not innate. They are constituted by the external world of words, images, and the loss that gives rise to the object *a*. When there is no paternal lineage giving the law of "no" to psychic oneness with the mother, the mother is not lost as primary object of *jouissance*. Inadequate difference from the mother means there is not enough distance from a compelling *jouissance* to establish one's own identifications. In this failure to sublimate the object *a*, the mana of metaphor collapses into metonymic proximity with the primary *jouissance* object *qua* real. The symbolic order boundaries one might label as the law of distance disappear.

Freud spoke of human pathologies, which Lacan called the differential categories of desire created by the way a paternal metaphor is (or is not) knotted in a given life to produce the neuroses (hysteria, obsession, phobia), psychoses, or perversion which structure the *sinthome* as a writing of the real that traces the particular path of the dialectic between desire and *jouissance* in a given life. More particularly, in Lacan's first formula for the paternal metaphor, written in the 1950s, one thing substitutes for another: $\frac{FN}{MD} \cdot \frac{MD}{x}$. The Name-of-the-Father substitutes for the mother's desire which is unknown, the Father's Name coming to mean dead speech (the Other), and the phallus coming to mean the value assigned an infant within the economy of the mother's desire $\frac{(Other)}{(phallus)}$. Lacan's goal here was to correct Freud's use of the Oedipus *myth* by explaining how human sexual difference is constituted. Lacan referred, instead, to persons—not myth—and to the fact that the relation of Mother ◊ Father (a kinship bond) does not translate the enigma of the sexual formula, Man ◊ Woman. Borrowing the word phallus which Freud used ambiguously in his early writings, Lacan discovered, instead, the effect of lack. Lacan first used this word to mean the unknown value that plays enigmatically in language, being, and relationships. And most children quickly encounter the *che vuoi*—What do I want? Who am I?—that poses a question about the value of one's worth at the heart of all quests. Since psychotics lack such *lack*, they remain bound up in a primary attachment to a real *jouissance* they can not lose. Neurotics, on the other hand, appear to move, substituting one thing for another. Lacan saw neurotic movements as static repetitions, however, as running in place, changing partners, but not fantasies. Weighed down by running to answer to the archaic desire of the Other, identifying with the dead *jouissance* of an archaic past, a neurotic remains complicitous with the value assigned him or her in the Other scene.

In psychosis, one might describe the unconscious as annulled insofar as nothing is lacking. The Other is present, not absent, that is. Psychotic language is drenched in *jouissance* minus desire, minus the lack that causes an awareness of others as desiring. If the relation of being to time is the timing of unconscious desire in neurosis, and if the lack of desire is the triumph of *jouissance* in psychosis, it makes sense that this subject's mooring in the symbolic order would disappear in psychotic episodes. When nothing is lacking in the *jouissance* of being, no unconscious *fantasy*—based on the divided subject—subtends the use of language. Rather a fundamental *lalangue* of delusion materializes language by *jouissance*, interweaving itself throughout psychotic speech. Thus, the psychotic "acts out" what the neurotic hides so well in multiple lies of repression and denial. Sustaining the Other's existence by his fusion with the Other's *jouissance*, the psychotic blurs distinctions between self and other, manifesting boundary limits only by miming others, or in passing directly to acts of violence. His deficiency lies in a difficulty in representing a self for others.

In Lacan's first formula for the paternal metaphor, the field of representations he named the Other is supported by the phallus, itself symbolizing a question mark about the mother's desire in reference to the Father's Name. Although the mother is certainly a signifier (in the symbolic) and a being with desire (in the imaginary), Lacan points out that her place in the symbolic and imaginary cannot be separated from the real of primordial effects that first constituted her child's *jouissance* at the level of *la lalangue* where the signifier of the mother's body is inseparable from the unrepresentable, unspeakable real of the drives. Contrary to Freud, Lacan argued that the mother must be lost as an object signifying satisfaction. When she intrudes, signifying herself as all to the child, she blocks the child's capacity to constitute desire as a lack-in-being by which he or she becomes able to (re)-constitute a "self" in relation to others, negotiating this "self" in language and in the drives as a desired or desirable "object". Put another way, subject position is merely a functioning of desire acquired by the tying together of a corporal *Gestalt* (the imaginary) with a proper name (the symbolic) for which "I" can then be substituted. A child's self image and proper name are infused with energy from the real in the form of impasses he or she, in turn, seeks to avoid by making unities in language and in identifications.

The Oedipal scenario Lacan paints goes something like this. An infant needs food in order to live, so it cries out for food. The response given to this "call" by an other begins to constitute the subject as desiring a certain consistency that gives a sense of well being or satisfaction. If the "call" is answered only negatively, autism may be the result. Later, we make others responsible for answering our precise demands, even though our expectations have already been primed by the fixing of *jouissance* in libidinal pleasures or displeasures which are repeated for ever after in a dialectic of anticipation and retroaction.

Lacan's second formula for the paternal metaphor shows the Freudian Oedipal complex to be a myth.[13] In *Television* Lacan defined myth as "the attempt to give an epic form to what is operative through the structure."[14] We know that epic generally means on a grand scale. And we know that Lacan defines structure in *Encore* as a direct equivalent of topology.[15] Thus, myth is the mock heroic epic that shows each person as a *sinthome* of her or his experience of sexual being, first constituted in unary traits of primordial identifications. These traits bond *jouissance* to language and to the palpable void created by the trauma that produce the real as an order of unassimilated knowledge. That this topological interlinking of words, images, and impasses of the unbearable to know composes the Borromean chains in overlapping, non-linear associations, accounts for the lapses and blind spots we call denial and repression. It accounts, as well, for the sporadic ups and downs of memory and forgetting. Thus, language is not sufficiently consistent to give a unity to being, either as a fictive name or as a set of signifiers.

Jacques-Alain Miller has clarified Lacan's second theory of the paternal metaphor. In his "Geneva Lecture" (1975), Lacan suggested that one might erect a logic of inconsistencies wherein the phallus is a predicate, not a nominative.[16] In this context each person's mock heroic epic shows that person dealing with his or her *sinthomes* in terms of being or having the phallus, wherein phallus means the value assigned to the sexual difference as a signifier in its own right. But how does Lacan's paternal metaphor reveal the Freudian Oedipal complex to be a *myth*? In his Course at Paris VIII in 1988–1989, Miller argued that one way the Oedipal can be understood after Freud is by "interpreting the cause."[17] "When Freud says that the father is already the phenomenon of sublimation, he is saying nothing other than what I am repeating there," Miller says. "And that is why we may accept that what we call the function of the father is language itself, as dead" (Miller, "To Interpret the Cause," 44). That is, language clothes our *jouissance* in semblances that make our identifications seem pregiven or "natural" fixities despite the fact that this libidinal glue blocks us from reshaping our thoughts or fantasies so we can (re)-constitute our desire and, thus, change.

In the 1950s Lacan had already begun to undercut his first theory of the paternal metaphor by arguing that the leftover effects of loss that he called surplus or excess *jouissance*—the *petit a*—introduced inconsistencies into language, being, and body. Lacan said such positivized effects of *jouissance* are *caused* by the functions of separation and alienation that produce the object *a* whose common factor is that it is bound to the orifices of the body. Moreover, the *a* throws everything off balance, elliptical, askew ("Seminar of January 21, 1975," 164). Indeed, Lacan developed his science of the real in trying to account for *jouissance* as meaning concentrated in traits or marks whose effects produces the affects Lacan calls the ups and downs of life.[18]

In Lacan's first formula for the paternal metaphor, we remember, the phallus stands for what is unknown about the mother's desire, i.e., it stands for the unconscious. Clarifying Lacan's structural reading of the Freudian Oedipal myth, Miller argued that the parental couple can be made into a matheme; i.e., a fixed relation one can write as a formula. But the only fixed relation a child can find in the parental couple, as the child tries to figure out who he or she is as a gendered, sexed, speaking being, is a link missing in language and representation. Lacan called this "missing link" the phallus. In moving from Lacan's first to his second theory of the paternal metaphor, Miller says the Lacanian phallus can be translated from an "unknown *jouissance* to the phallusization of *jouissance*, that is to [the] significantization of *jouissance*" ("To Interpret the Cause," 46). Insofar as *jouissance* of being makes up for being castrated, such a *jouissance* is correlated with ego conviction. Other names Lacan gave this *jouissance* are the passion of ignorance or the master discourse. We also seek a *jouissance* of meaning by a ciphering of the unconscious that seeks to ascertain what the voice carries of the real. Miller says a child tries to derive *its* knowledge of what a *relation* of Man $\lozenge$ Woman would be from the formula Mother $\lozenge$ Father (41). Both Mother $\lozenge$ Father and Man $\lozenge$ Woman work as relations or functions that enable analysts to structure something in knowledge that asks for an interpretation of the cause (42).

But between Freud's Oedipus and Lacan's first paternal metaphor $\left(\dfrac{NF}{DM}\right)$, a large gap appears. While Freud equated the parental couple (M $\lozenge$ F) to the sexual relation (M $\lozenge$ W), Lacan viewed the parental couple as an obstacle to sexual relations. He developed this argument in *The Ethics of Psychoanalysis* (1959–1960) by showing the dialectical tension between a primary lost object and the repetitions of *jouissance* aimed at Oneness with an "object" that is both forbidden, and not itself One to start with. The opposition between a desire for Oneness and the surplus *jouissance* left over by the loss of *jouissance* creates a third thing: the substitution of speech or language to replace the primordial mother with the father as Other. Here the Other means the speech or culture that signifies an obstacle to silent fusion with the mother as primary guarantee. Insofar as the mother is a signifier for the primary object whose loss causes desire, she also signifies the *loss* of the desired objects, associated with her body, that subtend language. Such loss lies at the heart of a cultural *malaise* as well and nothing can ultimately cure it. Certainly Freud's fantasized harmonious sexual *relation* between man and woman has never been a cultural panacea.

Unlike Freud's formula, Lacan's is not strictly sexual. (Miller, "To Interpret the Cause," 40). Rather, Lacan sees language as the cultural medium that allows order to be instituted around the desire for libidinal objects. By taking the differential phallic third as a point of reference—a name and an identity myth correlated imaginarily with gender—the bar between father and mother $\left(\dfrac{F}{M}\right)$ comes to equal substitution, while the primary mother equals the object *qua* lost: $\dfrac{F}{\cancel{M}}$. This simple formula denotes a temporal metaphorical structure. Although the primordial repressed part that causes desire is lost, its effects do not disappear. They are displaced into speech as the object *a* that materializes thought around *jouissance*. Thus, although a "subject" of desire is produced by and in language, it is not defined only by it. For the excess in *jouissance*—the non-utilitarian real part—has to do with the effort to have a relation with the Other, even though a hole in the Other places radical loss beyond the bar of the sexual divide. In Miller's clarification of Lacan's first formula for the paternal metaphor, he emphasizes that one starts with $\frac{F}{M}$: Father-bar-Mother. But in this "generalized formula," which unifies Freud's Oedipal theory and his castration complex, there is no fixed sexual symbol—such as the penis or the Father's Name—that *causes* the mother's desire ("To Interpret the Cause," 45–46).

In this simple formula, the bar signifies that the child *does not know* how to decipher what it means to be male or female based only on observing the relationship between its parents. Father and mother do not translate into a sexual formula for the child where girl clearly equals woman and boy clearly equals man ("To Interpret the Cause," 35–44). So father comes to mean language *qua* difference only in the sense of something that imposes an obstacle for the child, or a distance from the mother *qua* object of hoped for libidinal fulfillment. Structurally speaking, the paternal metaphor hypothesizes that a child substitutes language for *being* something other than a libidinal extension of the mother, in the form of an object *a* identified with her gaze, voice, breast, and so on. The child who is stuck to these partial objects elides the cut of separation, and remains the mother's real phallus. Such a child demonstrates the logic of autism or a preliminary psychosis. For distance is indeed a correlate of the difference that makes metaphorical substitution possible as a mental function. This particular function of desire derives from the loss of *jouissance* that makes lack a structure ($) that pushes one to build a fiction of *being* a self or identity.

In clarifying Lacan's second paternal metaphor, Miller writes this formula: $\frac{F}{M} - \frac{Phallus}{x} - \frac{O}{J}$. The *jouissance* left over from the loss of primary objects is itself enigmatic, an enigma that many people would rather worship than examine. Miller describes the *jouissance* phallus as an excess of affect in the body which, nonetheless, serves as a reality principle. That is, the *jouissance* phallus (JΦ) denotes the cultural identifications by which individuals keep from encountering the void in the Other [S($\emptyset$)] which is linked to the $\emptyset$ by an arrow in the sexuation graphs (Lacan, "Love Letter," 149). And *jouissance* enters the field of representations as a "quota of affect."

Miller clarifies Lacan's 1958 Oedipal formula for the paternal metaphor by arguing that the *jouissance* phallus represents the *quest* for a Oneness with a primary object and in this sense symbolizes the principle of difference that causes desire. Pushing toward the infinite—the limits of the knowable—*jouissance* gives meaning to biological sex by inscribing the organism with a limit in "psychic" (*tychic, tuchē*) sex. Lacan stresses that Freud sought to distinguish between psychic *Realität* and biological sense data (*Wirklichkeit*) every time he tried to delineate a phallic phase ("Le phallus, pierre de touche," 35).

Lacan used the word *sexuation* to describe the imposition of a *jouissance* metalanguage upon the body (Miller, "To Interpret the Cause," 46–48). Put another way, the loss of the mother as *the* primary object gives rise to the search for a guarantee at the level of identifications. Miller unites Lacan's first and second paternal metaphors by these mathemes:

$$\frac{FN}{DM} \rightarrow \frac{\Phi \text{ (inconsistent Other)}}{x \text{ (enigma)}} \rightarrow \frac{\varnothing \text{ (loss)}}{-\phi \text{ (lack)}} \rightarrow \frac{\varnothing}{(a)}.$$

We fill up the gaps in the Other with condensed bits of *jouissance* (*a*) that Miller calls libidinal consistencies. These stoppers guarantee a cohesion to our lives via the paradoxical pleasures of familiarity, thereby constituting the strange paradox of the death drive in which consistency and familiarity are more important to people than change, truth or freedom from suffering.

In the second paternal metaphor, Woman as *mother* becomes a signifier for the suppression of a *jouissance* of the One, which can be equated with the impossibility of infinity. Yet many of the figures erected in the name of Woman—whether idealized or degraded—appear whenever the real of loss is at stake. One thinks of frustrated male taxi drivers saying "Mother of God," "Holy Virgin," "cunt," and so on. Freud's inability to grasp why the pleasure principle ran up against the death drive in the form of repetition (in 1921) fascinated Lacan, whose discovery that Eros is built out of Thanatos, not in opposition to it, enabled him to unveil the structure of loss itself as a positive limit in being or knowing. This is only because loss of the primordial mother gives rise to the partial drives whose aim is to replace lost objects. No mother's desire will ever be reducible to behavior or a "natural" knowledge, then, because both male and female children will always be tied to some part of the maternal objects that first begot *jouissance* as a positive "quality" they seek to avoid, or to replace via substitutions.

Thenceforth, Woman is associated with the primary object at the level where the mother is the first good. Because of the confusion between Woman and mother, woman comes to signify a totality or an essence in masculine fantasy where she is partialized, fetishized, and sought on the slope of the real, *outside* representable meaning. Yet grammatical language can only function realistically—i.e., driven by fantasy—as long as the primary object is lost, is the metonymical lost *cause* of language. Displacements, which Lacan denoted by the object *a*, are thus libidinized images, things, persons, bodies, or events, each "object" functioning to stop up the hole in the Other. Thus, thinking moves along the order of the body, although philosophy supposes an order of the mind. Indeed, the heterogeneous *a* takes many forms, having no form common to it, although it is generally thought of orally (taking in) or shittily (expelling), its common factor being, rather, that it is bound to the orifices of the body, and so throws everything off balance (Lacan, "Seminar January 21, 1975," 164). At the level of the symptom, the *a* is the *subject* of metaphor that hides itself as the metonymic cause of desire, materializing being, body, and language by *jouissance*.

From Metaphor to Topology

In Lacan's theory of how one acquires language, not only is language not innate, neither are time or space. There are, for example, no innate Chomskian tendencies or capacities for language. The only innate language features arise from the biological organism with its vocal cords and capacities to produce sounds. Nor could one argue for the Chomskian distinction between competence and performance, a distinction which enabled the famous linguist to explain away whatever did not fit within his theory of innate linguistic structures. By evoking a Platonic notion of an ideal speaker-listener in a homogeneous speech-community, Chomsky and other cognitionists in his wake have relied on hypothesized perfect language conditions to account for the imperfect body of language.[19] Yet, in Chomsky's lineage, American linguists, cognitive psychologists, biologically inclined psychiatrists, and even object-relations analysts, still think that the human "capacity" for language is innate and its prime mover, biology. This evolutionary theory would sup-

pose that the "cause" of language resides in links between genes
and neural synapses in the brain as they have evolved over millen-
nia. Having pinpointed *material* causes in the organic history of the
human animal, partisan theorists assume that most people learn to
use speech and language more or less correctly. "Misuse" or de-
formation of recognizable syntax or semantics is labeled as a learning disorder, attributed to a biologically caused dysfunction of the
body *qua* organism (the brain, the hormones, and so on).

"Syntax," in a typical dictionary definition, is "the pattern or
structure of the word order in a phrase, clause, or sentence." In
Lacan's theory of language, syntax might better be thought of as
pre-conscious, based on the unconscious and *jouissance*.[20] That is,
consciousness (language or thought) is ordered by something other
than itself, by signifiers *already there* in suspension or in sufferance,
and by primordially repressed objects that cause desire and enable
drive because they are lost except as vague reminiscences that call
one toward the resonance of unary traits. Linked to a void of leftover
jouissance that occupies an empty place, these unary traits attach
themselves both to the world and to the void as one-stroke signifiers
that bind perception to consciousness, the latent to the manifest.
One may make sense of such an idea in light of Jacques-Alain Miller's comments on Lacan's *Television* where he describes laws of
the unconscious and of *jouissance*.[21] At the time of the interview,
which aired on French television for two hours, Lacan answered
Miller as to why he would use a Freudian word like "the unconscious." Although the word is negative, Lacan said, Freud did not
find a better one and there is no need to go back on it now (Lacan,
Television, 5).

Miller later suggested a way one could work with the word "unconscious" precisely *because* it is negative, reminding us that Lacan
defined the unconscious in *Television* as

> a very precise thing in intent, not just the negative of conscious-
> ness. . . . He reminds us there is no unconscious without language
> and speech. So, the path of Lacan . . . goes from . . . the supposedly
> known which is language, to the unknown which is the uncon-
> scious. You know the old theory of the unconscious by Lacan, the
> classical one, which . . . defines language . . . on the basis of the
> distinction of signifier and signified. This is Lacan's simplification
> of Saussure. . . . What Lacan adds to this separation is a relation
> of causality between the signified and the signifier (Miller, "A Read-
> ing," 18–19).

In *Seminar* XV, *L'acte psychanalytique* (1967–1968) Lacan named three poles that constitute knowledge in a Borromean unit, but are not a revision of the linguistic sign. The poles are: the symbolic order signifier that joins the world of language to that of imaginary images and objects; the unary trait which links the body to others via the functions of projection (expelling) and incorporation (taking in) that operate the process of identification; and the object *a* which Lacan described as a piece of the real falling onto the vector which runs from the symbolic to the imaginary.[22] Put another way, some piece of the real—either an absent cause of desire or a veiled object *a* that stops up the hole in the Other—always lies between one's actions and one's consciousness of one's acts. Moreover, at the level of referent, this nothing is *some-thing*: the void place Lacan called a positivized negative whose effect is that of the *more* than language in language that weighs it down.[23]

Alexandre Leupin describes this surplus in language or in the body as the *quality* of meaning Lacan called the *jouissance* (too much, too little, enough, and so on) that one encounters between secondary process (grammatical language) and primary process (desire).[24] But Lacan did not find a reason to make the *jouissance* of meaning the cause of the other two *jouissances*. Rather, the three *jouissances* stand at different intersections of the three orders, demonstrating three ways *jouissance* aims to embody the object *a* at the heart of every signifying unit. Yet insofar as the aim of the drive is not the Freudian constancy of entropy as a tensionless state, but the consistency of *jouissance*, no aim can find its final mark. No fantasy can tally with its ideal. No object can be "good enough." At best, pleasure must be repeatedly sought through the repetitious pathways of displeasure. Our hopes for totality, for ongoing pleasure, for final harmonies, are inane dreams that make us suffer and keep us from making any change at all. Yet we whitewash our hopes, give dignity to our life lies, and keep ourselves from realizing the price we pay for clinging to the familiarity of *jouissance* that blocks any exit from pain and discontent. Since fantasy, the drive, and desire can only seek their goals via the material of language—grammar supported by a primordial *lalangue* that parasitizes language—people are "used" dishonestly by the language which they assume informs or communicates, rationally and objectively. Although individuals believe they seek information or knowledge, they unconsciously seek to be satisfied by a return of the only *jouissance* they know: their own. Thus, people stick together around *jouissances* of belief, body, or interpretive communities of meaning.

If language is not a biological pre-given, then it becomes crucial to ask how it constitutes fixed illusions that harden into solid convictions and set beliefs. As he gradually moved away from Saussurean laws of linguistics (which he had redefined from the start anyway), Lacan not only reformulated the Saussurean discovery, he also gave further understanding to Jakobson's work on metaphor and metonymy. He also added unconscious *jouissance* and desire to Jakobson's efforts to categorize the pathways of communication in categories of adressor/adressee, etc. Language is not only *not* innate in a newborn, neither does its acquisition correspond to the kind of pre-ordained natural cooperation theory Kenneth Burke hypothesized in "A Rhetoric of Motives."[25] Lacan debunked the idea that the biological organism develops its own knowledge, as if there were a "natural" human propensity for intelligence. By going from the structure of psychosis to the "psychosis" of normativity, Lacan formalized a science of the real, subtended by a theory of the logical structures spawned by the paternal metaphor. In tackling problems of the truth functionality of contradictions and inconsistencies, Lacan widened the scope of what we consider rational by explaining the logic of what is generally written off as irrational.

Moreover, he explained the structure of psychic reality that determines a person's relationship to knowledge in terms of unconscious identification as masculine or feminine. Such self images, as we know, are established in the experience of relating to the phallic third term of difference *qua* difference between the masculine and feminine. While psychosis is the failure of an inscription for lack—of being all one sex—neurosis denying the difference and perversion repudiating it, each structure is laid down in a logic that is not arbitrary, but whose relation to *jouissance* determines how being, body, and meaning will interact. And since masculine or feminine identification do not correspond to gender, nor do they determine the gender of sexual object preference.

Lacan's theory evolves as an extension of Euclidean geometry into a topological structuralism of the subject wherein his break with classical psychoanalysis, as well as with classical philosophical theories of epistemology and ontology, comes to the fore.[26] And although the implications of his break are radical at the level of epistemology, Lacan's immediate concerns were always analytic treatment. Not only do his new views of subject and object answer questions about how the world becomes mind, and how mind, in turn, becomes matter, his answers also tell us how unconscious fantasies structure what we call mind or reason out of the desire that is each person's cause and the *jouissance* that maintains it or blocks it.

In one sense, the limit of language can be said to appear at the place where a seemingly unified subject falls out of grammar, showing the face of thwarted desire that subtends language. At this limit point, *jouissance* appears as palpable libido, emptying a weight of affect into secondary-process meaning. In mathematics, the limit symbolized by $+00$ can be taken as a correlate of the real of *jouissance*. That is, in a number series, if every number has a limit (i.e., is real), "it is in this measure that it is infinite" (Manseur, "($-\phi$) et jouissance," 89).[27] In Lacan's analytic terms, this means that castration ($-\phi$ or -00) has a functional limit in the life of a subject precisely *because* he or she can hypothesize an infinite sexual *jouissance*, lack implying infinite *jouissance*. But the impasses of the real mark a limit in desire at the point where knowledge of loss causes unconscious identification to be constructed around the issue of the whole or not whole.

When sexual difference is first perceived it "says nothing to the child," Freud wrote in 1925.[28] With the discovery of the Other's (mother *qua* Woman) absolute alterity, Lacan points out that the phallus takes on its meaning in relation to castration. Lacan's stress is not on anatomy, however, but on how one chooses to desire in interpreting the phallus as a universal value: "Castration can be written as the passage from Φ to $-\phi$."[29] That is, if one forecloses difference, one chooses psychosis. The other choices all accommodate the difference itself in differing ways of relating to desire.

In his sexuation graphs, Lacan shows that identification with the whole, with a universal proposition, is a lie based on an error concerning why law is necessary. He places this lie within the symbolic (*Encore*, 73). By thinking of oneself as an exception to the rule of lack, the masculine position in knowledge reveals its certainty in a master discourse based on the denial of the unconscious. The masculine illusion of wholeness compensates for identification away from the primal mother *qua* loss itself, away from the intimations of death that anxiety (whose object *is* the void) brings us. Lacan's point, a crucial one, is that masculinity is a stance taken toward knowledge, not a matter of gender or biological sex. Males who identify with group laws represent the *norme* of a society. Lacan described females who identify with masculine belief in the whole as *nor-mâle*.

Lacan uncovered this paradox: In life, as well as in mathematics, limits arise from the possibility of conceptualizing an "experience" or knowledge without limits. Frege denoted this fact by the number 1 (one), the Lacanian signifier of non-existence. Lacan equates Frege's number 1 with his One (*l'Un*)—a set of the whole—which opposes itself to lack ($-\phi$). But Lacan's lack, or castration, is not, then, equatable to Frege's zero (0). Rather, the limit of castration placed on infinity is the One which Lacan symbolized by this symbol for limit: the Φ of *jouissance* which fills in lack. The minus phi of castration ($-\phi$) explains what Frege could not answer: Why zero grounds the actual number one and then splits into a -00 rather than producing infinity as a $+00$. The One of totality (or absolute *jouissance* as exemplified by the mythic uncastrated father of the Freudian primal horde) is a lie because the all (*le tout*) marks an *impossibility* in mathematics, in language, and in being, not an infinity. Yet this avoidance of the real—by a belief in Oneness—places a certain dissatisfaction within the subject of grammatical language who wages a dialectical war between desire and *jouissance*. Seeking the infinite or ideal, and stymied by the real of its impossibility, "masters" will always be confused as to why things do not work as they expect them to.

Arguing that the human "subject" is logical, not biological, Lacan's long emphasis on the mathematical logic of "relationship" culminated in a *rhetoric of the unconscious*. Moving away from models of intuitive geometries, Lacan turned to topology insofar as it is dependent on Leibniz's logic of position (*analysis situs*). Working with the relationships of functions one to another, as in metaphor and metonymy, Lacan went beyond the imaginary aspects of his early schemas, grounding his later ones in the logic of the symbolic order (Leupin, *Lacan*, 12–13). From this he evolved a science of the real. In 1972 he began to elaborate his new topology of the three orders, situating the "subject" in varying positions, depending on whether "it" is momentarily centered or balanced in the imaginary, symbolic, or real. Thereby he elaborated a means for studying the relative positions of geometrical "beings" one to another in terms of quality, not quantity (empiricism). Leupin writes: "As such, this topology makes meaning (=quantity) dependent on structure (=quality). . . . Needless to say, this insistence on quality permits at the same time its formalization and its total transmissibility" (Leupin, *Lacan*, 13).

In his *Seminar R.S.I.*, Lacan demonstrated how the *real* makes the field of language inconsistent and incomplete, writing the axiom this way: $(\emptyset)$.[30] In his new topology, Lacan redefined his three orders as exigencies or *tori*.[31] A torus [⊚] looks like a doughnut or a car tire. Lacan found this figure important in his efforts to redirect thinking about the Freudian unconscious toward the idea of a real hole in being and body that places space both inside and outside a person, collapsing inside and outside into an extimate object *a* that *is* the subject. That is, the void in language, being, and body forms a torus where inside and outside define two voids—an internal and external one—that point to something real in form itself. That some*thing* that we see as a sphere, a spiral, and so on, is caused by an *ab-sens* at the very heart of meaning. Indeed, the similarities between the laws of form and the forms of the human body give one pause. That this hole functions as a palpable density is a radical concept, a hole acting as a compacity between all seeming unities and preventing the actual totalization of anything. Not only does the void evacuate non-utilitarian *jouissance* into language, thereby destroying imaginary illusions that like equals like, it also intersects with the unconscious as it appears at the edges of cuts that first gave rise to desire as a corporeal knowledge: an ability to distinguish between satisfaction and dissatisfaction when the infant momentarily *loses* the breast it imagines belongs to it, not to the mother, or loses a familiar voice singing it to sleep, and so on.

In this last period, Lacan taught that wherever thought fades or becomes feeble, wherever consciousness thinks itself at its own limits, one encounters unconscious desire hiding in the void, behind representations. And one can depict these moments in formulae that pin down certain fixed functions Lacan called axioms: repeating phenomena whose constancy is ahistorical and, in this sense, structural. "There is no such thing as a science of man," Lacan said, because science's man does not exist, only its subject does. . . . It is logic which here serves as the subject's navel, logic insofar as it is in no way linked to the contingencies of a grammar. The formalization of grammar must literally circumvent this logic if it is to be successfully carried out, but the circumventing movement is inscribed in this very operation."[32] So, for example, the matheme signifying castration $(-\phi)$ denotes one of the limits on *jouissance*. Such a limit correlates with desire, insofar as it arises from a lack in being. Desire does not emanate from innate elements with which being then coheres in some harmonious correspondence with an *a priori* reality of sexual *jouissance*.

Lacan's science of the real finds its "subject" of *jouissance* in the lines, points, intersections, and overlaps that *appear* in language as mysteries, confusions, mistakes, miscommunications, lapses, enigmas, affects. He argues that these ever-present inconsistencies tell the story of the return of the real. But most people do not consider castration, repression, or trauma as the agents that structure decision or choice because they think of knowledge as a *content* that fills a container they call mind. In that Lacan's Borromean chain operates as "mind" in associational linkages and co-joinings of relations and oppositions, one can talk about the "dimension" of a human subject whose language is the body's *jouissance*. But the subject is also marked by a *jouissance* of meaning, i.e., a continual use of language (Φ) to interpret the unconscious ($\$$) in order to fill up the hole (*a*) at the heart of the Other (S[Ø]).

Thus, representations (language and images) bind themselves to a void which is continually constituted and reconstituted out of loss of *jouissance*. That is, the first cuts that create losses give rise to unary traits—i.e., "divine details"—of words, images, and libidinal effects linked to a palpable void. Thus, the void itself is positively charged by *jouissance*, which continually empties itself into language. And each conjunction of the real and symbolic, the symbolic and the imaginary, and the imaginary and the real, shows the absence of the master signifier Lacan named the phallus (Leupin, *Lacan*, 15). That is, signifiers install order by substituting things for a master signifier that has disappeared from signifying itself as such. Yet one can retrieve the *effect* of things that have been substituted for by other things through traces of *jouissance* that are left in imaginary being, the body, or the meanings one makes of language—effects that are retrievable in dreams, fantasy, and symptoms. But they are not observable at the level of remembered experience or coherent narrative, only in the more than language in language that Lacan called a *jouissance* knowledge.

The Logic of Autism, Prior to Any Metaphor Whatsoever

Autism is a *rare* condition that usually appears at approximately eight months of age. One may ask what bearing this condition could have on Lacan's theory of language acquisition? The answer is that we can better understand the paternal metaphor by which Lacan explains what Freud was trying to get at with the Oedipal myth in light of his work on the structure of autism. *The Random House Dictionary* defines autism as "self absorption, esp. extreme withdrawal into fantasy." In 1990, Colette Soler proposed that autism is one pole of psychosis. Rather than defining it as biologically caused, she argues that it is an extreme point of negativity in which mirror identification with the mother (or primary caretaker) has been foreclosed. Unlike most autistic children, psychotics frequently participate in the symbolic order. But since the castration that constitutes lack as a differential key signifier for most people is *foreclosed*, we remember that the psychotic identifies rigidly with language and rituals. While doubt and the search for proof give a way of life to most people who *deny* any lack in being, or repress that fact, the psychotic functions as a subject of certainty, rather than a subject of doubt. But such rigidity prevents any easy movement within the order of the imaginary, described by Alexandre Leupin as "the system of projections and identifications [that] displaces the Freudian *ego*." While the psychotic lacks the distance from the real that would enable him to easily represent his body and being within the change and flux of the symbolic, the autistic child is not even divided by the mirror *Gestalt* or projective plane (Leupin, *Lacan*, 22). Thus, the autistic identifies wholly with the real of the drives, rather than the social structure of transference where self symbols are exchanged within a syntactical flow of words substituted for lack.

A psychotic who is troubled during the mirror stage (or an autistic who never reaches a mirror moment) manifests a difficulty in identifying with a signifier for the pronoun "I," for gender, or with a unified image of the body. Between the poles of autism (a prepsychosis) and a psychosis from which a person functions in the social world, one sees the sheer death weight of trying to maintain a consistent *jouissance*. Here the living being is the object of the drive, not its subject, the prevailing real producing all kinds of libidinal confusions and illusions in language and fantasy. To fight this discomfort, most people depend on the symbolic and imaginary to maintain a law of measure, equanimity, and balance through attachment to familiar beliefs. If, however, there is inadequate loss of the mother as primary object, or if the father puts forth no desire for the child to fulfill, the excluded real returns into the symbolic as paranoïa and onto the imaginary body as schizophrenia, with a vengeance that results in violent acts and endless suffering.

The autistic lives in the *real* of the void, a place where *jouissance* consistency makes of being the demand for nothing. Thus, autism is the condition of not using grammatical language at all or using it woodenly or incorrectly—i.e., the pure structure of metonymy in which words are used like things, unlike the structure of metaphor wherein words substitute for images and things.

In *Encore* Lacan defined language used in an effort to communicate with others as "discourse." Although all language is not used for that purpose, the bond or "social link" forged by discourse is itself the basis for a principle of law. In this sense law means exchange and is built upon a scaffolding of transference. Although autism forecloses the conventional imaginary of transference relations, there is a structural similarity between the pre-psychosis one might call autism and the episodic breaks undergone by psychotics. In both autism and psychosis, the imaginary is lived *as if* it were real. Since maintaining a consistent *jouissance* is the goal of psychosis, *jouissance* is not represented dialectically for the purpose of deciphering unconscious meaning. Such ciphering gives most people a way to distance themselves from the drives which demand immediate gratification. Both language and identifications are "dehumanized" in psychosis, then. Although a psychotic may well function in language *as if* he or she were in the social network, the tension manifest in the unmitigated pain of autism comes from a complete identification with the only bond the autistic knows: "Being as a purely negative libidinal servitude to the primary Other. Indeed, the primordial *jouissance* present in psychosis is locatable in the signifier for infinity and inexistence, in a place beyond the symbolic where there is no law of limit (Manseur, "$(-\phi)$ et jouissance," 89).

Anxiety and violence dwell at the surface of autism precisely because transference has not been built up as an imaginary bond that will allow substitutions of one thing for another. In autism, there has been no cut, no mirror stage, no separation from the primary real of bodily *jouissance*. No hole has been made in the Other that will allow the constitution of the void as a space in being. If autism is the most primitive pole of psychosis, as Colette Soler has suggested, one might speak of schizophrenia as a pre-mirror failure to identify with one's body as a whole image. In psychosis the drives divide the infant, rather than giving it a semblance of unity in representations that co-join the real and imaginary in two overlapping voids. When the real becomes unhooked from the symbolic and produces haunting voices and gazes wherein language and images are not repressed, they can not re-present a subject of desire that is negotiated between dialectical signifiers. Nonetheless, in treating psychosis, the signifier must remain the guide in the forest of psychotic language.[33] In autism, however, since no mirror-stage moment of identification ever joined an image of the infant to loss of that image, the body itself suffers the full force of being its own cause. The lack of distance between the real of the biological organism and the field of imaginary representations produces a horrific version of Condillac's "man machine." In psychosis proper the mirror effect constituted a tenuous imaginary which must, nonetheless, be imitated from the outside because no signifier for difference ever made a phallic split between the imaginary *qua* representation of name and sexual identity.

Although the primacy of primary *jouissance* disappears in most children, it does not disappear in autistic infants. When early experience of the gaze or the voice is too weighty, too negative, too poisonous, too absent for an infant to bear, that infant remains entrapped in the pure real of a negative *jouissance* which constitutes his or her identification in the Other. Most children who depend on language—that is, on identification with the symbolic father—are *free to invent the Other* out of repressed memories, giving a guarantee to being and knowing which anchors them (albeit retroactively) to the names of ideals: imaginary daddies in the guise of political leaders, heroes or heroines, authors, characters, artists, religious figures, ideological belief systems, and so on.

But how does this celebrated *manque-à-être* (lack in being) come to *ex-sist* for most people, when neither being nor lack are material pre-givens? Nor are they commensurate with the biological organism or "perception." As early as *Seminar* I (1953–1954), Lacan tells us that whatever is reduced to the eye, to the visible, is imaginary:

> In order to reduce us for a moment to being only an eye, we had to put ourselves in the shoes of the scientist who can decree that he is just an eye, and can put a notice on the door—*Do not disturb the experimenter*. In life, things are entirely different, because we aren't an eye. So, this eye, what does it mean? It means that, in the relation of the imaginary and the real, and in the constitution of the world such as results from it, everything depends on the position of the subject. And the position of the subject—you should know, I've been repeating it for long enough—is essentially characterized by its place in the symbolic world, in other words in the world of speech. Whether he has the right to, or is prohibited from, calling himself *Pedro* hangs on this place. Depending on what is the case, he is within the field of the cone or he isn't.[34]

In Melanie Klein's celebrated case of four-year-old Dick (whose "developmental" level she describes as being between fifteen and eighteen months), she portrayed Dick as using words in a deformed way, inopportunely. Dick is further characterized, in Kleinian theory, as being apathetic because he had encountered bad objects *in* his mother's body. Lacan contradicts the Kleinian view of Dick, pointing out: "this child has no desire to make himself understood, he doesn't try to communicate, his only activities . . . are emitting sounds and taking pleasure in meaningless sounds, in noises" (*Sem.* I, 81). Indeed, "well-functioning" psychotics manifest this same love of playing on the sounds of words. Such subjects prefer to use words non-dialectically rather than pursue problems of meaning or efforts at communication. Making meaning and exchanging with others both disrupt the consistency of *jouissance* that only silence or non-dialectical invention provide.

Lacan points out that Klein's patient grasped something of language, nonetheless, or Klein could never have made Dick understand her. Taking account of Klein's various statements about the "real" objects *in the world* available to the child, Lacan makes this point: "If we now sum up everything that Melanie Klein describes of this child's attitude, the significant point is simply the following— he makes no call (*appel*)" (*Sem.* I, 83). That is, he does not call out to the other. He is not *in* the social domain of transference relations. By drawing attention to the fact that the first signifier of most infants is a "call" to the other, wanting something from the Other, Lacan argues that *desire* is the basis of transference. Stressing that Dick—at four years of age—already had his own system of language, Lacan says that that system was quite sufficient for him. "The proof is that he plays with it. He even makes use of it to play a game of opposition against the adults' attempts to intrude. When adults ask him to reproduce words he uses correctly, he reproduces the 'correct' word in an unintelligible, deformed manner" (*Sem.* I, 83).

By distinguishing between "negation" as the denial Freud named *Verneinung*—which points to something already there to deny, i.e., an unconscious repression—and a negative manner, Lacan alerts us to a kind of negativity that is different from denial or repression. He finds the prototype of this kind of negativity in Freud's *Verdrängung*, the primordial repression which establishes a lining of the real in subject function. In other words, the prespecular objects that first cause the "call," thereby constituting the field of the real— the Ur-lining of the subject—can be organized in such a way that they will *not* cause desire. They will not give rise to a being that lacks. And such primordial negativity occurs even prior to the negation Lacan called foreclosure or *Verwerfung*: throwing out the signifier for a father's name from the symbolic. Indeed, the first resistance possibly causes the second one. But in both cases—psychosis or autism—whatever is foreclosed from the symbolic does not disappear. It returns in the real. That is, at the level of the real or trauma one does not escape effects just because they have not been assimilated or symbolized in conscious knowledge.

In autism, need is equated with demand such that nothing is subtracted from language or drive. Indeed, the autistic child cannot bear the intrusion of Otherness and the lack it brings with it. As impossible as it may seem, refusing relationships with others is a(n) (h)ontology that takes on its most graphic form wherein the "human" is constituted as a machine of destruction. Since autistic children are objects of the Other's *jouissance*, by definition, they are not re-presented or -signified in the Other. If the primordial object held out to an infant for its "satisfaction" is a malevolent gaze, a dismissive voice, an all-consuming invasive mother, or simply absence itself, it is only logical that this infant take these offerings of the primary caretaker's fatigue, distress, momentary disability, real dislike, or apathetic disinterest for what they are—*negative*. What is even more surprising in this logic of the real is that such an infant can make a system of meaning—of the *non-sens* meaning of the letter of "being"—from such offerings. When Lacan says that the autistic child does not drop the object *a*, he stresses that the object is the only thing that defines him with some guarantee of "being" *qua* consistency. Any infant must cling to something, even if it is a poisonous relation to the gaze or voice of the real that has constituted him or her as a creature of rage.

In introducing *l'appel* (the call to the other), Lacan tells us he is not slipping language into his theory (not even a higher level of language such as a metalanguage), but *la lalangue*, a primordial level of murmuring *beneath* language. Even pets, deprived of speech, make "calls" to you, says Lacan. "To the human call a further, richer development is reserved, because it takes place precisely in a being who has already reached the level of language" (*Sem.* I, 84). That is, a human cry is more than a meow, bark, chirp, and so on. What the autistic rejects is not language *qua* language, but the primordial structuring agents of separation: the gaze and the voice. For the autistic, these Ur-objects show the Other as a dangerous persecuting presence. Their negative power lies in that they function to structure the subject as an object of the drives. If the voice and the gaze are *causes* that structure desire for most people, one sees how the theory of an actual "bad breast" (versus a good one) could arise in a clinic such as Melanie Klein's where the analyst takes the visible organ to be the thing in itself, or a symbol of it.

Lacan's teaching is a topological structuralism, however, not a moralistic or imaginary set of prescriptions. Not only does the autistic not call out to the other, Colette Soler pinpoints a second autistic trait: the autistic's efforts to annihilate the offensive Other of which he or she is, paradoxically, the "victim." The refusal to permit any intimation of the Other's word constitutes a third trait of autism. Since the autistic identifies *with* rejection of a persecuting voice, he or she must refuse words themselves, for words confront this subject with a negative intrusion of the world of objects, with a threat of division he cannot permit. If identification with a negative voice or gaze conditions a refusal of the other's look, voice, or touch—of what are generally taken as signs of affection—the autistic's larger refusal to enter symbolic relations entails a rejection of the drive *qua* demand for satisfaction addressed to an other ($ ◊ D). The autistic cannot ask or desire because he or she does not trust (believe in) others. With a negative primordial Other as his or her guarantee, the autistic, by definition, forecloses the social Other, remaining an extension of the primordial Other who provides the only guarantee for being open to him or her (Soler, "Hors discours," 17–19).

Alienation and Separation

Lacan's discovery that humans are constituted as pre-determined effects of particular causes is new to epistemology. In the 1960s Lacan taught that culture is essentially installed by the two logical operations of "alienation" and "separation." In "Alienation and Separation: Logical Moments of Lacan's Dialectic of Desire," Bruce Fink points out that Lacan reconceptualized alienation as a *logical* operation on the level of the symbolic (language), rather than on the imaginary level, as Hegel had. While Hegel's concept of an alienated subject is consisted of the you/me, either/or model, the Lacanian "subject of desire" is defined at the point where he or she is not thinking, but is there as lacking or absent. Lacan translates Freud's *Wo Es war, soll Ich werden* to "There where it was," I would like it to be understood, "it is my duty that I should come to being."[35] Although one *is* there in a moment of *jouissance* which is itself re-presented *in* language, *Ich* will redefine *Es* in the analytic treatment.

The either/or dialectic of Hegelian alienation belongs to the realm of conscious reification or ego politics. But Lacanian "alienation" is essentially the result of an individual's encounter with language, from which one emerges as castrated by language or not. The phallus as Lacan defines it is not positive—i.e., the real organ penis—but negative, in the sense that it refers to something not quite visible or tangible. One is speaking, rather, of the veil of desire which responds to a lack in being. The phallic signifier, phallus, paternal metaphor, Father's Name, master signifier, or object *a* are just so many different names for the same effect: alienation or eclipse of the subject of *jouissance* behind language. Alienation is Lacan's name for the unconscious; that is, the *unknown* as a presence of imaginary castration, or something lacking ($-\phi$). Moments of fading in language and perception give one a momentary glimpse of the unconscious behind the world of visible consciousness, behind a random ordering of symbols, within a somewhat chaotic ordering of the so-called developmental stages (Lacan, *Four Fundamental Concepts*, chap. 5).

The neither/nor dialectic of "separation," which Lacan also called the cut, both marks the void by the negativity of loss *and* binds *jouissance* to the void via imaginary traits, signifiers, and libidinal effects inscribed in and on the body (Fink, "Alienation and Separation," 80, nn. 17, 18; 115–16). *Lacan described these effects of separation as the beginnings of the constitution of structure*, visible only in the unary traits (*lalangue or primordial jouissance*) that appear as excesses of *jouissance* in language. That is, unless a unary trait becomes a signifier—*jouissance* significantized, representing a subject for another signifier, the S_2 or binary signifier—meaning cannot come into existence (Lacan, *Four Fundamental Concepts*, 199). Thus one may define the Other as the "battery" or set of all signifiers where S_1 or the phallus is repressed by the subject of unconscious fantasy: $\$ \Diamond a$. Insofar as the S_1 is a signifier which has no corresponding signified, it institutes the unconscious by attaching the desiring subject to the Other via inaugural signifiers that constitute an ego ideal. Bruce Fink writes that "S_1 represents the subject (of the unconscious) for all the other signifiers. S_1 is the signifying chain's point of origin and the *sine qua non* of the constitution of the subject as a subject in language. Lacking this fundamental mooring, the other signifiers (designated as a whole by S_2)—to the extent that they are even assimilated—are condemned to drift without ever giving rise to meaning" (Fink, "Alienation and Separation," 88).

In *Extimité* Jacques-Alain Miller explains that the phallus is the signified for which the Father's Name is the signifier. On the one hand, language functions as a metaphor, referring to itself by the signifier of the Other. At the same time, language also functions in relation to a law (or serial ordering) Lacan called the Father's Name.[36] But even as early as the 1950s Lacan saw that one aspect of meaning is not representable as the signifier: the primordially repressed Ur-objects (the mammilla, the feces, the voice, the gaze, the urinary flow, the phoneme, the [imaginary] phallus, the nothing) that are in-*corp*-orated via the mother or her substitute. But only one of these objects *causes* or inaugurates human demand via the pathway of need where physical survival is at issue: the mammilla. The feces are located *elsewhere* in the mapping of psychic reality. That is, the first demand that an infant win approval in the eyes of others concerns the deposition and destruction of the feces. This act marks an infant as socialized. The contradictory aspect of the demand—Give this gift which is also disgusting—places the feces in the realm of the visible, under the mark of the superego.

Lacan depicts the realm of the scopic drive as one where judgments concerning ideal performance beget anxiety which returns throughout life in moments of logical time. Loss begets anxiety which makes one seek to fill up the void that marks the body with knowledge of loss. It is not as things in and of themselves that these Ur-objects constitute the real lining of the subject of desire, however, but through their effects as "objects," if only in the sense they give of an oscillation between satisfaction and dissatisfaction. Still, the drive aims at satisfaction although it always stumbles on a gap between the real effects of Ur-objects and the deception of imaginary lure objects that appear to be *das Ding an sich*. This missed encounter occurs, in part, because the real object *a* that causes desire has the property of being *separable* from the organ which seems to produce it.[37] Such separation suggests the incompatibility of loss with the things sought to appease it.

If the object causes desire and then defaults on payment, Lacan found Freud's argument that a nucleus of the unconscious is real logical. Formed as the *Urverdrängt* of primordial repression, this something lost is but a trait or mark of the effect of loss itself, which is inscribed as the *jouissance* of meaning, body, and the organism. Freud's *einziger Zug* becomes Lacan's imaginary bond or unary trait which retains a piece of the real at the moment of loss (the cut), thereby attaching the mark of a radically lost "object" to the void: i.e., joining two lacks. In other words, loss is posited *in language* as a palpable and dense (material) presence that one encounters in enigmatic impasses, in any suspicion of a "beyond" in language, as well as in symptoms written on the body. In this context, the signifiers of language *re-present* a subject as an object *a* one might call a signified. Insofar as signifiers retain re-pressed resonances of libidinal attachments that cannot be spoken at the level of memory or experience, the *jouissance* of meaning is what psychoanalysis tries to understand. One might call this a metalanguage of effects whose *jouis-sens* comes from its bond with a *jouissance* of being, thereby eroticizing lack/desire at the body's edges and rims.[38]

In Freud's theory of repression, he said the *Vorstellungsrepräsentanz* or the representative of a representation stands behind what is represented. But both Freud's concept and his term (which has been translated into English as the "ideational representative" of the drive) remained enigmatic for him. Lacan chalked this up to his seeking the link between representations and repression in perceptions or affects.[39] Lacan linked representations to repressions in another way. By viewing the *Vorstellungen* as *a priori* repressions of unary signifiers created by the primordial loss of "objects," Lacan showed that such cuts create a dialectic with loss itself. And this dialectic, symbolized by S[Ø], destroys the possibility of a true One-ness between a person and the words, images, or others that constitute his or her world. Neither perception, affect, language, nor anything else, can mean on its own. In *The Four Fundamental Concepts of Psychoanalysis* Lacan points to the *Fort! Da!* bobbin reel game Freud used as an example of how repetition is linked to representation, to argue a novel idea. This Freudian concept sheds more light on Freud's theory of primal repression, the *Urverdrängt*, than it does on representation, Lacan said. The *Repräsentanz* is not the bobbin reel as some composite symbol of the mother, as Freud suggests, nor any primordially repressed imago of a breast. Rather, the game itself mimes the effect of the mother's departure on the infant, the departure momentarily creating a ditch of loss that decenters the child, giving it a sense of being there or not being there. Rather than representing what is actually visible in the game, the departure shows what is *a priori*: loss catalyzing the real of anxiety which pushes the child to fill up the hole with an activity (Lacan, *Four Fundamental Concepts*, 63).

Representation is not linked to repetition at the level of the visible, then. In Lacan's teaching, Freud's theory becomes an imaginary interpretation in which images and repeated acts (such as the game) serve as a shorthand for Lacan's concept of function. Both cover over a gap or a *Spaltung* in the subject. In the bobbin reel game, the mother's departure causes the child to acknowledge loss

by identifying with another "object," but not because some primordial affective bond has been severed. Rather, the child encounters anxiety when he experiences the opening of the void. Such
an encounter with loss elicits anxiety as a "knowledge" about the
void which, in turn, gives rise to the quest for *jouissance qua* consistency via the repetitions intended to guarantee a continuity in
language and being as they constitute the body for a meaning "beyond" itself.

In the field of language the S_1 or master signifier is the "I think"
of the "I am's" more inclusive *savoir* (S_2). Desire lies between the
two signifiers for language and points to the subject's *cause* in fantasy and *jouissance*, not in communication or in relationships *per
se*. And the object *a* denotes an *écriture* that is absent as a visible
referent between word and thing, but palpably present as the mysterious cause of desire. Such an invisible cause is not, however,
simply the nothingness of empty space, but some*thing* precise produced by the cut that creates a quota of *jouissance*—nonsense, a
non-utilitarian libido—which only *seems* to emanate from the lure
objects one desires. Loss of *jouissance*, paradoxically, makes one
seek objects as a guarantee of grounding, not as an object *per se*,
although people generally think of objects as "the thing in itself."
Objects are actually semblances that hide a real void in language.
This becomes an even more perplexing notion when one notes that
master signifiers (S_1) can only be inscribed as such by re-presenting
the object *a* as a subject *for* another signifier, the S_2 or binary signifier. That is, S_1 alone cannot symbolize thinking, for it is retroactively defined by S_2 which takes "repressed" desire into account.
Psychotic speech does not function this way, however. It is bom-
barded, rather, with a plethora of S_1s. But most speech is not psychotic and so must work with repressed desire. Because of this,
"thinking" continually ends up in hermeneutical dead ends where
people find solutions to problems in the order of the visible where
seeing is believing.

In *Television* Lacan described *jouissance* as a "knowledge" system whose components are: a "battery" or set of signifiers, pleasure
and displeasure in the body, the shocks one gets from encountering
the symptoms whose *jouissance* provides a sense of meaningful
consistency to one's being. Jacques-Alain Miller points out in "A
Reading of Some Details in *Television*" that *jouissance* is a "knowledge" of the real, where "I think" coalesces with the Freudian
primordial father—the exception to the rule of castration—to become the Lacanian "more than you in you" (Miller, "A Reading,"

18–29; esp. 26). This real is proximate to the void of anxiety, but is not the void spoken of by Malcolm Bowie as a "boundless and inexpressible vacuity." It is, rather, a powerful encounter with the absolute weight of the void, emptying the *jouissance* effects of imagined oneness into language. And these effects constitute a knowledge that materializes language around the partial drives.

In "To Interpret the Cause" Miller said one might equate the alienated field of the Other with representations (O), but the *quota* of affect that governs the deployment of representations is *jouissance*: $\frac{O}{J}$. And the residue or excess between the two is Lacan's object *a*, the filler of the void (Miller, "To Interpret the Cause," 49). Combining Lacan's first and second paternal metaphors, Miller rewrote Lacan's formula for the primordial paternal metaphor this way: $\frac{F}{M} \cong \frac{O}{J}$. Something which is *not* a signifier—the mother as lost desire—is substituted for by something which *is* a signifier: The Father's Name. But the secret of the paternal metaphor, of Oedipus, is not that. Rather, any phallic anchor (be it a Father's Name as a signifier or an object *a* acting as a signifier) can make a fixed substance—a libidinal glue—out of the *jouissance* which fills the void. In the sexuation graphs in "A Love Letter" (*Encore*), Lacan designated that link as a tie between the symbolic and the real:

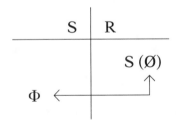

(*Feminine Sexuality*, 149). Miller's formula mentioned above shows that *jouissance* can be inscribed in the symbolic order because the mother is lost *qua* primary object ("To Interpret the Cause," 46).

Memory does not come *from* the mind, then, or from a grammatical language chain adequate to its own functioning. Memory comes from contingent associations. And inconsistencies in memory come from difficulties encountered in the ordering of desire around the impasses of *jouissance* which one might also call libido, or a quota of affect. In the real, memory is a knot of unassimilated meanings which persist, organizing unconscious desire, the fundamental fantasy, and the symptom around unsymbolized (traumatic) knowledge. Yet the real "returns" anyway in bits and pieces of *jouissance* that "cannot enter the place of the Other, cannot be marked and transferred as a signifier. And that is precisely what Lacan called small *a* . . . the *plus de jouir* as the difference between the libido and language which produces this small *a* as a residue, $J - O = a$" (Miller, "To Interpret the Cause," 49). Thus, the small *a* unites language to libido in the fetish objects marked by a surplus value. Although the object *a* usually succeeds in hiding the void in the Other, the *jouissance* of being, body, and meaning are continually disrupted by the impasses that "return" in moments of loss, displeasure, or "death" (Lacan, *Four Fundamental Concepts*, 55).

Being only *seems* ontological to us because it *appears* to give a person a place of position or identity without one's having to see the obvious: that each person can only find recognition of his or her being (as a particular constellation of signifiers Lacan called an ego ideal) from others. Yet narcissistic creatures though we are (*m'être*), we will do anything to hide the inverse face of narcissism: our shame (*hontology*) at being less than the ideal we pretend to be in our lies to self and other. Moreover, our happiness resides, not in others *per se*, but in the *jouissance* we recoup from them, although we treat this "knowledge" by denial, repression, repudiation, or foreclosure. Yet desire remains inextinguishable as it unfurls its relation to castration in the position one takes toward the phallus where one values oneself as masculine, i.e., in the symbolic, or feminine, i.e., in the real. Lacan argues that this drama culminates in neurosis (denying that the sexual difference is itself a distinction between the masculine and feminine), psychosis (foreclosing knowledge of the difference), perversion (repudiating belief in the difference), and the norm (the *père-version* or sexual "perversion" where the difference is acknowledged, but its cause is repressed).

When Lacan symbolized the experience of being this or that by the *game* Freud's nephew played with the bobbin reel, he showed that the reel's importance is not as an object. Any object—be it concrete or experiential—can be invested with a small part of the real that, in turn, imbues that object with the anxiety surrounding loss. Jacques-Alain Miller has called the Ur-lining of the real—the objects that cause desire—a pre-symbolic real (R_1). After coherent language is learned, a person inhabits a post-symbolic real (R_2) where the objects invested with *jouissance* show the tedious, deadly game of repetition as inseparable from the death drive (Lacan, *Four Fundamental Concepts*, 62).

A New Theory of Identification

Lacan reinterpreted Freud's theories of identification from *Totem and Taboo*,[40] "Psychology of the Group and Analysis of the Ego,"[41] and "The Ego and the Id."[42] From these he built his theory of identification around his interpretation of the Freudian death drive. Taking Freud's mythical primitive father of "Totem and Taboo" as the first object of identification—the real father who "enjoys" beyond the law of limit as a *veritable parasitical presence* in our "minds" and bodies—he argues that a primary *jouissance* is emblazoned in a montage of images, sounds, and experiences surrounding the primary object. Thus, frustration, castration, and privation are constituted in a triadic relation to the object, prior to a secondary sublimation one might equate with the paternal metaphor.

But the Lacanian real father is not the pre-Oedipal mother of Kleinian theory, nor any actual father as a conscious being or an imaginary figure. Nor is he an object *a*, cause-of-desire. Rather the obscene "father" enjoyment—the Ur-symbol of exception to the rules—encapsulates identification with the *jouissance* of the death drive taken as that which hurts us even as we cling to the *semblant* of appearance over the truth of our lives. In this sense, the primordial cause of being and desiring is the void: $\frac{\varnothing}{(a)}$. The symbolic father $\left(\frac{O}{-\varnothing}\right)$ comes after, in the guise of whatever symbol of order provides a source for identifying with the rules of the group in which one defines oneself as *all*.[43]

And the contradiction between believing one is an exception to the rule of loss because one is, paradoxically, identified with a group of the supposed whole (all those who deny lack: $\exists x \ \overline{\Phi}x$) and the reality of there being no all or whole that will annihilate the void at the heart of being, places the masculine on the slope of the death drive, along with its accoutrements—violence, aggression, power, and control. Jacques-Alain Miller has explained that the residual quantum of affect Freud described is Lacan's object *a*. Not finding a place in the Other, the "object" is displaced into language and the body, concentrated in pockets of excess *jouissance* that *repeat* deadly rituals. These rituals, nonetheless, give the illusion of a consistency in being. Insofar as the function of the object *a*—in and of itself an inexistent, empty form—is to delimit the anxiety produced by an emptying out of *jouissance* from the void, it is heterogeneous. Any fetished or cherished object, be it a ritual, a walk down a certain street, a *Glanz auf der Naze*, and so on, can constitute the object *a* as a stopper to the void.

In "The Analytic Experience" Miller extends Lacan's theory of libido. "Repression is a *separation* of the idea [representation] and the quantum of affect [the object *a*], with only anxiety standing apart as the affect that does not mislead."[44] That is, repression is not simply a denial or a disassociation. Repression is a real cut or split between an idea and a *quantity* of feeling. In Lacanian psychoanalysis, such a theory gives rise to a very different kind of clinical practice than those praxes in which analysts advise people to "talk about their feelings." For what disturbs and troubles—the repressed truth—is precisely *what one cannot say*. Lacanian analysis separates the object *a* from the void it fills in a series of cuts into an analysand's narrative. This procedure gives rise to fantasies that support destructive *jouissance* which, in turn, informs blind drive. That is, as we go through multiple identificatory fusions, we become subjects of the drive Lacan described as a collage (*Four Fundamental Concepts*, chap. 13). Analytic treatment aims at breaking up the destructive collusion between the object *a* and the "better than nothing" pleasure one takes in the illusion that all is well with one's world.

Primordial identification with the real of absolute *jouissance* produces the Freudian primitive father that Lacan "translates" as a libidinal object: a profound identification of oneself as an object of *jouissance*, not as a subject of language. The subject as object of the partial drive goes through the Freudian drive circuit—source, goal, aim, and thrust—on the side of the real, of a material sense of Oneness (*Four Fundamental Concepts*, chap. 14). But Lacan does not see the drive as achieving satisfaction in some mythic evolution from orality to anality to a harmonious genitality. Rather, the drive's aim is to make a unity between desire and the realization of a *fantasy*. But the drive repeats failures instead, because the desire for pleasure that Lacan calls Freud's primary process and the reality of repetition that Lacan calls Freud's secondary process coalesce in the solitary *jouissance* of one's fixities.

But what has this to do with the paternal metaphor? Slavoj Žižek, for example, explains Lacan's notion of the Name-of-the-Father as the dead symbolic father, or the father of dead letters.[45] Not only is language made of the archaic memories of already dead tongues, Jacques-Alain Miller clarifies Lacan's re-reading of Freud further to say that one name of the object *a* is the real father as a living presence of death. The real father is to be found in the burning coals of dead letters that pierce desire and language with *jouissance*.[46] If *jouissance* is first linked to the world via the insignia of images and words, then the primal sexuality of any being is marked by the impossibility of Oneness, by the loss of the primary object. The craziness in psychosis is the radical foreclosure of this loss. Thus, the first human identification (constituted by the infant's repeated demands for satisfaction) is with the real father *qua* rejection of limits. Yet, the first limit encountered is the mother as primary forbidden object: What is forbidden is that some other being eradicate our own losses once and for all. The incest taboo, structurally speaking, is ahistorical, then, ensuring that most infants acquire language within the framework of Oedipal law.

At the level of a secondary *jouissance* or reality principle (Φ), the symbolic order prevails over the primordial relation to the mother. In differentiating themselves away from their mothers, sons identify with symbolic order myths that delineate some concept of the whole. $\exists x$ is the matheme for the subject whose *existence* is based on the illusion of being an exception to the rule of castration, a function which is, in fact, foreclosed ($\overline{\Phi}x$) (*Feminine Sexuality*, 149).

In Lacan's teaching, the superego (or ego or id) are not agencies of some predetermined psyche that exists apart from the drives or language. The superego starts as an *Ur-object* of the real that constitutes the ego and the id insofar as the voice and the gaze of the primordial Other are the first agents of castration or judgment. In later life a neurotic tries to obey the Other's desire which is, nonetheless, opaque to him or her, while the psychotic follows the dictates of the Other's *jouissance*.[47] As we have already said, whether we speak of neurosis, psychosis, or perversion, we refer to different outcomes of the way the orders are knotted by the paternal metaphor. We remember that the three exigencies—real, symbolic, imaginary—constitute the "mind" as a necklace of signifying chains ordering each person's desire, first in reference to the phallus, i.e., as a symptom of a mother's unknown desire correlated with the *signifier* for a father's name. But this "relation" from Lacan's first formula is not adequate to explain how a mother's unconscious desire plays such a powerful role in constituting subjectivity, precisely when it is ungraspable as clear conscious knowledge. Concepts such as *lalangue* or unary signifiers try, at best, to describe reminiscent traces of desire. But these are not empirical facts or retrievable events. Thus, the mother's desire can only be understood by the law of the signifier: when it is taken with the signifier for her partner—the father.

But no opposite and equal function obtains. Rather, both sons and daughters are referred to the signifier for that part of the mother's desire that goes beyond her child. And since both sexes identify first with the mother, the issue of gender will always concern identifying *with* her or *away* from her. Insofar as daughters identify *with* her, this means being part of a group of people who have ex-sistence beyond the symbolic order of rules and closure. Sons who identify *away* from her, do so by identifying with a group of the (imagined) whole, bound by certain societal rules. If no signifier for difference *separates* the child from its mother's desire, then castration does not occur; lack is not introduced into being. *Jouissance* or libido holds sway such that meaning cannot be created in a substitutive flow of dialectical movement, metaphor being the way meaning is built by one thing *substituting* (exchanging) for another: $\frac{2}{1}$ (Miller, "To Interpret the Cause," 45). Whenever the referent is not represented in the imaginary as a signifier for sexual difference, the void produces *jouissance* that must be constantly evacuated in order to clear space for producing any meaning (Miller, "Language: Much Ado about What?" 34).

Derrida claims one can knock out the sign for opposition between two binaries thereby *cancelling* out opposition or "differance," collapsing opposites into the same. The traces of language and noise that build knowledge out of language into a logocentrism are supposedly subverted in this way. Yet Lacan sees language as functioning dialectically only when the phallic signifier for difference (the bar of substitution) has been learned as sexual difference. One might call this signifier an "introject" that allows humans the freedom to move in language, even to *play* within language. If this difference is not put in place to start with, a tragic being evolves, one who is subjugated from infancy to words and sounds enunciated by a superego maternal voice. Consequently, the psychotic produces meaning like an automaton. Because words are equated with drives, they are not pliable.

The fact that subject structuration comes from how one is programmed for sexual difference imposes a spatial effect within the linearity of a person's use of grammar. Lacan described this effect as the unconscious working in language to insert the timing of desire by the function of substitution. The time of *jouissance* persists in language as a stoppage, limit, or blockage to its smooth flow. *Jouissance* is not *unconscious*, then, in the sense of the *Unbewusste* or not known. Rather, the *jouissance* of being and the *jouissance* of the body insert symptomatic inconsistencies and enigmas into language, showing that language is always inadequate to the task of representing thought. Moreover, the primordial objects that cause the desire that materializes language around desired objects allow language to function only by the temporality of anticipation and retroaction. Thus, repression refers to the experience of rediscovering desire that has been pressed under before. Insofar as loss and gain are always in play, Lacan says the symptom is always being written in language, a writing of ups and downs ("Seminar of 21 January 1975"). That is, the unconscious is not timeless at all, as Freud supposed, except in the sense that language, identifications, and symptoms are nailed down, fixed. And the subject is not an individual, but an instant in time.

When language refers the child away from the signifier mother as primary object of desire, toward the signifier for a father's name, a fourth term is created: the subject as a *point* one can identify at the intersections of the orders in each person's signifying chains. In a manner of speaking, the "subject" *qua* symptom registers the catastrophe everyone experiences who loses the primary object, a loss which gives rise to fantasies of how to recoup *jouissance* from the world. Thus, fundamental fantasies structure our subjective positions in life as unconscious movements toward *jouissance* (Miller, "To Interpret the Cause," 43). But one does not move directly toward *jouissance*. Lacan gives this reason. Finding no *fixed* or symmetrical relationship between father and Man, or mother and Woman, Lacan suggested a third term of reference: the phallus defined as an object of desire or mark of lack-in-being that defines each person in reference to castration (Miller, "To Interpret the Cause," 46). But, if the mother's desire is unknowable at the level of lack (phallus), then the secret of Freud's Oedipus can be found in Lacan's second paternal metaphor where something that is not a signifier is substituted for something that is. Lacan denotes the inscription of *jouissance* in the symbolic order by the signifier of the phallic *jouissance*.

$$\frac{F}{M} \rightarrow \frac{\Phi}{x} \rightarrow \frac{O}{J} \quad \text{(Miller, "To Interpret the Cause," 46).}$$

In the first paternal metaphor, Lacan's phallus supports language to say that something is unknown: a signified without a signifier, an enigma. Later, in "Subversion of the subject and the dialectic of desire" Lacan opined that one can only receive one's own message from the Other by reading backward in the chain of signifiers.[48] Thus, at the point where a subject is *signified* as a symptom, as a metaphor of the paternal enigma, this first formula shows the phallus functioning as an x, as a question mark or mystery concerning the mother. An infant cannot define him- or herself in terms of what the mother wants precisely because the phallus stands for this truth: something always lacks in desire $(-\phi)$. And this something missing in knowledge plagues every person whose "cause" is always already lost, unsayable (everyone except the psychotic who believes his *cause* is not lost). Given this reality, Lacan argued that meaning cannot be ascertained outside discourse, which defines the social "link" in terms of language used in the service of transference relations. That is, even though the real resides outside the social link, it still inhabits language as an excess in meaning, an *hors-sens* (*Encore*, "A Jakobson").

The phallus is not only the knowledge one lacks about what the mother wants, then, but also a question about what she enjoys. What failed identification, what ideal, govern what she says to her child? Does she enjoy martyrdom, inducing guilt, maligning (or lauding) her husband? In one sense the phallus denotes the structural function of lack and the "object" one hopes will fill the lack. In signifying that the subject lacks knowledge about what the Other really wants of him or her, the phallus hides as a question mark in the forest of what is said.[49] This is quite a different notion of the phallus from Malcolm Bowie's view of Lacan's 1958 reading of Freud's phallus as organ or symbol: "There is something desperate about this apotheosis of the phallus. It is of course agreeable to see the relations between Mind and Word turning for a visionary moment upon a single hinge."[50]

At the level of signifiers (insignia of the imaginary and symbolic) the ideal ego unconscious formation has become a principle of resistance, a function usually ascribed to the ego. If the signifier for lack $(-\phi)$ gives rise to the symbolic order—

$$\exists x \quad \overline{\Phi x}$$
$$\forall x \quad \Phi x$$

—one could describe this order as the distance from the primary *jouissance* that bolsters the ego's resistance to knowing about primordial identifications. Perhaps what we generally call perception—or perspective in art—is actually a measure of distance from the primary object, a distance that is lacking in the structures of autism and psychosis. It is not the actual father who is at issue, then, but the foreclosure of the signifier for one's lived existence as based on identification with a father and with a lineage or history of the father's name. It is not, then, the father's *proper* name that is in question.

The Second Theory of the Paternal Metaphor

We come again to Jacques-Alain Miller's elaboration of a second formula for the Lacanian paternal metaphor. Unlike Lacan's 1958 formula, there is no consistent Other in this second formulation. Eric Laurent wrote in "The Uses of Phantasy" that the second formula concerns an inconsistent Other, perhaps in the sense of Bertrand Russell's inconsistent logics, but not consistent with Russell's meaning of "consistent." The Other produces a negative phallus (castration) and a remainder (the object *a*). One can write the effect like this: $\dfrac{\emptyset \quad \text{Other Discourse}}{-\phi \quad \text{Phallic Signifier}}$ (Laurent, p. 36).

That is, *any lack* has a sexual meaning if loss is taken to mean the loss of *jouissance*. Even sexuality itself becomes one more substitute for filling the void of anxiety. In this context, the father's name would function as an object *a*, rather than as a signifier or a name. We remember that an object *a* marks a place that is empty at the level of symbolized meaning. But this very emptiness causes fantasy to circle around it, making the referent of all language the void. Put another way, the Father's Name functions as a signifier for lack (alienation, castration) in the symbolic only if the father does not act like a real father who is beyond the law of castration (as did Schreber's father, or certain "fathers" of countries such as Hitler, Hussein, or any other such dictator).

A real father denotes a person (male or female) who enjoys in flagrant rejection of the laws that constitute the distance, boundaries, or conventions that order the symbols of the symbolic. The second formula for the paternal metaphor—the formula, as well, for the repression (*refoulement*, *Verneinung*) of the object *a*—places this object under the inconsistent Other $\dfrac{(\emptyset)}{a}$. This formula denotes the human effort to deny castration or lack via *jouissance* or sublimation (Laurent, "Uses of Phantasy," 36). The difficult point in this second formula is that no father (either as a signifier or name) can be taken as a guarantee of limit or law. Not only is Woman not a guarantee, neither is the father in whose name we speak, whether it be the father of a family, an ideology, a belief, a theory, and so on. Rather, to some degree, every desiring person forecloses law in favor of *jouissance*, taken as a guarantee of being and knowing.

This formula $\frac{(\emptyset)}{a}$ means that no knowledge, person, method, or ideology can truly provide the certainty that would ensure objectivity or truth (except in terms of certain physical or mathematical laws). Supporting the place of the inconsistent Other where something is missing, one finds not a positive phallus (Φ), but the sign for castration ($-\phi$). Because something *is* lacking in knowledge and being ($\$$), persons are driven to represent themselves one to another, or to themselves, as fully present and autonomous subjects. The truth of the matter is that any subject *qua* person is suspended in representational networks (S_1) of their own master signifiers. Two signifiers—S_1 and S_2—represent the field of language, but only because lack ($\$$) makes it impossible for fantasy ($\$ \Diamond a$) to fill the void with a *semblance* of being a subject of consistent *jouissance*.

In his first theory of the paternal metaphor, Lacan tried to delineate differential clinical structures on the basis of belief in the father *qua* symbolic father. The neurotic was an atheist or an agnostic, a disbeliever in God who tries to evade the problems of the Other while holding on to the Other's desire. The pervert was a true atheist, one who has no symbolic father at all, only the gaze of the real father. The psychotic, the only *true believer*, believes in the gods who inhabit the field of the real, speaking in omniscient voices and casting looks that scald. Belief shows that we necessarily think we have innate language or innate knowledge precisely because we "have" a structural deficiency we must deny. But even in his first theory of the paternal metaphor, Lacan was already arguing that behind the metaphor of the father, taken as subject of the law, the metonymy of castration is hidden in the name of the phallus (Laurent, "Uses of Phantasy," 34).

Miller's clarification of the second paternal metaphor is founded in part on Lacan's "Geneva Lecture," where he argued that one can organize the phallus as a predicate on the basis of already existing mathematical knowledge of inconsistent logics (*Analysis*, 7–26). The fact that the Other as father—either as name or as signifier

of a law—is not a sufficient guarantee on which to base either knowledge or belief, answers yet another question for Miller: Why is sex
a trauma that links language to desire and lack, thereby constituting
differential clinical categories? Why would sex be so traumatic as
to create each person as an effect of the real, cut in many places
by the montage of the drives?

The answers are to be found in the second paternal metaphor in
that it shows the subject as an effect not only of identifications, but
most particularly of Oedipal ones. Three fates await an infant as it
assumes a myth of identity as a gender fiction. All three fates are
derived from a position taken vis-à-vis the phallus: castration brings
neurosis; foreclosure brings psychosis; disavowal brings perversion. In the context of the second paternal metaphor, a child does
not seek to know what is "inside" the mother, then, as Melanie
Klein thought, but rather to make the father's name function as a
signifier that will guarantee a sense of worth to his or her being in
the Other. But signifiers have two sides. One produces imaginary
and symbolic messages for another signifier concerning some issue
of desire. The other produces traumatic (*jouissance*) knowledge
that pertains to loss, and thus enters language as silence, enigma,
symptom. But desire partakes of both sides of the signifier. The
neurotic identifies with the Other's desire via the *jouissance* of
meaning—taking "pleasure" in deciphering his own unconscious
without seeing the double bind. A dialectical effect is constituted
for the neurotic by identification with a problematic symbolic father
who, nonetheless, *stands for* the law or social bond Freud called
the superego. In trying to foreclose the symbolic father, the obsessional opens desire directly onto the omnipresent lack he tries to
exclude, a lack with which the hysteric identifies.

In psychosis, where desire is for a totalized *jouissance* of Being,
desire is static and petrified, its signifier a lack of lack. In explaining
the meaning of Lacan's concept of the foreclosure of the Name-of-
the-Father, Miller writes the matheme for psychosis this way: O ≅
J (Stevens, "Two destinies for the subject," 26). In identifying with
the real of *jouissance* in the field of speech and language, the psychotic will always be caught up in the drives in a painful way. The
Otherness or difference that constitute the order Lacan calls symbolic (its rules and conventions) will always seem alien and unclear
to psychotics who can only follow rules via the mimesis of imaginary models. Thus, the psychotic's only guarantee of a semblance
of unity is through *jouissance*. While most people are used by language or changing conventions and are carried along by a seem-

ingly "natural" flow of substitutions and displacements, in psychosis, rigidity itself forms the knot that substitutes for cuts or splits never made in the Other. For neurotic subjects, splits in the Other are filled up with pseudo-consistencies (objects a) that, in turn, offer a semblance of totality and the comfort of imaginary closure. When such closure functions, one believes there is a unity among image, language, and body. But in psychosis there is no semblance of a consistent identity, no solid name, no final trust in language, for this subject cannot depend on the mother's desire as a signifier that allows distance. Indeed, the psychotic cannot relinquish proximity to a primary libidinal object—deployed in language or body—because it is his or her *only* guarantee of being.

Instead of finding comfort within language, the psychotic encounters hostile gazes and voices that speak *as if* they were split off from his or her thought. In a psychotic *episode* voices or gazes become literally detached from thought and function as hallucinatory persecutions or commands. But even though most persons are not psychotic, traits of voices, gazes, and so on appear in their language as the multiple insignia of partial objects that cause desire. If a young child chooses to identify with the primary object *qua* totality of *jouissance* instead of with the signifiers and the object a which cut into body to constitute a lack in being, psychosis waits in the wings. Yet this is rare. Indeed, most people are not even deeply neurotic—by which one infers a norm—but are unthinking, blindly ignorant subjects, carried along by their own dialectical movement between desire and *jouissance* wherein substitutive repetitions, identifications with words and with images and things, leave little space for genuine questions or authentic doubt.

One can denote the structure of neurosis by this matheme—$\dfrac{\$}{-\phi}$. Herein, desire ($\$$) is supported by castration situated in the position of truth ($-\phi$) (see "A Jakobson" in *Encore*). The neurotic equates the lack of knowledge about the Other's desire with the primordial lack that begets desire in the first place. Such a union creates an identification with the imaginary wherein a signifier from the Other's desire becomes the unary trait that dialecticizes identificatory meaning thus: $\dfrac{I}{\$} \rightarrow \dfrac{S2}{}$ (Stevens, "Two destinies for the subject," 98). The seemingly least troubled of discourses, the one where denial works well and certainty prevails, is the master discourse of "normative" neurosis—i.e., relatively untroubled individuals who make meaning spontaneously, fluidly, easily, by identifying ego with the social codes of their group context. Insofar as language is supported by a lack—that is, no signifier assures one of a finished identity or totalized meaning to "self"—"going along" with others requires little effort for the *norme-mâle* and his female counterpart, the *nor*-mâle. Both speak a master discourse, set forth in "A Jakobson" as: $\frac{S_1}{\$} - \overset{\frown}{\underset{\smile}{}} \frac{S_2}{a}$ (*Encore*, 21). Socially current values produce *jouissance* as the cause of desire, and desire itself is repressed as cause.

Confrontation with division—be it of language, image, need, or drive—unveils unconscious desire as primary process. But we see clearly that Lacan's primary process is not Freud's primary-process condensation and displacement except insofar as desire has the structure of displacement. Rather something unknown— a gap, ditch, or empty place—appears in language, thought, or body, making a rupture between seemingly unified perception and conscious unawareness. Bringing a seemingly non-temporal locus into language, such ruptures cause fading, forgetting, slips of the tongue, dreams, laughter, silence, excessive responses, and so on. When the metaphorical duality of language is momentarily unveiled, the splits in being disappear, allowing us to glimpse ourselves (or others) as lacking. We "see" that at the center of being each one seeks *jouissance*—not objects—to fill the hole that keeps us from being One with ourselves. Lacan used the expressions "excluded interior" or "excluded on the inside" to describe this phenomenon.[51]

Identification and the Object *a*

Jacques-Alain Miller explains this paradox of "internal exclusion"—where the inside and outside meet in a point Lacan called extimacy—as internal to the very *structure* of being which, by necessity, we repeat to enable the thinking that defines us as beings of desire and pursuers of *jouissance*. Yet the moment of repetition re-introduces conflict as a split, showing loss at the center of repetition. "Pleasure principle" "reality principle," or "death drive" are different names for the same function: the quest to maintain or attain *jouissance* as a "libidinal" glue meant to guarantee permanence, certainty, and objectivity through repetitions of known modes of satiety. The object *a* on which one depends to close out loss is intended to guarantee this consistency and stability *once and for all*.

By accepting the impossibility of a totalized, exclusive identification with the desired primary object, most children accept, instead, identification with cultural values whose ideals they try to meet (Lacan, *Four Fundamental Concepts*, 199). But forever after humans seek a primordial *jouissance* in their relations that is only acknowledged at the level of profound affects, not understood. But one does not usually think of *jouissance* as an *a priori* knowledge about the value of one's life, a knowledge that is both rational and logical. Psychotic or neurotic, we cannot know who or what we are as extimate objects, as responses of the real, for *jouissance* is veiled by the misrecognitions and lies that come from identifying with ideals.

In Lacan's first formula for the paternal metaphor, desire as signified by the mother appears in the child's question, "Who am I?" In his second formula, Lacan equated language and the reality principle of repetition with the *jouissance* phallus (Φ) (*Sém.* XX, 73). One wonders why he made this change in his thinking about the phallus. A possible answer lies in Lacan's development of Freud's third theory of identification, where Freud questioned the idea that we identify with some preformed ego. In scrutinizing Freud's theory here, Lacan finds a hysterical identification with the *split* in the subject itself: $\frac{i(a)}{a}$. One seeks to make one's being commensurable with one's ideal of being, an impossible feat. Yet narcissistic convictions allow people to believe their own lies about their worth as adjudged in terms of "self" fictions. Miller explains Lacan's matheme as meaning that the image of another person as ideal clothes or covers over the real of one's own ex-sistence as object (Miller, "Extimité," 128). Miller develops Lacan's matheme thus: $I \rightarrow \frac{i(a)}{ego}$ (Stevens, "Two destinies for the subject," 99). That is, *identification with* the imaginary constitutes the completion of the master discourse or *père-version* in an identification with the social order *qua* norm: $\frac{O}{a}$ (Miller, "Extimité," 128). Narcissistic identifications stop up the void opened by the intervention of the object *a* in language, body, relationships, and all other seeming totalities: $\frac{\emptyset}{(a)}$. Identification with conventional wisdom and with the "in" group one chooses enables people to deny the divine details that build "being" on the scaffolding of loss, detail by detail. Yet, at some level, "normative" people "know" they are stopping up loss. Religion, myths, the love of fiction, film, and sport are all denials of the unbearable obvious. We are not whole within ourselves. There is no autonomous self whose life course is charted free of others.

To sum up, it takes three stages to get to Freud's third identification where a fundamental split constitutes what Lacan calls the *père-version* or social norm ($\$$), based on repression of unconscious desire. The *first* identification is to the real father *qua jouissance* that grounds an infant in seeming internal libidinal consistencies which are not consistent after all, and so must be sought by the repetition of master signifiers; i.e., unary strokes, that make an identification between *jouissance* and desire. The *second* identification with language and symbolic law is what Lacan called the signifier of a father's name ($S_1 \rightarrow S_2$, the Other or the symbolic order). This second identification gives individuals a sense of getting somewhere, a purpose in life, a place within a social order. The *third* identification with the group or leader (the law of the "norm") might be called a transference onto immediate others. Such transference is itself a way of denying one's unconscious foundations in the past and in unconscious fantasy. In this third identification the lack of a signifier for a "natural" sexual rapport is correlated with gender identity myths in ways that make social roles all important in the sexual masquerade.

In the third identification, the normative masquerade unveils the effects of an "Oedipal" trajectory wherein desire can be seen as structured. While "self" identification is clearly structured for most people, the issue of sexual object choice is not so certain. Indeed, actual object choices may be made late, or may change. Gender ambiguity is certainly a serious concern for the psychotic for whom identity difference was never learned as sexual difference; i.e., as symbolic. When an imaginary identity recedes in a psychotic episode, revealing sexual difference as foreclosed *in the real*, one witnesses psychotic women in the throes of the ultimate pain of the real, while psychotic men are feminized (the *pousse-à-la-femme*), tied as they are to the mother and to the oral drive. One can see that what has been foreclosed from the ego is distance from the mother's *jouissance*. Indeed, no identificatory fantasy is open to the male psychotic except a nostalgia for oneness with the mother, with God, music or some divine or sacred figure. Tormented by the necessity to create a fantasy that will align sexuality with organs and gender myths, psychotics find no basis for a fundamental fantasy that aligns body and world. Schreber solved his problem by delusion, by remaking his "self" identification into an impossible figure—himself as the wife of God. Fantasy bears on the possible, then, while delusion concerns impossibilities.

The issue of the relation of gender to sexuality is paramount for the neurotic, whose dilemma is that of being torn between mixed identifications with the father as Man and the mother as Woman. The hysteric always wonders whether she is a man or woman, whether she merits a *name* commensurable with her deficient narcissism. Rent between identifying with an impotent father and an all too present mother, the obsessional's question—Am I alive or dead?—is more primordial than the hysteric's: Am I a man or a woman? By definition the "normative" neurotic, the one for whom repression functions well, flees differences from others in identification with the law of the "social good." Answers, solutions, beliefs, are all antidotes to questions and doubts that circle around repression of the unconscious—all these give rise to the pseudo-debates of the pub, the church, or the country club.

In Lacan's second paternal metaphor, identification turns toward the object *a*, not the signifier. For example, in the third identificatory direction, men and women live by the conventions of their beliefs, posing questions only insofar as the object *a* produces an excess in the *jouissance* surrounding the sublimation of a father's name. Is the president truly honorable, honest, etc? "Knowing" unfolds in discourses spoken by *masters* of opinion, *professors* of knowledge, *hysterics* whose mastery lies in subverting conventional certainties, or by *analysts* who do not presume to know what the analysand wants. Does one "know it all" as an ego accoutrement of the ideology of opinion, wherein confidence fills up the lack in being? Or does one "know it all" in an identification with fixed *jouissance* that makes certainty a psychotic trait? Or does one reveal the uncertainty of neurosis that underlies an overkill in "knowledge" where one finds the hysteric's subversion, or the obsessional's ritual doubt?

Lacan surprised us by placing sexuality on the slope of being where *jouissance* blocks truth, fading behind the object *a*. Yet truth has the *structure* of fiction—which elaborates unconscious fantasies—and, as such, lies along the path of desire insofar as desire sets into motion the partial drives that aim for *jouissance* ($\$ \lozenge a$). All such efforts at satisfaction tell one story. The object *a* has more than one meaning. Primordially repressed Ur-objects that become partial drives function first to evoke desire. Built up in signifying matrices, they return heterogeneously in the real, introducing fading and cuts into all objects sought for satisfaction.[52] That is, desire is first constituted in reference to partial drives—oral, anal, invocatory, and scopic—that constitute each person as a sexed being. Body is libidinized by the object *a* at its rims, edges, and surfaces. Not only is there no sexual ratio or signifier for a man or a woman, there are only the objects each desires. Moreover, the lack of wholeness in being that sexual desire unveils comes not only from a permanent divide between one person's "sex drive" and another's, but more profoundly from the real of sex which is itself unrepresentable. Yet we try to depict sex as a whole, in words or images of gender ideologies, in speaking of body types, or in semiologies of erotic organs linked to desiring codes, and so on.

Lacan said in 1969 that the terms supporting neurosis are knowledge (the Other/S_2), *jouissance* (J) and the object (*a*) as they make knots in the signifying chain in three logical moments, creating a first outcome of sexuality attained in adolescence.[53] As pure subject of the drive, an infant is first constructed via the paths of alienating language, *jouissance* (libido), and a gathering together of whatever constitutes the object *a* meant to stop up the void. In Lacan's teaching the Oedipal structure concerns how one copes with *jouissance* and desire, then, not Freudian sexual complexes concerning whether a woman lacks an organ or a man has one.

Lacan's topological logic or science of the real explains the connection between language and desire. An individual is paradoxically enabled to believe him or herself whole only if there has been sufficient intervention in the mother-child dyad in the first place to displace the child's dependence on the mother—rooted as it is in pure *jouissance*—onto other things. The first distance between the orders (serial orderings) is created by the necessary cuts that constitute certain objects as lost: the breast, the gaze, the voice, etc. Paradoxically, the desire for these objects introduces the infant to an awareness of loss as loss of *jouissance* for which he or she compensates by identifying the symbolic mother with frustration (imaginary lack), the real father with interdiction, and the imaginary father with privation.[54] To compensate for the fragmenting experience of separation *qua* cut, the infant forges unary links—a kind of real signifier that retains some trait of the imaginary and symbolic—that project onto the world a "sense" of what was lost. These unary links—Freud's *einziger Zug*—produce *jouissance* as a positive thing, not a philosophical negativity of nothingness or simple emptiness.

Perhaps the idea that sexuality is constituted by a logic of the cut, wherein "sex" is partialized in the drives and language, will make sense if one keeps in mind that Lacan's topology is based on Leibniz's *analysis situs* wherein meaning (=quantity) is dependent on structure (=quality). Put another way, an infant chooses to "be' in the social link via lack, or to "be" petrified.[55] If he or she chooses petrification, the status of being psychotic, that infant is identified with nonsense signifiers that fail to re-present him or her as a subject of desire for another signifier. Relying on Jacques-Alain Miller's 1984–1985 course "Orientation lacanienne," Bruce Fink explains the link between being and meaning this way: "Meaning (or signification) is only possible when there are two signifiers in question, one signifying a subject—no matter how devoid of being he may be—for the other. Meaning is produced only in that part of the Other's circle or 'field' where we find S_2. The autistic child's blockage at S_1 means that neither the subject nor the Other can come into existence, each requiring as it does the other's existence."[56]

The question at stake in psychoanalysis is this then: "Language divides humans into subject and object, subject of a demand addressed to the Other, object as an answer coming from the other. There is no division such as male and female language."[57] Both males and females are either subjects of desire in speech or objects of the drive in the quest for satisfaction. The sexual division in speaking beings is introduced by the real of the drive as it brings a certain kind of *jouissance* into sex which depends on the "object" we desire in (or from) the Other. If *jouissance* brings satisfaction only insofar as the other provides the "correct" response to the demand that constitutes the drive ($\$ \Diamond D$) as a demand for *jouissance*, one wonders how Jacques Derrida, George Lakoff, and many other important scholars can suppose that mastery over metaphor has been achieved.

For language *is* metaphor that is always at risk because metonymy enters its field as libido via the splits caused by desire. When confronted with "objects" that don't comply, language plays tricks rather than signifying things. For one must use words, only words, to bring the other to do what one has to do—just enough, not too much—for one's own *jouissance* (Apollon, *Lacan and the Subject of Language*, 119). Insofar as the desire for immediate *jouissance* is the law of perverse fantasy ($a \Diamond \$$), one is not surprised that a basis for all fantasies is primordial layers of desire turning around issues of law. Where the phallic effect has not intervened at all, as in psychosis where *jouissance* is the principle of ordonnance, psychotic poles are defined, as we know, by what is not missing: the distance from *jouissance* we call social exchange. Yet any tiny infant lives in a state of pseudo-psychosis, trying to escape the exquisite pain of identifying with the primordial real. An infant's "developmental" challenge lies in trying to stretch images and language over the chasm between the real and imaginary, trying to cover the brutal law of the unmediated real with the law of the symbolic. It does not lie in some supposed biological or cognitive climb up a ladder already mapped by the biological body.

In "Language: Much Ado about What?" Jacques-Alain Miller referred his audience to the beginning of the analysis of language in Bertrand Russell's 1905 theory of description that appeared the same year as Freud's "Three Essays on Sexuality."[58] Russell tried to disambiguate language with such model sentences as "The King of France is bald" (Miller, "Much Ado about What?" 26). A first conclusion is that language produces its own references, sometimes to nonentities such as a bald king of France. Miller's point is that the whole enterprise of a philosophical logical analysis of language is grounded on nothing more than errors of reference. Indeed, language—meant to refer to things—generally fails to do so (27). Such references do not function by correspondence, but by what Miller calls a disappearance theory of language. In his picture, one would not say that language expresses something, but that language nullifies the referent because one speaks of the real which is impossible to represent. So, in speaking of the real, one erases it (29–30).

The simplest example of a classical Freudian analysis reveals the difference between the Lacanian direction of interpretation and a post-Freudian one, where exchanges like the following are typical correspondence-theory interpretations: Patient: "My husband repeated grow, grow; change, change to me all the time." Doctor: "Well, don't you see that he really wanted you to grow a penis, like the penis he could never accept his mother did not have? Grow, change did not refer to your character, but to the phallic mother. It was his way to tell you to protect him from being the homosexual he really wanted to be."[59] Such examples illustrate the nonsense in the biological Freud.

In "Science and Truth," Lacan says:

Let us recall that Freud unties the knot in his discussion of the

lack of the mother's penis, where the nature of the phallus is revealed. He tells us that the subject divides here regarding reality,
seeing an abyss opening up therein against which he protects himself with a phobia, and which he at the same time covers over with
a surface upon which he erects a fetish, i.e. the existence of the
penis maintained albeit displaced. Let us, on the one hand, extract
the (no) [pas-de] from the (no-penis) [pas-de-pénis], to be brack-
eted out [à-mettre entre parenthèses], and transfer it to the no-
knowledge [pas-de-savoir] that is the hesitation step [pas-hésita-
tion] of neurosis. . . . Let us, on the other hand, recognize the subject's efficacity in the gnomon he erects, a gnomon that constantly
indicates truth's site to him. Revealing that the phallus itself is
nothing but the site of lack it indicates in the subject.[60]

   In the site of lack, one carries the weight of a family's joy and
disappointment. Moreover, only the analysand *has* the knowledge
of what that means to him or her. The analyst does not. Put another
way, the unconscious is the knowledge that something is lacking
in knowledge, not on the mother's body. This is not to say that
children do not imagine that the mother has a penis, or that perversion does not replace this supposed penis with a fetish object in
the imaginary whose cause is in the real. But Lacan argues that in
a biological generalization of his theory, Freud mistook organs for
knowledge. Moreover, Freud's idea of knowledge concerns the
cause of being. In the notes to his translation of Lacan's "Science
and Truth" Bruce Fink writes that Lacan's "Let us . . . extract the
pas-de from the *pas-de-pénis* . . . and transfer it to the *pas-de-savoir*
. . . that is the *pas-hésitation* of neurosis" refers to page 198a, lines
15–16 of Aristotle's *Physics* where Wicksteed and Cornford translated Aristotle as saying "It is clear, then, that there are such things
as causes, and that *they can be classified under the four heads that
have been enumerated.*[62]
   All of this brings us to Lacan on the issue of cause. "I am not the
cause of myself," he says in "Science and Truth" (13). What is the
cause? Unconscious fantasy is structured by a battery of signifiers—
by language—and by the object *a* that causes us to desire. But the
object *a* is not a new name for the cause as concept or as a thing-
in-itself. And while the object *a* offers the illusion of consistencies,
it is "discontinuity, and not regularity that is essential to the notion
of causality" (Miller, "To Interpret the Cause," 33). When something lacks in the signifying chain, cause shines through as an object
a, as an irreducible residue of indecipherable knowledge. Lacan
taught that a question arises when loss penetrates meaning, when

an impasse blocks symbolization. Such moments tell us that language means more than it can ever say.

Notes

1. Jean LaPlanche, "The Unconscious: A Psychoanalytic Study," trans. P. Coleman, *Yale French Studies*, no. 48 (1972).

2. Anika Lemaire, *Jacques Lacan*, trans David Macey (Boston: Routledge & Kegan Paul, 1977), xiii.

3. Jacques Lacan, "The agency of the letter or reason in the unconscious since Freud," *Ecrits: A Selection*, trans. Alan Sheridan (New York: W. W. Norton, 1977), 160.

4. G. Manseur et al., "($-\phi$) et jouissance dans les structures cliniques de la névrose," *Hystérie et obsession: les structures cliniques de la névrose et la direction de la cure*, ed. J. Adam and H. Wachsberger (Paris: Navarin, 1985), 89.

5. "La Troisième Jouissance," Lettres de l'école Freudienne," no. 16 (1975): 178–203.

6. Ana Martinez Westerhausee, "Le phallus, Pierre de touche de la question de la réalité Freud," *La lettre mensuelle*, no. 97 (March 1991): 34–36.

7. Jacques Lacan, "Desire and the Interpretation of Desire in *Hamlet*," ed. Shoshana Felman, in *Literature and Psychoanalysis: The Question of Reading Otherwise, Yale French Studies*, nos. 55/56 (1977): 11–52. The seminar of April 29, 1959, from *Le séminaire VI (1958–1959): Le désir et son interprétation* (unpublished seminar).

8. *Encore*, "A Love Letter," *Feminine Sexuality: Jacques Lacan and the école Freudienne*, ed. Juliet Mitchell and Jacqueline Rose, trans. Jacqueline Rose (New York: W. W. Norton, 1982), 141–161; *Seminaire de Jacques Lacan* (1972–1973). *Encore* text established by Jacques-Alain Miller (Paris: Seuil, 1975), 73–82.

9. Jacques Lacan, *Le séminaire XXIII (1975–1976): Le sinthome* (unpublished seminar).

10. Jacques Lacan, "Massachusetts Institute of Technology," 2 décembre, 1975 in "Conférences et entretiens dans les universités nord-américaines," *Scilicet*, nos. 6/7 (1976), 56.

11. Jacques Lacan, "Seminar of 21 janvier 1975," *Feminine Sexuality* ed. Juliet Mitchell and Jacqueline Rose, trans. Jacqueline Rose (New York: W. W. Norton, 1982), 167–71; from unpublished seminar R.S.I. (1974–1975). *Ornicar?*, no. 3 (May 1975), text established by Jacques-Alain Miller, 104–10.

12. Jacques Lacan, "On a question preliminary to any possible treatment of psychosis" (1958), *Ecrits: A Selection*, trans. Alan Sheridan (New York: W. W. Norton, 1977), 199–200.

13. Eric Laurent, "The Uses of Phantasy," *lacanian ink*, no. 1 (Fall 1990): 29–38; 34–36.

14. Jacques Lacan, *Television: A Challenge to the Psychoanalytic Establishment*, ed. Joan Copjec, trans Denis Hollier, Rosalind Krass, and Annette Michelson (New York: W. W. Norton, 1990), 30.

15. Jacques Lacan, *Le séminaire XX (1972–1973): Encore*, text established by Jacques-Alain Miller (Paris: Editions du Seuil, 1975), 100.

16. Jacques Lacan, "Geneva Lecture on the Symptom," *Analysis*, no. 1 (1989): 7–26.

17. Jacques-Alain Miller, "To Interpret the Cause: From Freud to Lacan," *Newsletter of the Freudian Field*, vol. 3, nos. 1/2 (Spring/Fall 1989): 30–50; 31. "Cause et Consentement," Course at the Department of Psychoanalysis, Paris VIII, 1988–1989 (unpublished course).

18. Bruce Fink, "Alienation and Separation: Logical Moments of Lacan's Dialectic of Desire," *Newsletter of the Freudian Field*, vol. 4, nos. 1/2 (Spring/Fall, 1990): 78–119.

19. Noam Chomsky, *Aspects of the Theory of Syntax* (Cambridge, Mass.: MIT Press, 1965), 3.

20. Jacques Lacan, *The Four Fundamental Concepts of Psychoanalysis* (1964), ed. Jacques-Alain Miller (Paris: Editions du Seuil, 1973), 39–40; 56.

21. Jacques-Alain Miller, "A Reading of Some Details in *Television* in Dialogue with the Audience" (Barnard College, New York, April 1990), *Newsletter of the Freudian Field*, vol. 4, nos. 1, 2 (Spring/Fall, 1990): 4–30; 18.

22. Jacques Lacan, *Le séminaire XV (1967–1968): L'acte psychanalytique* (unpublished seminar).

23. Jacques-Alain Miller, "Language: Much Ado about What?" *Lacan and the Subject of Language*, ed. Ellie Ragland-Sullivan and Mark Bracher (New York: Routledge, 1991), 21–35.

24. Alexander Leupin, Introduction, *Lacan & the Human Sciences*, ed. Alexandre Leupin (Lincoln: University of Nebraska Press, 1991), 1–23.

25. Kenneth Burke, "A Rhetoric of Motives," *The Rhetorical Tradition: Readings from Classical Times to the Present*, ed. Patricia Bizzell and Bruce Hertzberg (Boston: St. Martin's Press, 1990).

26. *The Seminar of Jacques Lacan*, Book II: *The Ego in Freud's Theory and in the Technique of Psychoanalysis*, 1954–1955, ed. Jacques-Alain Miller, trans. Sylvana Tomaselli (New York: W. W. Norton, 1988), 23.

27. Jacques Lacan, *Le séminaire XX (1972–1973): Encore*, text established by Jacques-Alain Miller (Paris: Editions du Seuil, 1975), chap. one.

28. Sigmund Freud (London: The Hogarth Press, 1986), "Anatomical Distinction," *SE*, 19: 252.

29. Roger Wartel, "Fetishes-Fetish," *lacanian ink*, no. 3 (Spring 1991): 17.

30. Jacques Lacan, *Le séminaire XXII (1974–1975): R.S.I.* (unpublished seminar).

31. Jacques Lacan, "Conférences et entretiens dans des universités nord-américaines," *Scilicet*, nos. 6–7 (1976): 7–52.

32. Jacques Lacan, "Science and Truth," trans. Bruce Fink, *Newsletter of the Freudian Field*, vol. 3, nos. 1/2 (Spring/Fall 1989): 4–22.

33. Colette Soler, "Hors discours: autisme et paranoia," *Les Feuillets du Courtil: Institutions pour enfants*, no. 2 (1990): 17–19.

34. Jacques Lacan, *The Seminar of Book I (1953–1954): Freud's Papers on Tech-

nique, ed. Jacques-Alain Miller, trans. John Forrester (New York: W. W. Norton, 1988), 80–81.

35. Jacques Lacan, "The Freudian thing," in *Ecrits: A Selection*, trans. Alan Sheridan (New York: W. W. Norton, 1977), 128–29.

36. Jacques-Alain Miller, *Extimité*, Course at the Department of Psychoanalysis, (1985–86), unpublished course.

37. Jacques Lacan, "The subversion of the subject and the dialectic of desire," *Ecrits: A Selection*, trans. Alan Sheridan (New York: W. W. Norton, 1977), 315.

38. Paul Verhaeghe, "L'impasse de la forclusion comme symptôme de la clinique 'structurale' des psychoses," *Quarto*, nos. 28/29 (October 1987): 86.

39. Sigmund Freud, "Papers on Metapsychology," *SE*, 14: 1–162.

40. Sigmund Freud, "Totem and Taboo" (1912–1913), *SE*, 7: 123–243.

41. Sigmund Freud, "Group Psychology and Analysis of the Ego" (1921), *SE*, 18: 65–144.

42. Sigmund Freud, "The Ego and the Id" (1923), *SE*, 19: 65–144.

43. Serge André, *Que Veut une Femme?* (Paris: Navarin, 1986).

44. Jacques-Alain Miller, "The Analytic Experience: Means, Ends, and Results," *Lacan and the Subject of Language*, ed. Ellie Ragland-Sullivan and Mark Bracher (New York: Routledge, 1991), 92.

45. Slavoj Žižek, "With an Eye to Our Gaze: How to Do a Totality with Failures," *Newsletter of the Freudian Field*, vol. 4, nos. 1/2 (Fall/Spring 1990): 67.

46. Jacques-Alain Miller, *Ce qui fait insigne*, Course at Paris VIII, 1986–1987 (unpublished course).

47. Alexandre Stevens, "Deux destins pour le sujet: identifications dans la nérvose et pétrification dans la psychose," *Les feuillets du Courtil* (Institution pour enfants), no. 2: 25–40; see also *NFF*, vol. 5 (Spring/Fall 1991), in English translation.

48. Jacques Lacan, "Subversion of the subject and the dialectic of desire," *Ecrits: A Selection*, trans. Alan Sheridan (New York: W. W. Norton, 1977), 312.

49. Bernard Baas and Armand Zaloszyc, *Descartes et les fondements de la psychanalyse* (Paris: Navarin Osiris, 1988), 48.

50. Malcolm Bowie, *Lacan* (London: Fontana Press, 1991), 142. See also *Ecrits: A Selection*, 291.

51. Jacques Lacan, *Le séminaire VII (1959–1960): L'éthique de la psychanalyse*, text established by Jacques-Alain Miller (Paris: Editions du Seuil, 1986), 122.

52. Jean-Pierre Klotz, "Sex and Identity," *Newsletter of the Freudian Field*, vol. 4, nos. 1/2 (Spring/Fall 1991).

53. Geneviève Morel, "Sur le concept de névrose infantile," *Quarto: L'enfant et la psychanalyse*, no. 39 (May 1990): 34–37. See also Jacques Lacan, *Le séminaire XVI (1968–1969): D'un Autre à l'autre* (unpublished seminar of May 21, 1969).

54. Russell Grigg, "Lacan on Object Relations," *Analysis*, no. 2 (1990): 42.

55. Jacques Lacan, "Position de l'inconscient," *Ecrits* (Paris: Editions du Seuil, 1966), 841.

56. Jacques-Alain Miller, "Orientation lacanienne," course of 1984–1985 (unpublished course).

57. Willy Apollon, "Theory and Practice in the Psychoanalytic Treatment of Psychosis," *Lacan and the Subject of Language*, ed. Ellie Ragland-Sullivan and Mark Bracher (New York: Routledge, 1991), 118–19.

58. Sigmund Freud, "Three Essays on Sexuality" (1905), *SE*, 7: 123–243.

59. Lucy Freeman, *The Beloved Prison* (New York: St. Martin's Press, 1989).

60. Jacques Lacan, "Science and Truth" (1965), trans. Bruce Fink, *Newsletter of the Freudian Field*, 3, (Spring/Fall 1989), 24–25.

61. Aristotle, *Physics*, trans. P. H. Wicksteed and F. M. Cornford (Cambridge and London: Harvard University Press, 1929), 28 n. 46.

Index